The Practical Guide to
Man-Powered Weapons and Ammunition

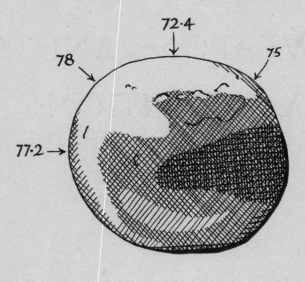

72.4

78

75

77.2 →

Towards the end of the eighteenth century cannonballs came to be made of cast iron. They were not very spherical and today we are surprised at the extent of their irregularity of shape (see page 5).

This 3 lbs 15 oz cast iron cannonball was found in a house in New Zealand, possibly dating from 1840-1870. Diameters are given in millimetres. It is in the possession of Dr G. Anderson.

The Practical Guide to

Man-Powered Weapons and Ammunition

Experiments with Catapults, Musketballs, Stonebows, Blowpipes, Big Airguns, and Bullet Bows

Richard Middleton

Skyhorse Publishing

Skyhorse Publishing books may be purchased in bulk at special discounts for sales promotion, corporate gifts, fund-raising, or educational purposes. Special editions can also be created to specifications. For details, contact the Special Sales Department, Skyhorse Publishing, 555 Eighth Avenue, Suite 903, New York, NY 10018 or info@skyhorsepublishing.com.

www.skyhorsepublishing.com

10 9 8 7 6 5 4 3 2

Library of Congress Cataloging-in-Publication Data

Middleton, Richard, 1957-
  The practical guide to man-powered weapons and ammunition : experiments with catapults, musketballs, stonebows, blowpipes, big airguns, and bullet bows / Richard Middleton.
      p. cm.
  Previous ed.: The practical guide to man-powered bullets : catapults, crossbows, blowguns, bullet-bows and airguns / Richard Middleton. 1st ed. Mechanicsburg, PA : Stackpole Books, 2005.
  Includes bibliographical references.
  ISBN-13: 978-1-60239-147-5 (pbk. : alk. paper)
  ISBN-10: 1-60239-147-5 (pbk. : alk. paper)
  1. Weapons. 2. Air guns. 3. Bow and arrow. I. Middleton, Richard, 1957- Practical guide to man-powered bullets. II. Title.
  U873.M53 2007
  623.4'41--dc22

                          2007029921

Printed in Canada

Contents

A WORD OF WARNING

When I was young and had nothing better to do, and finding there wasn't one in any of the bookshops, I wrote a book about catapults. It didn't stop there: it never does. People who build catapults invariably go on to construct all manner of other doubtful objects; I did it myself and this is the somewhat expanded version of that book.

Since I knew from bitter experience that they always went wrong in some fashion and it always hurt, I rather thought that an enterprising lawyer would hop about with excitement and bring some legal action against me.

Therefore I issue this very plain warning. I'm not a qualified engineer, but I'm as careful as I know how to be and I check my materials with every technical textbook I can lay my hands on to make sure they'll do the job I ask of them. And yet I still get hurt.

Whenever you're trying to control or harness large amounts of energy, the energy will find the weak point in your design or calculation and it will let you know in the most direct possible way. Something you hadn't anticipated will break. If it's a catapult, a roofing bolt screwed into the endgrain of an elmwood handle (see Fig. 4.13) might split free despite the strength of elm and come screaming back into your eye socket at a hundred and fifty miles an hour. There'll be a moment's shocked pause while you think "Oh. Damn!" to yourself, and then you'll go hobbling along to your local Accident and Emergency Department where there's someone whose job it is to sew people up after they've tried to free a bit of wood from a table saw without switching the motor off. And after that you'll either eschew these things altogether and vow to concentrate on growing obscure varieties of fuchsia, or you'll wait three weeks and be back at it again until the next time something goes horribly wrong.

I still can't anticipate what's likely to go wrong. Although I've survived the building of a number of airguns, I'm always fearful that I've miscalculated the strength of the tube I'm using for a compressed air reservoir, or that there's a scratch-mark I hadn't noticed and I'm about to discover, the hard way, that I've actually made a pipe-bomb.

My favourite legal disclaimer is from a website www.ourfamily.com.sg/ Faired.html:
Disclaimer: The boat plan shown here is not professionally designed blah blah blah. If you sink or suffer mental anguish or whatever, don't come crying to me.

It sums up my position nicely. I've had a lot of fun writing this book and I hope you have fun reading it but it is not a step-by-step guide to making any of these weapons. If you use this book as anything other than an account of my own experiments you're likely to get hurt, probably quite badly. Most importantly of all, if you're going to make airguns, go and read every textbook on pneumatic machinery and pneumatic seals you can find, and don't base anything just on what I've put here. I have checked everything as thoroughly as I know how but I'm not a professional pneumatic engineer and I'm not advocating that anyone, based on my experiments, follows my example. It is too easy to get yourself maimed or killed.

Now there's one other point, and it's a legal one. I happen to live in a country where you may own any of these weapons, even powerful airguns, without a licence. Most countries are not this liberal. I used to live in England where it was so crowded that shooting any gun even in the countryside was a potential hazard, and the authorities quite wisely limited the power of air rifles to a muzzle energy of twelve foot-pounds. It's more than ample to knock over a rabbit in the cabbages, and if you needed a more powerful airgun you simply applied to the Police for a Firearms Certificate. I can't check every legal code in every country, so if you plan on building any of these things, it's your business as a citizen to ask your authorities if it's allowed or what licences you need. You'll seldom find your country's laws – especially about airguns – corresponds with any other country's. And don't offer any weapons for sale until you've checked the law where you live. I happen to know something of the reasons for the formation of Proof Houses. Too many guns have burst and killed unsuspecting purchasers.

Finally, beware of the Internet. There are an awful lot of people - bless 'em - making ingenious things like this round the world, but not all of the things they make are especially safe, so for your own sake do your own research and find out what the tolerances are for any materials you use, and don't rely on any single source.

And I do hope I don't need to echo the basic safety rules of gun-handling. Even a crossbow string, zipping along the stock, will fairly sting any protruding fingertips. And a blast of compressed air alone, without a bullet, can deafen or blind someone. Jolly well be careful.

Introduction

The function of a bullet is to impart a blow. The weapon is the interesting means by which a missile is sent on its way, but the work itself is done by the bullet.

Human-propelled bullets are low-velocity bullets, and low-velocity bullets require explanation but not apology. The justifications lie in the immutable laws of physics. Explaining physical laws is clearly something our schools fail to do, or young Bob's flat tyres, as he labours to school past my house on his bike, would be pumped up of a morning.

One of the instruments for measuring projectile velocity – indeed the first, used by Benjamin Robins and Professor Hutton in the eighteenth century for musket balls and cannonballs respectively – is the ballistic pendulum. The bullet is shot at a heavy pendulum bob, and the momentum of the bob is calculated from observing how far it swings after the bullet has collided with it. It is a very easy instrument to make; for years I had a seven-foot pendulum of surprising accuracy, if I ever had the patience to gather a statistically valid sample of shots, hanging from the ceiling in my garage, with a bob weighing twelve pounds. Since I also had an electronic chronograph, I could and often did shoot different projectiles with known energy at this pendulum, and it was very noticeable that when struck by a .22 airgun pellet at 620 fps it swung about half an inch, whereas when struck by a .451 calibre lead ball from a catapult at 196 fps, it swung an inch and a half. The interesting fact is that both of these missiles have exactly 12 foot-pounds of energy.

This, then, is the first justification for the low-velocity bullet. Suppose, instead of a 12-pound pendulum bob I wanted to swing a 12-pound cat off my thyme bush, where it was performing such deeds as cats do perform on thyme bushes, I could move it an inch and a half with the slow catapult ball, but only half an inch with the airgun pellet. The example is rather unlikely owing to several obvious factors – the rarity of 12-pound cats being only one of them – but the principle is sound. If I were to want to move my cat the same distance with the airgun pellet, it would need a velocity of 1,964 fps which is the phenomenal energy of 120 foot-pounds. Ignoring the rude remark of my veterinary surgeon friend – that the cat would not move at all – we can see that the amount of energy required by a projectile to fetch a given clout to the target is inversely proportional to the weight of the bullet. For a given momentum, if the bullet is ten times as heavy, it needs a tenth of the energy to have the same effect on our 12-pound cat.

As a necessary digression, the removal of cats from gardens is better achieved with a larger, lighter missile having less momentum, penetration being highly undesirable for certain tasks. Discussing this with my shooting colleagues I received a letter from Dr. Lambie which is worth quoting in full:

Now here is a subject on which I regard myself as a minor authority. Many years ago while on a campsite in Spain a friend and I (just returned from a failed expedition across the Sahara - 1976 poured with rain non-stop from central Spain to Wadi El Huzef in southern Morocco) camped on site in Granada in Spain and our foul mood was made worse by a yapping nasty little cur from a tent several pitches away. My friend, a military man, was all for bludgeoning the brute to death but we were obliged to stay on the site while the Land Rover was repaired so good relations had to be maintained. Anyway I thought a discreet shot with the catapult would do the job, but a stone or hard object would have left a mark, so we came up with alternative ammunition in the form of one of those tight round pine cones which have small sharp protrusions over their surface. The first hit on the cur's flank at 10 yards was remarkable because the spinning cone not only struck with force but also momentarily tore at the fur and held firm for a second before falling off. The pain level was therefore much higher than a straight hit. Yelping piteously the brute returned to its owners who emerged to see their pet seemingly frantic with pain but no signs of bodily damage. Realising we were onto a good thing we crept up on the whimpering creature, that now only dared venture a few yards from its tent, and gave it another salvo. This time the yelps brought people out of other tents and we were concerned because one of the cones had clung persistently to its backside; but fortunately it fell away as it ran back to its tent.

The following day the cur kept its distance but we caught it on a verge outside the site and gave it several salvos – the howling was horrible and the owners shot out of their tent as though flushed by a lion. This time it was so demented it tried to bite its master and was completely inconsolable. After that it stayed in its tent and we saw no more of it. Needless to say we experimented on other dogs of varying sizes and the effect was the same except for an Alsatian which came for us, but a full hit on the chest at short range drove it back into retreat making sickening growls interspersed with shrill yelps.

The now famous 'dog nut' is widely used in the Newark area and as far as I know has been the standard way of pacifying unruly dogs since the mid 1970s.

Yours, George

The second reason we are drawn to slow bullets is that it always takes more energy to achieve high velocity, than it does to achieve the same momentum with a heavier bullet and a lower velocity. It is curious, but that is all, that I happened on the figures for a 12 foot-pound airgun and a 12 foot-pound catapult not by theoretical physics but by happy coincidence. I do shoot such pellets from an airgun, and I also have a .451 calibre spherical bullet mould, and in their respective weapons each does indeed produce 12 foot-pounds of energy. The airgun pellet is obliging enough to weigh exactly a tenth of the weight of the lead ball. This illustrates just how expensive high velocity is; with the same energy, the airgun pellet moves a little more than three times as fast as the heavy ball, yet the ball carries ten times the mass.

When we were testing his Borneo blowpipe, a friend and I found we could neither of us get any velocity higher than 203 fps, and that out of an 8-grain pellet. The best we managed with a 20-grain pellet was 176 fps, which was double the muzzle energy. (We had to use pellets because the long dart tripped the chronograph sensors at an angle and gave unreliable figures.) The Borneo darts weighed 26 grains, and we worked out that the Borneo tribesman, whose lungs were trained to the job, could have achieved 203 fps with these darts if he approached double our best energy input. But if he wanted the dart to go faster – say 300 fps – he would need to produce almost four times as much energy as we were able to. We are apt to forget that energy is required to shoot the bullet from our weapon; and it takes a great deal less energy to give a heavy ball a given momentum than it does a very light pellet. If the energy is limited to that which we supply with our muscles, this becomes quite significant. Fortunately for the tribesmen of Borneo, their darts rely on poison and not on muzzle energy.

The third attraction of the low-velocity bullet is reduced drag. Benjamin Robins found that the drag on a bullet is proportional to the square of its velocity up to a speed of about 800 fps. As it approaches the speed of sound, 1,080 fps, the drag rises dramatically, and creeps to somewhere around three times as much. In 1901 Fremantle published the velocity of the .303 bullet measured at every 100 yards up to the range of 2,000 yards and from this data we can learn all manner of interesting things. The bullet weighed almost exactly half an ounce, being 215 grains, and this is highly convenient because a half-ounce (218.75 grains) lead ball is one of the best low-velocity bullets to use whether from a catapult or a crossbow. Fremantle's table gives a great many details which do not concern us, but from his velocities it is easy to calculate how much energy is lost every 100 yards, this energy loss being the result of drag. At speeds above that of sound, the drag is about 17% every 100 yards, while below the speed of sound, it is only 7½% every 100 yards. That is to say, if the .303 bullet is going faster than 1,100 fps, 100 yards later it will have lost about 17% of its energy; while if it is going below 800 fps, after 100 yards it will only have lost 7½% of its energy.

Now this might lead us in the direction of very slow bullets indeed, but it is necessary to have a certain amount of speed or the target will up and stretch itself and leave the field before the arrival of the bullet. Besides, as we discover by the very practical means of building a series of low velocity bullet-shooting weapons, there is always an optimum weight; a weight of bullet which, if either exceeded or reduced, results in a less efficient transfer of energy. Imagine, for example, a fibreglass, recurve target bow with a 44-pound draw weight. Being no particular respecter of the products, admirable though they may be, of Mr. Yamaha, I altered such a bow to shoot bullets and got a one-ounce bullet to fly briskly at 182 fps, producing 32 foot-pounds. This, could I but shoot it accurately, might be a useful sort of thing to have. But it is hard to imagine the same weapon shooting a one-pound iron cannonball to any useful purpose. As a matter of fact, and as we shall see with all of these weapons, bullets have their greatest energy when they weigh somewhere around an ounce; a bit more with some weapons, a bit less with others.

But energy is not everything and lighter bullets, weighing a third of an ounce, may be more useful because a large sacrifice in energy gives a modest, but important, gain in velocity, and velocity is still essential in a missile. Velocity is important because velocity determines exactly how far a bullet will fall in the course of its flight. At 600 fps a bullet shot in a vacuum will have fallen half an inch at 10 yards' range. At 300 fps it falls two inches over 10 yards' range. For the drop, of course, is not a constant one; the drop is accelerating, and if the bullet is flying for twice as long, it falls four times as far. Given that range estimation is the hardest task of the marksman, high velocity greatly reduces the main error. After four twentieths of a second a bullet will have fallen 7.7 inches but after five twentieths, it will have fallen 12 inches, easily enough for a miss. At 300 fps it is the difference in range between 20 yards and 25 yards, and in the field it is difficult to be sure that our range estimation is even this accurate.

When low-velocity bullets were the order of the day there was neither a methodical approach to their study nor the technical means whereby such studies might be undertaken. The study of the muscle-propelled low-velocity bullet is in its infancy but accurate measurements are now within everyone's grasp. Not least by way of warning other experimenters, I detail here my many experimental failures as well as my few successes.

The world's politicians, with the lack of insight that characterises the breed, increasingly reflect only the viewpoint of city-dwellers, which is to legislate against anything as politically incorrect as shooting. It would be unkind to reflect that the five permanent members of the United Nations

Security Council between them supply the other politicians of the world with 88% of their gross overburden of military armaments. But we permit our politicians to make our laws and it does seem that we who suffer from an interest in shooting will have to explore short-range, and perhaps home-made, weapons to a greater degree than before.

Richard Middleton
New Zealand, July 2005

A Note on Measurements

A reference in the text to a bore or calibre of, for example, ".22" means .22 of an inch.

Bores and calibres measured in millimetres are referred to as "9 mm".

Useful Definitions and Explanations

Bullet weights and sizes – see table on page 8
Acceleration – see pages 2-4, 13
Beam theory – see pages 32-33
Drag – see page x
Energy – see pages viii-xi, and pages 2-4, 61
Mass – see pages 2-4
Momentum – see pages viii-xi, 2-4, 12-14
Purchase(s) – see pages 59-60
Spin – see pages 3-4
Trajectory – see pages 3-4
Velocity (high and low) – see pages viii-ix

Abbreviations

fps – feet per second
g. – gramme (metric measure)
gr. – grain (Imperial measure: 7,000 grains = 1 pound, so 437.5 grains = 1 ounce)
in. – inch (Imperial measure)
lb. – pound (Imperial measure: 16 ounces)
M. – metre (metric measurement: 1,000 millimetres)
mm. – millimetre (metric measurement)
mph – miles per hour
oz. – ounces (Imperial measure)
psi – pounds per square inch
yd. – yard (Imperial measure: 36 inches)

Chapter 1

Ammunition

Originally 'ammunition' meant military stores. I use it here in its more widely accepted meaning 'projectile'.

The function of ammunition is to do work – destructive work – to a target. The weapon is the means by which energy is transferred to the ammunition but the work is done solely by the ammunition at the end of its flight. The ammunition is, therefore, much more important than the weapon – the arrow is more important than the bow, the bullet more important than the rifle. Alas, our eyes twinkle more at the sight of a gun than at the sight of a bullet.

High velocity is difficult to achieve with muscle power alone. Low-velocity projectiles, whether arrows or bullets, do effective work to the target either by penetration or by the blow of what police reports are pleased to call a 'blunt instrument'. Arrows designed to kill small animals have enough momentum to kill merely by the blow they impart, and in my youth I used an arrow with a blunt head for rabbit shooting, which to those untutored in the power and accuracy of a bow was surprisingly successful and effective. An arrow with a blunt head does not bury itself in the undergrowth in the way that a pointed arrow does, and blunts are much easier to find after the inevitable misses; furthermore, when hit by a blunt a rabbit is invariably killed outright.

Archers hunting large animals require good penetration because there is insufficient momentum in an arrow to kill anything bigger than a rabbit. Among hunter-gatherers a very fine-tipped arrow is sometimes used which, concentrating all its energy into a single point, has very good penetration: the killing is done by poison smeared on this fine tip. An alternative preferred where big-game hunting with bows is still permitted, is the broad arrow-head, which cuts through vital blood vessels and organs and kills in the same way that a sword-thrust once did. This, too, requires the concentration of the available momentum into a small surface area for adequate penetration: and it must have an exceedingly sharp cutting edge.

We have here bumped into the word 'momentum'. This is a precise physical term. It means, very simply, the mass of the projectile multiplied by its velocity. It is not the same as energy. To anyone reared on the arts as opposed to the sciences, the significance of that statement may be lost, but it is worth dwelling on.

Momentum is the mass times the velocity, and there is a law of physics which states that in any collision, there is an equal amount of momentum beforehand and afterwards. Physics teachers in these troubled times of national curricula are apt to be conservative to the point of dullness, and experiments which demonstrate momentum involve such innocuous wooden trolleys as do not offend politically-correct Educationalists, rather than such airguns and bullets as would enthuse those who have to endure Education. The physics is, however, exactly the same, and it is rather important. Kinetic energy, measured in foot-pounds, is discussed endlessly, but at lower velocities momentum has more effect, and the two are very different.

If a wooden trolley weighing six pounds rolls at a velocity of 10 fps, and a stationary wooden trolley is placed in front of it, there will be a collision. If both wooden trolleys stick together – physics teachers like to smear the connecting ends with modelling clay to ensure that they do – then the total mass will be doubled, and the momentum being the same after the collision, they will then trundle along together at 5 fps.

Should our physics teacher momentarily step out of the room and we promptly perform the altogether more interesting experiment of replacing the first trolley with a catapult ball, the transfer of all the momentum still remains obedient to the laws of physics. Suppose we took a fairly weak catapult, and shot a heavy one-ounce glass marble at 97 fps from it at our stationary wooden trolley. Assuming the marble stuck into the modelling clay – by no means a foregone conclusion – the trolley would now weigh six pounds and one ounce which is 97 ounces, and since the momentum before and after the collision has to be the same, the velocity would be 1 fps. The cunning reader will deduce that I haven't chosen these figures at random.

The concept of energy also fascinates shooters and also lurks in the realm of physics. The energy of a moving object is defined by its velocity, times its velocity, times half of its mass. We note the interesting fact that to find the energy, we have to multiply the velocity by itself. The energy of a projectile, whether a glass marble or a wooden trolley, is proportional to the square of its velocity. This is therefore very different from its momentum, which is directly proportional to its velocity. Unlike momentum, energy transfer is always

$$energy = velocity^2 \times \frac{mass}{2}$$

$$momentum = velocity \times mass$$

inefficient. To get energy into a bullet, a great deal of energy has to be supplied; indeed, much more energy than the bullet will possess. The enormous bang when a rifle goes off is energy, and that sound energy is not used to propel the bullet. All rifles are inefficient; powder rifles waste around 70% of the energy of the gunpowder.

The reason is to do with acceleration. It takes time to accelerate things and it takes energy to accelerate things. To get a powerful car to go from 0 to 60 mph may take six seconds, which the advertisers are very keen to tell us: what they refrain from mentioning is that this sort of acceleration uses huge amounts of energy, and if you have such a car and accelerate as hard as this, you will find yourself constantly putting fuel in the tank. A less powerful car will still get to 60 mph, but it will take a lot longer than six seconds to do so, and use less fuel in the process. What is more, if you drive along the road steadily at 60 mph, you will – by comparison – use hardly any fuel. With muscle power we limit both the time and the energy we can supply for this business of acceleration. Shooting a bow or a catapult is the work of an instant, and the single quick muscle-stroke limits the resulting velocity. Higher velocities from muscle power are only possible if a lot of time is spent feeding in more energy, which we can do, for example, by pumping up an airgun; and airguns are even less efficient than powder rifles, involving wastage of 80 to 95% of energy.

Returning to our trolleys and glass marbles, the energy of the six-pound trolley travelling at 10 fps is, more or less, nine foot-pounds. The energy of the one-ounce glass marble travelling at 97 fps is also, more or less, nine foot-pounds. But the interesting thing to us is what has happened to the target – the trolley – after each collision. When struck by another trolley, travelling slowly, the energy after the collision is roughly four and a half foot-pounds. When struck by the glass marble, the energy after the collision is only a tenth of a foot-pound. Notice this fact: before the collision there were nine foot-pounds of energy in each projectile. In the rolling trolley there was nine foot-pounds of energy, and in the glass marble there was nine foot-pounds of energy. The difference lies in the momentum. The slow trolley had a lot of momentum where the fast marble had hardly any. And it is the momentum, not the energy, which is transferred to the target upon a collision.

Naturally ammunition that does not hit the target cannot transfer momentum to it. We are not concerned with explosive shells and proximity fuses so the first function of our ammunition is to be accurate.

Projectiles are kept on course in one of three ways. First, rifle bullets are spin-stabilised, although it is rarely appreciated that they do not follow a straight line of flight. Not only does the trajectory curve because of the pull of gravity, which is universally accepted, but if the bullet is a little bit eccentric, it will have been spun by the barrel about a centre other than its centre of gravity and, like a slightly unbalanced spinning top, it will follow the line of a very elongated helix or spiral. The effect can be seen in Second World War air photographs, the fighter aeroplanes of that time having a camera triggered by the guns being fired. As some of the bullets were tracers, the photographs show long, spiralling tell-tale trails behind them. There is also lateral drift of a spinning bullet, and the subtlety of aerodynamics is shown by the fact that a spherical ball will drift in the opposite direction to an elongated bullet, if both are spun in the same direction.

Second, arrows are fin-stabilised and although arrows with feathers do spin, it is not the spin that gives them their stability, but rather the large aerodynamic drag at the rear keeping them in line. Natural feathers always have a curve and every fletcher knows that the curve of all three feathers must be the same or the drag at the back will be uneven and the arrow will fly in a haphazard and unpredictable manner. Arrows with a broad cutting head such as are used on large game need very large feathers at the tail to compensate for the aerofoil effect at the front of the arrow: five inches long and three quarters of an inch high usually guarantees stability in flight, and though the arrow flies in a very dull and lifeless manner, and the high drag reduces the range, such arrows give great accuracy at the short ranges used by hunting archers.

Third, catapult and crossbow and musket bullets are – well, not stabilised at all. They rely on being spheres to suffer no unpredictable buffetings through the air. It is this last category which mostly interests us, although as we shall see when we come to consider making unconventional weapons, there may be good reasons why we might consider shooting darts or even arrows from big-bore airguns.

Ammunition for both the catapult and the bullet-shooting crossbow travels slowly. Nevertheless, irregular shaped stones, as we discover on our eighth birthday, do not fly true.

Ball bearings are commonly sold as ammunition for catapults; usually three-eighths of an inch in diameter. They have three disadvantages: they are very expensive; they are small and do not afford a firm grip to finger and thumb as they nestle in the pouch; and they lack mass. It is this last fact that reduces their value as ammunition, despite the advantages of perfect uniformity and residual environmental safety. Mass, as we have just seen, is critical to momentum. Glass marbles are also used as ammunition, commonly those of around 16 millimetres diameter. Whilst giving a substantial body to grip, and being reasonably (though not perfectly) uniform in both roundness and mass, they still are not very heavy. Oddly enough they weigh almost exactly the same as the little steel ballbearings.

In India, small units of clay with a little vegetable oil mixed in to prevent brittle drying, all weighing the same as each other, are rolled by hand into a ball and are left to dry in the sun to be used later as ammunition for the stonebow. Provided the dry weights are reasonably large they may prove effective and, requiring no apparatus for their manufacture, are pleasantly free of expense. They are said to be effective on small birds, but civilized nations eschew the shooting of small birds, and quite right too.

Until the Industrial Revolution, ball for cannon was made of hand-chipped stone, labour being cheap and the raw material abundant. Eventually, towards the end of the eighteenth century, cannonballs came to be made of cast iron; to the modern mind of surprisingly imperfect diameters, and therefore often not very spherical. This was one of the reasons for cannon having a large windage. A cast iron ball wedged in a cast iron barrel having access only from the muzzle was a handicap in a battle. Since most gunpowder was slightly damp in the field, and possibly damper at sea, the chance of a misfire was too high to ignore. The Brown Bess musket misfired once every thirteen shots, though this may have been more closely related to the flint-lock ignition system than to the state of the powder.

Bullets for muskets were made of lead. Metal detectorists tell me that it is almost impossible to walk a ploughed field in England without finding a musket ball, and those I have seen have a very thin coating of toxic oxide. Before we discuss how to make lead bullets, a word of caution. The President of the Faculty of Occupational Physicians of the Royal College of Physicians, who might be in a position to know, once told me that lead poisoning is a real occupational hazard, and it really does occur among paint-strippers and stained glass workers and others who work with molten lead, if they are careless of safety. It may be simple to melt lead on a gas cooker, but the stench is dreadful, and lead fumes are invisible and therefore a real hazard. A safer method is to cast bullets out of doors, and a barbecue (if it is never again to be used for cooking) can supply the heat. Lead oxides appear on the surface of the molten metal in open crucibles and are highly and cumulatively toxic; nor do they disappear if the barbecue goes unused for a year or two. It is as well to dispose of the slag with the greatest possible care. I take it to a lead-works where it is eventually recycled. It is also perilous to neglect clothing. I have cast bullets wearing sandals, and don't much recommend it. Molten lead splashes readily, and leather motorcycle gloves, despite being hot and uncomfortable, are sensible, as are stout boots and spectacles of some kind.

Lead being malleable and ductile we could conceivably take lumps of identical weight, and hammer them until they became spherical. If we choose to make hollow slugs for our big airguns, we use the malleability to squeeze the lead through a die, although the power to do so is unlikely to be achieved with less than a hydraulic press. Ballbearings were once made by rolling them in a tube containing many thousands, loosely trundling round together for days and days on end in a slurry of wet abrasive powder. In the same way that pebbles are rounded on a beach by the action of waves, all the corners and irregularities are knocked off, and steel being a homogenous material (that is, lacking the grain direction which tends to make most pebbles egg-shaped rather than spherical) they end up with no corners at all.

Mould making

My brother-in-law once told me that he remembered having read somewhere how one might cast bullets with a plaster of Paris mould, and despite this being not exactly a well-referenced source, I made such a mould, casting it around glass marbles. Left for a couple of days to dry out before the marbles were removed, the hot lead immediately provoked an outburst of steam which blew the mould apart, and I had no success whatsoever. I abandoned the attempt and have nothing of any use to offer on the subject.

I have a number of commercially made bullet moulds, and frankly recommend buying one and having done with the business, for they barely cost an hour's wages for standard sizes, or double for one made to a specified size. These commercial moulds are made of aluminium. A century ago when aluminium was uncommon, pistol bullet moulds were made of brass, usually with short handles of brass as well, which suggests that our ancestors had thick and horny skin on the palms of their hands, or that they wore gloves, or that they were rather dimwitted. Brass handles get hot very quickly. Today's moulds have wooden handles and wood is a poor conductor of heat; something of moment when we consider that the melting point of lead is 325°C.

Metal moulds for spherical bullets can be bought quite cheaply in gunshops in calibres up to .575. Of the common sizes, a .451-calibre ball weighs about a third of an ounce and a .527-calibre ball weighs almost exactly half an ounce. It is possible to order a heavier bullet mould, and to wait a very long time indeed for delivery. The easiest way to make an odd size is to buy a small one and to grind each half of the hole bigger.

However, there is nothing to stop us getting two small blocks of aluminium and starting from scratch. Aluminium is particularly good because it acts rather well as a heat sink. A mould needs to be hot for the lead to flow into it, but it also needs to conduct heat away quickly or the bullet takes a long time to solidify in the mould.

I have a mild steel mould made for me by an engineer who was curious to know if it could be done on a lathe; each bullet must be left in the mould to cool for ten seconds after casting, and I can only make twenty balls in an hour with it. Why so slow? My engineer was not sparing with his steel and steel is a poor conductor of heat. Initially, we ladle molten lead – using a dessertspoon wedged and bound in a wooden handle – into the mould. Before the mould warms up a small dribble falls through the hole in the top and perhaps forms half a sphere in the mould chamber, but almost at once the hole becomes blocked with solidifying lead, and no more can flow through to form the top half of the ball. The problem is solved by applying a blow-torch to the mould for a few minutes. But once hot, steel remains hot. Accordingly, every ball cast has to be held while the steel cools to the point where the lead solidifies, before the mould can be opened.

An aluminium mould, by contrast, can be heated adequately in a few seconds with a powerful blowtorch, and sheds the heat to the surrounding air so quickly that almost as soon as the lead is poured, the mould can be opened and the ball dropped out.

Besides, aluminium is soft and easy to work, and steel is not. I have made moulds on a lathe, but to no benefit because I had no spherical follower, and a simple grinding bit in an electric drill is just as inaccurate and saves the purchase of the lathe. For both these reasons, therefore, if you are disposed to make, rather than to buy your mould, use aluminium. I am disposed to view what I do as fun, and there is great pleasure to be had in the accomplishment of shooting bullets cast from a mould I have made myself. Indeed I would say that making a bullet mould is a pleasant activity, but then Hodgkin says that making bowstrings is a jolly business; something which perhaps is intended to be read ironically, since the frustrations of working with a tangle of threads, into each of which an equal tension must feed, reduces me without fail to violent swearing.

We need two pieces of aluminium which each have at least one perfectly flat surface. An inch by an inch-and-a-quarter is probably enough, and five eighths of an inch thick; for bear in mind that not only does each half have to contain a perfect half-sphere, it has also to have room for pegs from the flat of one half to mate perfectly with holes in the flat of the other half. Nevertheless, the smaller the aluminium blocks, the less heat will be required before perfect bullets can be cast.

On one flat surface, we draw with dividers – so that they scratch the circle – the diameter of the bullet we wish to cast. We can calculate the size pretty exactly from knowing that a standard Brown Bess musket ball, of which there were 14½ to the pound, was 0.683" in diameter. Suppose, as well I might, I wish to make a twenty-bore ball. The volume of a sphere relates to the cube of its diameter: it is $\frac{4}{3}\pi r^3$. 0.683 x 0.683 x 0.683 (we don't need π) will give us 0.3186; if we multiply this by 14½, to give us a pound, we have 4.6199, and if we divide

$0.683^3 = 0.3186$
$0.3186 \times 14.5 = 4.6199$
$4.6199 \div 20 = 0.231$
$\sqrt[3]{0.231} = 0.614$

that by twenty, because we want a twenty-bore ball, we have 0.231. The cube root of 0.231 is 0.614, and this is the diameter in inches of a lead ball weighing a twentieth of a pound, or 350 grains. If we work in metric, the diameter is 15.58 millimetres.

We also know that a twelve-bore ball (12 together weigh a pound) is 0.729 inches in diameter. This presents a slightly awkward fact to be discovered by anyone mathematical, in that these figures can only be approximate diameters, since if a lead ball 0.683" in diameter weighs $14^1/2$ to the pound, a twelve-bore ball should be 0.72747" and not 0.729" in diameter.

Empirically, then, we find that the following give approximately the weights we might require, or are moulds commercially available:

Quantity per pound	Weight (grains)	Diameter (inches)	(mm)
11	636	.75	19.05
12 bore	583	.729	18.52
14	500	.692	17.55
$14^1/2$ (musket)	483	.683	17.35
16 (one-ounce)	437	.661	16.79
$16^1/2$	424	.655	16.64
18	389	.636	16.15
$18^1/2$	378	.63	16
20 bore	350	.614	15.6
24 (pistol)	292	.577	14.66
$27^1/3$	256	.5	12.7
32 (half-ounce)	220	.527	13.39
50	140	.451	11.46
$75^1/4$	93	.394	10

So, choosing our diameter accordingly, the first thing to be aware of is that the lead will have to be poured into the mould, and to save cutting off a sprue, or stalk, of lead (which is the casting of the hole going into the mould) from every single bullet, it is as well to make the circumference of the circle brush the top surface of the mould.

Now forget the circle for a while, and concentrate on drilling two holes all the way through both blocks of aluminium. I like to make these 2.5mm diameter. In one block I tap a 3mm metric thread, and screw into it, very tightly, a couple of tiny bolts which protrude sufficiently to locate into the opposing holes [Fig. 1.1]. Either the threads will have to be carefully filed off to fit these holes, or the holes will need to be enlarged. At this stage it is also sensible to think about how the blocks are to be mounted in the wooden

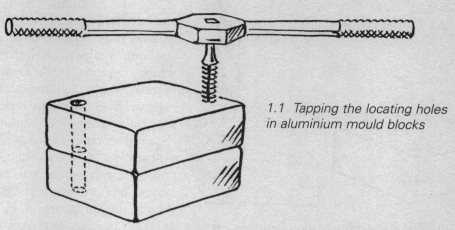

1.1 *Tapping the locating holes in aluminium mould blocks*

handles; having tried various designs, for simplicity's sake I favour a hinge at one end of the handles. If wood is plentiful, the 2.5mm holes can be drilled straight through the wooden handles and the aluminium blocks screwed directly to the wood – it will eventually scorch, but not for many hundreds of bullets. Otherwise, these holes can be extended into a couple of flats of steel which can in turn be mounted onto the wood handles; steel being a poor heat conductor, the wood will be better protected from scorching.

1.2 *Drilling the datum and pouring hole*

Next, drill into the combined blocks the pouring hole [Fig. 1.2] which serves as a datum mark for both blocks. Then part the blocks and with a large diameter bit drill a short blind hole into the aluminium where the future bullet will lie [Fig. 1.3]. Using a ball-grinding bit (sometimes called a spherical burr) in an electric drill, enlarge the hole into a hemisphere, as accurately as possible keeping to the inscribed circle defining the final diameter of the ball [Fig. 1.4]. Use a low drill speed and plenty of pressure, or the grinding bit will wheel itself out of the hole (I guarantee it) and gouge unpleasantness out of the mating surfaces.

It is a great help if a washer can be found which has the exact outside diameter of the intended bullet: this can be applied to the hole repeatedly to find those parts which need to be ground out to make a more perfect sphere. I have had no success with making a cutting tool having itself the finished hemispherical shape.

1.3 Drilling the pilot hole

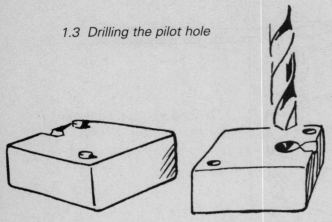

This, in part, is because the centre of the hemisphere receives only slight abrasion from a spinning hemispherical cutter, and whilst routers are known for woodworking, aluminium is a comparatively hard material. Even so, only care and patience is required to create something that is very close to a hemisphere. Parabolic mirrors of six and eight inches diameter are regularly hand-ground by amateurs making large astronomical telescopes – something requiring far greater accuracy than what we attempt here.

The temptation during this operation will constantly be to blow the swarf out of the developing hole, and no warnings ever devised have prevented people from doing this. I suspect each of us simply has to experience the shock of a sudden eyeful of tiny, razor-sharp shards of aluminium and be the wiser afterwards.

Do not, at this stage, do anything to the second aluminium block; this should merely have a short hole drilled in it to represent the second half-ball. A combination pouring-cone and sprue-cutting device must now be made. I like this to be of mild steel, which will cut the lead easily [Fig. 1.5]. It pivots on one block with a 6mm bolt going into a tapped hole in the half-mould. A little carelessness ensures that this hole is drilled where the future bullet-hole will lie, resulting in a truly amazing amount of cursing before the block is flung, worthless, across the workshop and a start on a new one is made.

Now the two halves of the mould are put together, the locating

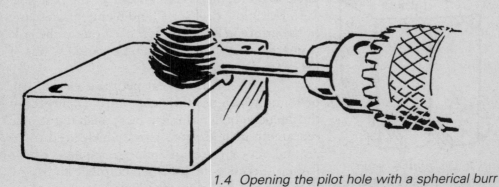

1.4 Opening the pilot hole with a spherical burr

pegs-and-holes firm against each other, and the entire device is clamped shut in a G-clamp, heated good and hot with a blowtorch, and a spoonful of lead melted and poured into the mould [Fig. 1.6].

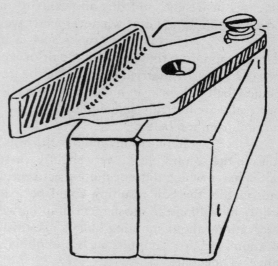

On separating the two parts of the mould we then have a cast of the dome of one half, and its circumferential circle sitting on the surface of the virgin half-mould. While the cast is sitting there, it is an easy matter to scribe with a needle a circle round the outside of it so that this, the virgin half, can be ground out to a close match using the spherical grinding bit.

1.5 Combined funnel and sprue cutter

Use a small diameter one for the initial grinding, a larger one later, and use a gyrating, rotary motion to bring the hole as close as can be guessed at to the half-sphere. Accuracy is likely to increase with practice, and to increase dramatically with larger bullets; the temptation is to make several different size bullet moulds, and far be it from me to discourage this entertainment.

Mankind has such a strong creative urge that often the making of these things becomes more enjoyable than the shooting of them. Astronomers report the same thing – people find the making of a telescope so pleasurable that they subsequently devote more time to building further instruments than they do to observing the heavens. This stage of the process takes rather longer than I have described, since the aluminium will need to cool before it can be handled, but this is something we each discover for ourselves, instantly and painfully, when impatience leads us to seize the mould just after the molten lead has been poured into it.

Then follows a steady repetition of the whole process of casting a bullet, a careful examination of the bullet, and grinding a little more from the half-moulds until the bullet is both spherical and of the correct weight. Shot from a catapult a little irregularity does not catch the breeze so's you'd notice. With bullets larger than half an

1.6 Lead cast of first half-ball ounce, it takes a good deal of grinding to make modest

increases in weight, and this allows us to make bullets which are very close indeed to spheres, and of whatever exact weight we may require.

How long to make such a mould? A leisurely day, including perhaps mounting the mould in a pair of wooden handles [Fig. 1.7] such that they can be easily married for pouring the lead, and equally easily split to drop the new ball out. Bear in mind that molten lead really does give off fumes and they really are horribly and cumulatively poisonous, so the less time spent over the cauldron, the better.

In one of my moulds the pegs from one block, which locate into holes in the second block, were slightly off-set, resulting in a ball made of two half-spheres which did not quite meet centrally. But because lead is malleable and ductile, the ball resulting could be made as near spherical as necessary simply by rolling the misshapen lump between two flat plates of iron. I have reservations about shooting bullets like this at high velocities down the barrel of a gun, but for catapults such a knobbly ball, shot at low speed and short range, is adequate.

Accuracy, penetration and momentum are intricately linked and we always and ever have to find a point of compromise. Accuracy from a low velocity weapon at short range is adequately attained by spheres of uniform diameter and weight. Large pebbles flung from slings fly straight but David carefully selected a round one to smite Goliath. Critical to our understanding of this is again the importance of momentum.

According to Newton momentum is maintained unless there is some force acting upon it. A half-ounce lead ball, flying through the air at over 100 miles an hour, has a lot of momentum, and since our shooting is at very short ranges, we can expect that the force applied by even a brisk wind is far too small to have any great effect upon it – and such is the case. Even with a smooth-bore barrel our low-pressure airgun (Chapter 9) shoots a half-ounce ball repeatedly through the same hole at 10 yards. At 100 yards, of course, it

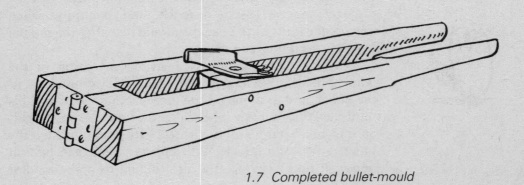

1.7 Completed bullet-mould

is a different matter due both to tiny inaccuracies in the ball and inaccuracies of aim through the barrel having a larger diameter than the ball itself. Musket fire will not hit a man at 150 yards. But we are not interested in hitting men, nor in ranges of a 150 yards.

The target rifleman, knowing his exact range and wishing to do no more than make a hole in a piece of paper, will sacrifice power, velocity, penetration and money to that end. A golf ball weighing 1.62 ounces can be struck to a speed of 250 fps – a useful 98 foot-pounds of energy – but two things prevent golfing tackle from being used as weapons: the lack of penetration and the lack of precise accuracy. Having once been hit by a golf ball at the end of its flight, I can say that its size, a little over an inch and a half in diameter, prevents its penetrating a human head – mine – but perhaps that is not the object of golf. The target archer cannot be quite so careless of penetration; an arrow which does not stick in the close-bound straw of the target does not score. The archer therefore has to have an arrow weighty and sharp enough not to bounce on impact.

Ignoring poor marksmanship, which largely depends on practice, the combination of ammunition and weapon will limit the useable range. All weapons tend to disperse their ammunition; the useable range is never further than that point at which the dispersion exceeds the size of the target. Nelson's warships shot cast iron balls a tenth of an inch smaller in diameter than the bore of the cannon, and at a mile distant, the ball might fall anywhere along a line half a mile wide. Accordingly, Nelson was in the habit of advising his captains 'to get so close to our Enemies that our shots cannot miss the object', and frequently this meant so close that they were touching one another.

Shooting a musket ball from a catapult ties in with the experience of hunting archers who rarely shoot beyond 20 yards, indicating the importance of stalking to anyone wishing to shoot low-velocity ammunition. Lateral dispersion is the concern of the weapon, but vertical dispersion depends on the time which has passed since it left the weapon. An important concept, which as a youth I never quite grasped, is that the bullet doesn't fall towards the ground at a constant speed: it accelerates. It accelerates downwards at 32.16 feet per second per second. This means that if you dropped a bullet out of the leaning tower of Pisa, as Galileo once did, after exactly one second the bullet would be falling at 32.16 fps. After exactly two seconds it would be falling at 64.32 fps. After exactly three seconds it would be falling at 96.48 fps. As the leaning tower is 179 feet high, the maximum time it can spend falling is three and a third seconds, and therefore the greatest speed it can attain is 107 fps.

These delightful figures mean that we can tell exactly where our bullets are at any time after we've shot them. The drop in feet may be calculated by multiplying the time (measured in seconds) by itself, and then multiplying this figure by 16.08. Or as a mathematician would have it, $S = \frac{1}{2}g\,t^2$. Why the drop is called S, I have never fathomed.

> S = drop (in feet)
> t = time (in seconds)
> g = gravitational acceleration (32.16 fps/sec)
> $$S = t^2 \times (g \div 2)$$

After a quarter of a second our missile has fallen 12 inches. Suppose we are shooting a catapult ball at 180 fps, which is quite likely. A quarter of a second after we've shot it, the ball will have travelled about 15 yards. So we know that at 15 yards, we need to aim a foot above the target to hit it.

The significance of this is that a bullet's drop is not related to the speed, but to the square of the speed, which means that if the bullet is travelling half as fast, it will drop four times as far over a given distance. Therefore slight increases in bullet velocity are worthwhile if for no other reason than assisting range estimation. In the field, it is difficult to estimate precise ranges. Towards the extreme range of a catapult, a 10% error at 30 yards is of course 33 yards. At 200 fps, a catapult ball drops 69 inches at 30 yards and 84 inches at 33 yards, which is significant.

Target archers usually draw their arrows to the chin. The line of sight is about five inches higher; specifically, at eye level. Target arrows fly at about 170 fps. A ringsight, fitted to the riser (or handle) of a target bow such that the arrow hits the centre of the target at 15 yards, will mean that the arrow will also hit the centre of the target at about five yards. The arrow only rises above the line of sight by a peak of about an inch for the whole of the interim distance. Why? Because the eye of the archer is looking along the tangent of the curve of the flight of the arrow and, since this curve approximates to the curve of a circle having a very large radius, it is pretty nearly a straight line.

The human-powered bullet therefore operates under the restraint of physics. It is hard to give it high velocity, because there is little time to effect an acceleration and because the amount of energy we can supply is limited, unless we reduce our rate of fire. But momentum is easily transferred to it simply by increasing its weight. A high momentum efficiently transmits a blow to a target, but a low velocity gives a high trajectory and limited penetration. We therefore have to shoot it at short range, and choose our targets carefully.

CHAPTER 2

Fibreglass bullet-shooting crossbow – a chapter of disasters

The advantage of shooting arrows from a bow is that the arrowhead, lying to one side of the bow, guides the remainder of the missile past the bow on its way towards the target. The disadvantage is that the spine, or bendiness, of the arrow must be a precise match to the strength of the bow for there to be any prospect of accuracy, and this means that the missile is an expensive, and therefore must be a recoverable, item. At today's prices, a single target arrow will cost the same as three pheasants from a butcher's shop, and given the fact that three pheasants cannot always be shot before the one arrow is lost, consideration must be given to what economists call the cost-benefit ratio.

Cheap missiles, namely bullets, can be expendable, but first the problem of the bullet clearing the bow must be addressed. If the string is always held in the same place, and the bow held securely, this ought to be straightforward to achieve by means of making a crossbow [Fig. 2.1]. I have discovered it is not automatically straightforward, alas, and this chapter stands as sorry evidence to this effect.

Daniels, Payne-Gallwey, Higson and latterly Credland and Littler have all written extensively about the English bullet-shooting crossbow and though I am not in the business of stealing their research, we need a summary.

Briefly, then, it had a steel bow, canted upwards at the limb-tips so the string would clear the tiller, with a draw weight of about 250 lbs. The string of this form of crossbow was drawn from its resting position five to seven inches backwards. Two small cross-trees separated the string into an upper and lower skein, so that a pouch for the bullet could be sewn to the centre of the thrust-line. A loop from both top and bottom string bestrode the pouch, and it

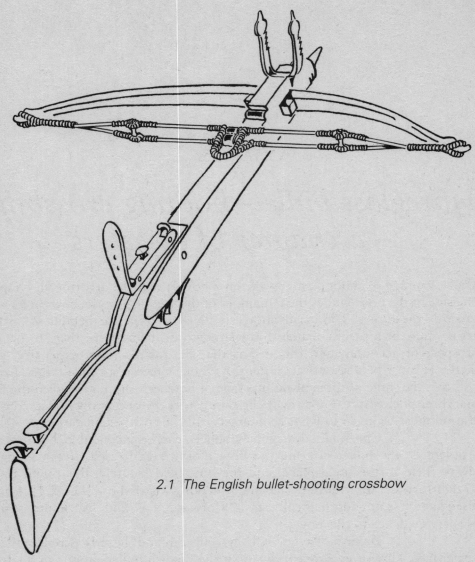

2.1 *The English bullet-shooting crossbow*

was the loop that was drawn back to a catch, which in so doing closed the pouch upon a lead ball usually weighing half an ounce. A large lever facilitated bending the bow; this was only pulled back just before a shot was released, to save the bow being fully strained for any length of time. The string usually had to be pulled back by hand to fit the loop to the nut, even when the lever was brought forward prior to spanning the bow. On a strong bow, this could be very difficult, as can be found when shooting restored examples. I once examined one with a longer-than-usual draw length, the back of the bow being 12¼ inches from the nut and the bracing height 3 inches, and it had a one-inch loop.

The draw weight I was unable to measure, but in the event it proved rather too strong for the tiller – at the third shot after reconditioning, the hand of the stock broke, occasioning many remarks of that character usual to such a misfortune. It must be attributed to the woodwork being two hundred years old.

The accuracy of the bullet crossbow startles everyone. *Sporting Magazine* of 1859 details a retired army captain who *'could pierce a playing card at 50 yards and kill a dozen pigeon at 30 yards or more,'* and Daniels gives the famed report of the novice hitting a knife-edge at 15 yards. George Agar Hansard describes a wager in which, in about 1828, a confident *'individual at Liverpool'* allowed a glass to be shot off his head at 16 paces. More recently in 1966 G. Millard shot six bullets into a 2-inch circle at 50 feet, while on 27th October 1973 Dr Flewett, who has possessed several such crossbows, rested his elbows on a stool and at twenty-five paces shot five bullets into a one-inch circle. This last I can personally vouch for, and I have the cardboard target, dated, with the holes neatly flattened [Fig. 2.2]. English bullet-shooting crossbows really are this accurate.

Like any other weapon, accuracy depended not only on how well the bullet crossbow was made and the skill of the marksman, but also on the care exercised in loading. There is a fairly hefty kick (though not at all painful) on release, and it takes a good many shots before one acclimatises to a particular bow and can draw on its potential.

It was not, however, very powerful, despite all its colossal draw weight. I recently chronographed a bullet crossbow Dr Flewett had just restored. It was engraved 'Patrick Liverpool' and was evidently made for a boy; it had a 26$\frac{1}{2}$-inch bow half an inch thick at its centre, a 3$\frac{1}{4}$-inch bracing height (measured to the back of the bow), and it was drawn 4$\frac{1}{2}$ to 5 inches, the nut being 8$\frac{5}{8}$ inches from the back of the bow but the loop being an inch from the string. It proved to have a 'muzzle' velocity of 159 fps with a 238-grain bullet.

2.2 Five shots in a one-inch circle shot at 25 paces by Dr W. Flewett with an English bullet-shooting crossbow

Sir Ralph Payne-Gallwey's shot a distance of 300 yards, and another of Dr Flewett's crossbows shot 280 yards, the latter measured with a wooden wheel fitted with a cyclometer on a disused aerodrome where he performed the experiment. Using the knowledge that a half-ounce bullet loses 6% of its energy every 10 metres, the late J. R. Wiggins and I calculated that Sir Ralph's bullet crossbow had a launch velocity of 206 fps (see Chapter 12).

For three reasons, the antique English bullet-crossbow did not reach its potential as a design. First, though its draw weight was large, the draw length was short. The physicist, heeded only by the ancient Chinese, constantly reiterates that we must enhance the draw length at all costs (including if necessary at the cost of draw weight) because acceleration is the transfer of energy, and a short draw length allows only a short time period to transfer energy to the bullet. A long draw, enhancing the time available for acceleration, results in greater missile velocity. Again, if I can sneak a nod in the direction of the physics lab, acceleration is measured in fps per second, and if we allow a lot of the last second of this acceleration, we get a lot of feet per second velocity as the result of it. Those of us who once had a passion for powerful motorcycles recall journalists expressing their awe at nought to sixty in three seconds, so if we allow more than these three seconds we know the motorcycle will be going at a higher velocity than 60 miles an hour.

Second, the bow was made of heavy steel, and a great deal of energy was used in returning the mass of bow to the braced position. A light, well-designed wooden bow can shoot faster than a heavy steel bow. I have one that does.

Third, light-weight string material was not available. The strings were heavy, the leather pouch was heavy, and the loop with which the string was held at full draw was heavy; this last unnecessarily so, for any weight at the centre of the bowstring acts as if it were bullet weight, and detracts from the efficiency of transfer of energy to the bullet. Why unnecessarily? Because whereas the bowstring needs to be strong enough to withstand the shock of the bow coming to rest, the loop need be no stronger than the draw-weight itself. Sir Ralph made his loop very stout, and whipped it even more stoutly, and his bullet bow turns out in practice to be little more powerful, though a very great deal more accurate, than today's catapult. But power is not everything, and a ball travelling at 206 fps which arrives within the circle of an inch of its aim is not to be despised.

If it is to remain a reasonably straightforward weapon the bullet-shooting crossbow has to use a stationary bow – that is, one which doesn't rotate about its centre – and therefore it has somehow to be arranged to be centreshot. English bows were of steel and were said to be tempered with a beeswax candle. The method sounds highly improbable but in fact it is not at all unlikely that a beeswax candle was involved. The bow was probably heated to red heat and quenched in water or oil. It may then, cold, have been rubbed over with beeswax, and heated until the wax just caught fire, before being left to cool slowly. Exactly this technique, using mutton-fat, is still sometimes used in a country gun-maker's to gauge the correct temper for the springs for shotgun locks. Payne-Gallwey recommended that we make a wooden model of a bow with canted limbs and send it to Liége in Belgium for specialists to forge a copy in tempered spring steel. If this option still exists, it is an expensive one and probably limited to someone of Sir Ralph's means. It has occurred to a number of practical souls to take a leaf from a car suspension spring and grind it into a bow, but I know of no examples where one was then used to shoot bullets. I do, however, know of such a practical soul subsequently shooting himself through the web of his hand while loading said crossbow, and mention the fact by way of warning. My local former Police Firearms Officer, who happily granted licences for deer-hunting rifles, told me the story and is very chary about crossbows because of the high incidence of accidents associated with them.

I, imagining myself to be both original and immune to these accidents, decided one bright morning that an alternative to steel would lie in the heavy glass-fibre bows which are cheaply available for commercially-sold crossbows. I was wrong on both counts. I have had no success with glass-fibre, and it has to be said so right at the beginning to preclude false hopes, but as we learn more from our mistakes than from our successes my failures are worth documenting.

A typical example is that made by Barnett and sold as a 'magnum prod'. The word 'magnum' derives from a two-quart bottle of wine, its relevance being questionable, though I do have a photograph of the leg of a 22-year-old Oxford man prior to a crossbow bolt being extracted from it 'under alcoholic sedation'. The circumstances of this accident, drily reported by the doctors at John Radcliffe Hospital, do not fully support this incident being classified solely as a hazard of crossbows. The word 'prod' is based on an error of palaeography: the word is thought by scholars to have been 'rodd' and did not refer at all to the bow of a crossbow. However, not all of today's crossbowmen are devotees of academic accuracy. I refer to it as a bow.

The Barnett bow I used had a draw weight of 150 lbs at 14¾ inches of draw length. It was 26 inches between the nocks, and in its relaxed state had the deflexed, recurved figure of a 'cupid' bow. It was of uniform thickness, 7mm, and of close to a uniform width of 32mm, there being very little taper towards the tips of the bow. Such dimensions meant that it was really rather inefficient; if of uniform width, it should taper in thickness according to a rather complicated formula governed by the fact that the stiffness of a beam relates to the cube of its thickness and the cube root of its length. Twice as long means eight times as bendy; twice as thick means eight times as stiff. If of uniform thickness, it should taper in width to a point at the tips. In an obvious move to improve matters some of the width from the lower edge of the bow towards the tips was filed off; this is a good deal easier than the precise thinning by which we could alternatively alter the bow's tiller. I was careful about taking too much off the tips, which are recurved, because narrow recurved tips are notoriously unstable, and given the heavy draw weight, it is all too easy to ensure that the bow throws off its string, as well as its bullet, at each shot. By this means I rather hoped to arrange for the stress to be taken along more of the bow's length than its centre portion, and lighter tips always fly forwards more quickly. It meant I had to discard the moulded plastic tip-covers, which in turn meant giving careful thought to smoothing and perhaps cushioning the string loops. This turned out to be much more important than I had imagined, both because glass-fibre is a heavy bow material, and because unidirectional glass-fibre is – er – unidirectional, and not a homogenous material as is steel. The mass of the bow material is important because when the weapon is shot, energy is required to move the limbs of the bow forwards and this energy is not available to shoot the ball. Heavy limb-tips moving forward very quickly possess a great deal of energy and a very great deal of momentum.

The Chinese pellet-shooting crossbows used a recurved bow mounted at a pronounced forward slope in the tiller, such that the string sat taut above the line of the tiller which itself was markedly curved. Their limb-tips were, however, left very wide.

It becomes significant to refer to the geometry of a bow. In any braced bow, the string will run along a perfectly straight line between the limb-tips. As the bow is drawn, the four points of contact – namely the two limb-tips, the hand holding the bow, and the fingers holding the string, will lie on a perfectly flat plane.

If we follow the Chinese plan, and cant our glass-fibre bow heavily forwards, this natural plane of forces no longer applies, and since the bow will be rigidly clamped at its centre, some twisting of the limbs themselves must take place. In practice this is small, it requiring comparatively slight pressure to push the string itself to one side of the plane of forces.

However if we propose to use the double-string of the English bullet-shooting crossbow, it becomes quite an important matter. Using an endless string, no matter how tightly whipped, the discharge of the bow results in the string experiencing a massive jolt, and this jolt hits the upper half of the string before the lower half [Fig. 2.3]. Do not believe that the time gap is so small as to have no effect. If the total string is of the correct strength, the time gap may be all that is required to subject the top shank of the string to the

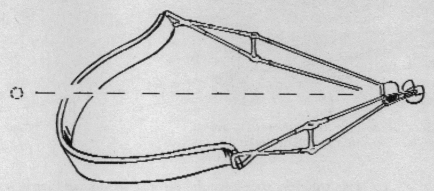

2.3 The bullet crossbow requires a canted bow for the ball to fly free

whole jolt first and, if it is half the strength needed to withstand this jolt, it will break. I failed to recognise this possibility, so my first string broke and so too did an expensive electronic chronograph, which – my wife heartlessly observed – afforded me the useful opportunity of learning how to import spare parts from Canada to repair it.

Doubling the thickness of the shank, by doubling the number of strands, does not necessarily solve the problem. Irritatingly, on being shot, one half-shank stretches and approximates to a straight line, while the other half takes on a more angled appearance and, as can easily be recognised from the tone of the half-shanks if plucked (as if tuning a violin) is under a great deal less tension.

My third solution was to make each half-shank separately, with its own separate endless loop. The final knot, tying first strand to last strand, of the endless loop is positioned carefully so it gets thoroughly and tightly whipped. Ideally one uses what fishermen call a blood knot which is as strong as the string itself, but you can never get this exactly as long as is wanted so I settle for a sheet bend, for although this is only 60% as strong as the string, there will be so many other strands apart from the knotted one that it isn't very significant.

The entire centre part of the string was made in the fashion described by Payne-Gallwey, but at the string ends, there are four loops, two for each nock of the bow. By staggering them, so that the inner loop of one side was from the top shank, and the inner loop from the other side was of the bottom shank, the strings are made sequentially of identical length on a single string-making jig [Fig. 2.4]. The upper string required wrapping at its ends with leather, to thicken it and compensate for the fact that it lay slightly further forward of the lower string when the forward-leaning bow was braced but at rest.

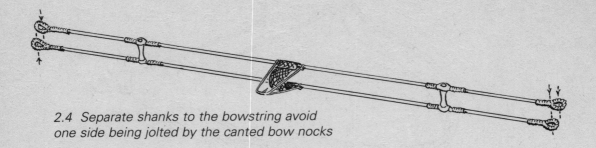

2.4 *Separate shanks to the bowstring avoid one side being jolted by the canted bow nocks*

This solution does have the distinct advantage that it is easier to get an even strain on the individual strands; otherwise this is a problem in thick bowstrings. In this context, it is worth adding that even strain is difficult to achieve if the loops are not made at the exact point where the strands each make the sharp turn round the hooks of the string jig. Since it is impossible to whip these sharp turns in situ, they must (as W. F. Paterson advocates) either be coxcombed with a needle – coxcombing being a blanket stitch [Fig. 2.5] – or protected from abrasion at the bow nocks by putting a small slip of fine glove leather inside the hooks of the string jig and sewing it in place as a protective sheath round the loop. It pays to check, twice, with the owner of the glove before removing any leather from it. A glove short of a thumb can, I assure you, provoke a whole repertoire of discouraging remarks.

It may be worth adding that with thick strings there are advantages in first twisting the strands into threads. Tim Baker has shown that the greatest strength is to be found in plies of up to, but no more than seven plies twisted together, but avoiding four plies. His research shows that maintaining an even tension on all the strands is critical to string strength. If, as is likely, we wish to make strings having 30 strands for each half-shank, there is sense in first twisting together five-strand plies, and using six of them for each shank. It is, of course, a good deal easier to get even tension in six plies each of five strands than in thirty separate strands.

But there is one other thing which needs to be emphasised, not least because it normally goes unmentioned. As a rule of thumb, a longbow needs a string with a breaking strain of four times the draw weight of the bow at full draw. Recurve bows need a string somewhat stronger, as do short bows. It is this

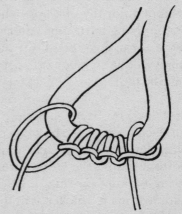

2.5 *Protecting the string loops by coxcombing*

shortness which is emphasised in a crossbow. Crossbows are a great deal shorter than longbows, and the strings must therefore be a great deal stronger, in proportion. How much stronger? I go for a string of about twenty times the draw weight. It might be thought that this is nonsense, that the breaking strain of a piece of string, including a bowstring, has nothing to do with its length – and of course this is true. But, as J. E. Gordon points out, and as the cross-bowman – me – has discovered empirically, it is not the breaking strain that concerns us, but the breaking energy.

We are not about to load weights with great care on our string. We are about to subject it to the most enormous jolt, and since bows are made of matter, and the matter must itself accelerate as well as the arrow, it is impossible to divert into the arrow every bit of the energy used in drawing back the bowstring. Some of that energy must go into the bow limbs, and the bow string must ultimately bring those limbs to an abrupt halt. The energy required to break a short string of a given breaking strain, is a great deal less than the energy required to break a longer but otherwise identical string. Even among 'non-stretch' strings there is a cushioning effect, and the cushioning effect of (for example) a long bowstring vibrating a little forwards and back after the arrow has left it, quite apart from the greater amount of even temporary stretch possible in a long string, is vastly more than it can be for a short crossbow string. Even the crossbow string vibrates. By fixing a piece of paper to the side of the front of the tiller so that it is torn by the string on release, it can be found that the string comes forwards of its at-rest position by as much as 55 mm, a fairly startling two inches and more.

Yet I have a small yew-crossbow string which has survived even though lightly built. That and the high performance of the yew suggest that the glass-fibre bow is pretty inefficient, having limb-tips so heavy as to retain much of their energy, which far from going usefully into bullet velocity is being wasted on trying to break the bowstring. Since a steel bow has even more mass than a fibreglass bow, we can only speculate about the additional problems occasioned by the bows available to the intrepid Sir Ralph, and guess that he had good reason for the heavy strings he used.

A heavy string acts, as now we all know, as if a third of its weight were attached to the arrow, and since we want a fast arrow (or in this case, bullet) we must make our string as light as possible. Sir Ralph wrote that his Belgian-barrelled bullet crossbow shot with greater force than his English bullet crossbow, and he attributed this to the string of the former bearing directly on the mid-point of the bullet. The physics suggests that the explanation lies in the weight of the string, which, having various additional pouches, loops and pillars attached to it, cannot be as light in mass as can that of the simple string used where it is the barrel that contains and controls the movement of the bullet. However, of course, his Belgian bow shot a heavier bullet than his English bow, and as we discover with regard to catapults, increasing the mass of a projectile tends to increase the efficiency of transfer of energy from bow to bullet. In passing, it is worth noting that barrelled bullet crossbows are not as accurate as double-stringed bullet crossbows, the tight fit required of accurate barrelled weapons (including rifles) being inimical to the poor thrust of a bowstring.

Therefore we make a light string, ignoring all the above, and see if we can get away with it. We probably can't, and the string will probably break, and then perhaps we will want to make a stronger string. All this I state from exhaustive experience.

The design of the tiller presents new problems. From my experience of building little yew bullet-bows (see Chapter 3), I thought I would prevent the weapon from becoming too unwieldy by arranging for the bow to slip easily in and out of the stock. I like to cut a deep lateral groove precisely fitting the bow at full draw, from the top of the tiller. Padding it with a slip of leather, I simply press the yew bow in from above. Provided the fit is tight, and is checked before every shot, this is a functional way of housing a yew bow. There must be enough wood in front of the bow so that it does not split off during the jolt on being shot, but this needn't be more than three inches of wood, perhaps two inches if the wood is sufficiently strong. Elm, if it can be obtained, is difficult to split and an excellent wood.

Holly is also the traditional choice of wood for a crossbow tiller. At least, so I was assured by a highly respected academic. So, scaling up as the medieval mason scaled his cathedrals up from his parish churches, I built a holly tiller for my glass-fibre bow of 150 lbs draw, to the same design as a smaller, lighter yew bullet-bow. Equipped as I now am with the bitter wisdom of chastened first-hand knowledge, I would offer the theory that holly is not a good choice for such a tiller, nor is a deep lateral groove an appropriate housing for a fibreglass bow of this weight.

The following occurrences are possible when shooting a newly-built crossbow:

1. The arrow (if not a bullet-bow) flips over rather than is driven forwards by the string, and hits the face of the crossbowman.
2. The bow leaps out of the lateral groove in the tiller and flies through the air.
3. The bullet strikes part of the bow furniture, unexpectedly hits a brick, and passes among the observers.
4. The front of the holly tiller splits off and flies through the air, pursuing the bullet and pursued in turn by the bow.

5. The reinforced front of the repaired holly tiller does not split off, but the whole of the rear portion of the tiller splits off instead.
6. A shard from one of these explosions, perhaps a cracked lever, perhaps the bullet on the rebound, perhaps one arm of the bow, smites the crossbowman in the face an inch from the eye, resulting in a flow of blood for seven hours and one of the most conspicuous black eyes in the history of that amusing medical condition.

It is of course possible to imagine worse, but the above list is not compiled from the imagination but rather from the singular taskmaster of experience. Every single one of these calamities has happened to me. The lesson to draw is that we are dealing with very great amounts of energy, and the controlled but abrupt release of large amounts of energy demands caution. At the time of writing, we read of the death of someone merely using a jig to put the string on a hand-drawn compound bow. The apparatus he was using broke, and it is thought a part of it hit him with sufficient force to cause a subsequent brain haemorrhage.

While it does indeed work to shoot a light yew bow from an open but well-fitting slot in an elm tiller, I am ill-advised to expect a glass-fibre bow, releasing six times as much energy into a bullet, to behave in the same way. Although I can still strive to make my crossbow come apart for ease of carriage, a rather more secure housing for the bow than an open slot in the top of the tiller is called for.

Further to illustrate the danger of building one of these weapons – and build one we must, if we want one, since they cannot be bought any more – I finally corrected all the major errors of my earlier attempts and being now thoroughly cautious, arranged to shoot the newly-built bow from behind a wooden screen, the crossbow being clamped in a Workmate bench with a long cord tied to the trigger.

The first bullet flew true between the prongs of the foresight, but on hitting a box of packed rags it rebounded, causing a 4-millimetre indentation in the wooden screen exactly five inches above the line of sight. The second bullet disappeared and was never seen again. The third bullet tore the sewn nylon webbing pouch, so enormous was the acceleration afforded by the crossbow and so great the inertia of the bullet. I re-sewed the pouch, but the pouch dimensions turned out to be fairly sensitive in a canted bow. Where previously the bullets were flying above the bow housing, they now started to crash into it, and the only bullet which could be induced to fly free of the forward part of the bow was one weighing 340 grains, which flew at 211 fps. Every half-ounce lead ball now became a half-ounce splattered lead hemisphere by the time it had left the front of the crossbow, and inspired confidence only in its ensuing inaccuracy. The experience does make it clear that with a canted bow, the structure of the string, the bracing height, the angle of loose of the catch, and the bullet weight are highly sensitive. Clearly, too, these factors are so interwoven and so complex that one would be rash to dissect them into individual factors and attempt to prescribe a formula that will work.

Unfortunately I next committed the cardinal sin of the experimental scientist, which is to vary more than one thing per experiment. My new bowstring was a little longer than the preceding string. There was of course a reason, and the reason was that a longer string allows a lower bracing height, which in turn allows a still greater draw length for the same strain upon the bow limbs. This allows a greater amount of energy to be released by the bow when shot. The part which I had overlooked was that the Barnett glass-fibre bow is recurved, and it is sold with a comparatively short string which therefore effectively removes the recurve: the string does not rest on the recurved portion when the bow is braced, but rather sits proud of it. My new bowstring, being longer, rested for an inch on the recurves, and what I did not realise was that this was putting a lot of longitudinal stress on the shoulders of the bow nocks, the string loops in effect acting like a chisel.

My final (as it was to turn out) experiment was to see if, using this new string, I could shoot a light .451-calibre ball, weighing only 140 grains. The theory was that there may be some dynamic movement of the pouch on release from the nut directing the half-ounce ball downwards at the exact moment of release, and that this downwards movement was what was causing it to crash into the metalwork at the front end of the bow. There were good reasons for this belief: the pillars I had made between the strings, the pillars holding the pouch open, were so short that the larger half-ounce ball was now held pinched in the pouch when the string was resting at brace height. This should not be so: the ball should be pinched into the pouch only when the string is stretched back to the nut [Fig. 2.6]. Otherwise, on being released the ball has to prise its way free from between the strings, and of course if the bow is canted (which was the case in this experiment), the last string the bullet touches will throw it away from the original free line of flight.

The result seemed to bear this out, in that the ball did indeed fly free of the front of the bow. But the small ball had not absorbed enough of the available energy so the heavy limbs still possessed far too much and were therefore still moving so fast that the string loops split the glass fibres down their length at one of the bow's nocks. The top string loop, made of Fastflight®, snapped while the lower string was pulled an inch deep along the length of the bow limb, permanently ruining it.

Thus ended my experiments with solid glass-fibre.

In retrospect a better plan would have been to take machined

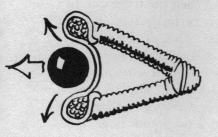
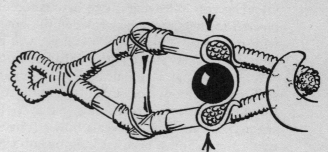

2.6 *The length of the pillars must allow the bullet to fly completely free of the pouch.*

strips of maple and uniform strips of glass-fibre, both sold for the making of laminated handbows, and to build two identical limbs to be mounted on either side of a crossbow tiller or stock, with a clear gap between them. Exactly this option is adopted by target crossbow makers in Western countries, other than Switzerland where the steel bow is retained. The design presents few difficulties and its execution requires only the skills of bow lamination, and the construction of the metalwork to ensure a clear central gap. Any archery book can be consulted as to how to make the bow, but for very short bows it is simpler to make a straight bow rather than a recurved bow. There is a tendency for a heavily-recurved bow to shed its string on release, and as we have discovered, bullet crossbows have about them an adequate number of hazards in their manufacture. The recurved bow might be left until some experience in bow-building has been acquired. Besides, a very short bow is pretty fast of itself since the limb tips move four times as fast if the bow is made half as long. To buy the strips of glass fibre, which is unidirectional, and milled flat pieces of maple, we have to go to a specialist archery supplier and there we can buy booklets on making the materials into bows.

Briefly, the process requires utterly clean surfaces and utterly regular pressure during gluing. I clean all surfaces with acetone immediately before gluing, and use fresh Araldite 2005, carefully weighed on a chemical balance. Any slack in any of the procedures results in the bow shearing apart at full draw, as I discovered in my early days as a bowyer. The strips, usually 2 inches in width, are laid along a flat piece of 2-inch-square wood, and a strip of waste wood a quarter-inch thick and 1¾ inches wide is laid on top to concentrate pressure along the middle of the laminations, which otherwise tend to thicken in cross-section towards the centreline of the bow. The whole is wrapped very tightly in rubber strips cut from a car inner tube, the strips for convenience being about a yard long and an inch wide. These are stretched heavily as they are wrapped, the whole developing great pressure on the bound laminates. Impatience leads to unwrapping the bow too early, and it then fails. I finally found success in leaving it two days before unwrapping. Then the limbs can be tapered to their tips, and provided the bow thickness is perfectly even, which with machined components it can be, will give a perfect bend, or tiller, to the bow. The process is straightforward but requires a very methodical approach.

If each half bow is mounted separately on either side of a gap such that the bow can be held perfectly square to the line of pull, the bullet should fly perfectly centre-shot [Fig 2.7]. The mounting will need to be very strong, and arithmetic reveals how strong. If we build a 60-pound bow with two 13-inch limbs, each sticking out of a one-inch mounting, the pull on the end of a bow limb is fully 60 pounds, and not, as might be thought at first glance, 30 pounds. This is like unto a lever, and therefore the 60 pounds is magnified twelve times into the mounting. Therefore the edge of the mounting facing the shooter, who requires some protection, must be strong enough to withstand 720 pounds. The German Kugelschnepper which was the forerunner to the English bullet-shooting crossbow, had a steel tiller, and now that box-section mild steel is readily available, together with very cheap electric welders, it may be easier to weld up a tiller than to make one of wood. I am a moderately competent welder, but hesitate to guarantee my workmanship to that standard, so I have never tried this with such a strong bow. I have made one this way for a wooden bow, and though it looks a little agricultural, it does work [Fig. 2.8].

A bow drawing up to 150 pounds can be drawn by hand with no mechanical leverage at all. A fit man can lift his own body weight, and this

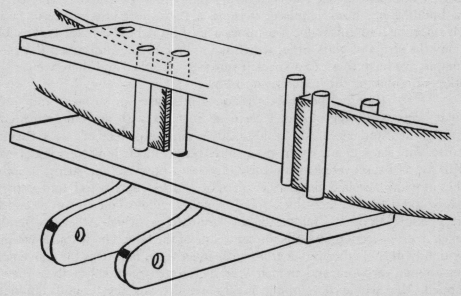

2.7 Possible 'Biplane' welded steel mounting for a centre-shot bow

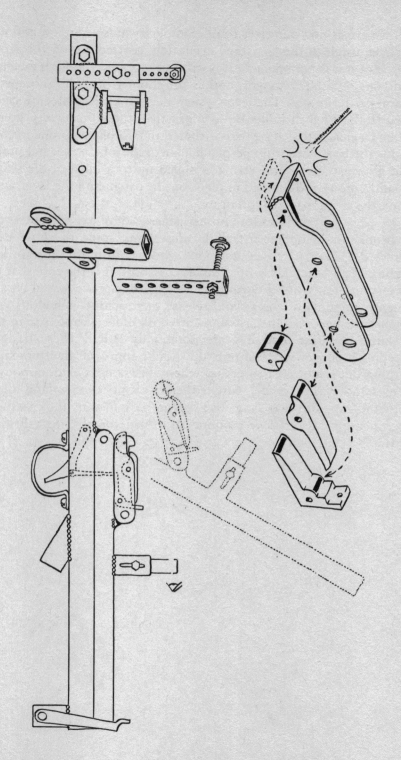

2.8 Welded steel tiller, lever and release mechanism for an 'agricultural' bullet crossbow

is all we are asking ourselves to do. Simplicity aids accuracy, and it is easier to make the catch of the crossbow accurately centred and in the same place for every shot if it is permanently housed. But repeated shooting means repeatedly lifting our own body weight, and as the shooter becomes more exhausted, so accuracy deteriorates. The lever system devised in the sixteenth century, epitomised in the English bullet-bow, is practical though the very greatest care is needed to ensure that the pivots – there are two of them, one in the stock and one for the box – are truly perpendicular to the stock. Normal practice was to build a lever whereby the string is pulled up to a third of the way back with the hands alone and hooked in place on the catch, and the lever was only used to pull the string back to full draw.

It remains for another generation of experimenters to overcome the problems. I content myself by describing some of those that must be addressed. There is, of course, one good reason for abstaining from the building of any such glass-fibre bullet crossbow. It is the case that the building and testing of any novel weapon is a dangerous process, and crossbows store immense amounts of energy and release them with tremendous violence. The fact that the bow and the crossbow are both older weapons than the gun does not dilute the fact that they are potentially lethal. These things really are exceedingly dangerous, and nobody should approach their construction with anything but the utmost care; and when once constructed, nobody should use them without the utmost care either. A King of Scotland died from an exploding gun, and two Kings of England have died by the crossbow. Modern experimenters are no less immune to violent deaths than British crowned heads.

CHAPTER 3

The yew-wood bullet crossbow

In my childhood my father indulged himself by giving me private lectures at post-doctorate level in optics. Innocent of understanding, I learnt nothing about optics, but I did learn that he needed someone – anyone – to receive the benefit of his knowledge. English clergymen have an analogous need which is guiltlessly to divest themselves of branches of yew trees overgrowing their churchyards, and being known in several parishes as a maker of bows, I became the recipient of a large amount of pruned yew boughs mostly of firewood grade. Vicars are remarkably fascinated by archery, and yew is so mythical a wood that no-one with a sense of history can simply discard it. When I lived in England the walls of my house were wainscoted with yew, so little could I bear to burn it.

A longbow can be made from two billets of yew spliced at the handle. Most bowmaking books tell us how to effect this joint, though its success depends more on the gap-filling qualities of the glue than on the gap-filling qualities that these instructions have in respect of our knowledge. Each piece of wood needs to be the length of the limb plus the length of the splice: 38 inches per billet is usually the minimum for a decent longbow, but of course shorter pieces can make shorter bows. Yet there comes a point at which, however sound a piece of wood, it is too short for even a spliced longbow.

The qualities necessary in yew wood for longbow making are that it is straight-grained, free from knots, and has a thin layer of sapwood. Bows can be made of other woods but they require much more skill on the part of the bowyer to overcome the problems posed by deviations from these desiderata.

The longbow design is dictated by a number of facts. The Americans, particularly Paul Comstock, Tim Baker and Jim Hamm who are largely responsible for the three volumes of *The Traditional Bowyer's Bible* –

a book for which the embryonic bowyer will do well to swim the Atlantic –
have shown that for the standard draw length of 28 inches, a straight bow 66
or 67 inches long will shoot faster than any other length. Yew wood of bow
quality is rare, and bowyers have always taken the logical view that a little
extra length in the bow buys safety at the expense of only a small amount of
efficiency. Otzi, the copper age Ice Man, had with him an unfinished yew bow
one-and-an-eighth times his own height. Edward IV ordained in 1465 that
everyone between 16 and 60 years of age should have a bow measuring
between the nocks his own height plus a fistmele. My fistmele, which is the
width of the palm plus outstretched thumb, measures a tenth of my height.

Doubling the thickness of a bow makes it eight times as stiff, so
heavy draw weights are achieved by a little extra thickness, but this of course
increases the stresses in the wood. A bow twice as thick is, quirkily, only four
times as strong but since it is eight times as stiff, every bowyer I know will
unhappily agree that it's twice as likely to break. Since a bow twice as thick will
recoil only twice as fast, a little extra length is good insurance. Rather than
worrying about beam theory, we can convince ourselves that making an over-
long bow is the same as not pulling the string back quite so far. Beam theory
does say that a bow twice as long is half as strong but eight times as bendy, but
unfortunately the shape of a bow limb makes everything so complex that even
as brilliant a physicist as Dr. Paul Klopsteg declared the stresses due to bow
length alone cannot really be analysed.

Despite its simplicity, beam theory is so confusingly stated and
so replete with algebra as to bring a cloud of unknowing over the most diligent
student. Studying my various engineering textbooks I am never certain I have
fully understood it, so I am always reduced to clamping wooden laths to table-
tops and dangling 2-pound weights off them to measure the deflections. This
can be done with a piece of common pine 3/4-inch wide, and such weights as
can be quietly taken from the kitchen without disturbing their guardian. I used
a 1-kilogram weight, which is more-or-less 2 pounds. A 1/2-inch thick bit of
pine 3/4-inch wide and 32 inches long, deflected 2 inches with a kilogram on the
end. Reduced to 16 inches, it only deflected a 1/4-inch. Gluing two such bits of
pine sideways together, to make a strip 1 1/2 inches wide, gave a 1-inch
deflection for a 32-inch length, while gluing two bits together to give 1 inch
thickness gave a 1/4-inch deflection for a 32-inch length. Those who object that
the glue will have stiffened things up had best look up 'neutral plane of
bending' somewhere [Fig. 3.1].

One could of course double the width of a such a bow to make
it twice as strong but we seldom come across a piece of yew which is obliging
enough to yield bow-grade wood both long enough and wide enough to give
us this option. Yew, as an interested party once wrote, does not grow that way.

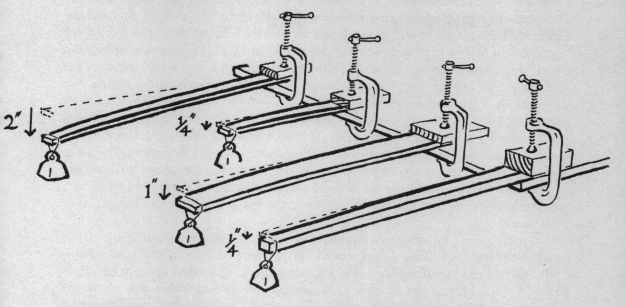

3.1 Half as long is eight times as stiff. Twice as wide is twice as stiff. Twice as thick is eight times as stiff.

Yew does, of course, grow in short lengths with beautiful unblemished sapwood and no knots at all, even if these short lengths are usually slightly bent or twisted. Bent wood is workable and, if it bends away from the final bend in the bow, it is advantageous, since this allows pre-stressing of the wood, and that gives us a little additional velocity. Too much of this bend is disadvantageous in that it results in pre-stressing to the point of over-stressing, and over-stressed yew breaks with a very loud bang.

A sideways bend in a piece of yew is often a profound disadvantage. The forces in a bent bow are such that at full draw, both hands of the shooter, and both limb-tips of the bow, lie on a single plane. If the handle of the bow is cacked over to one side, the bow full-drawn simply twists in the hand so that these four points do indeed lie in a plane. Some bentwood bows will oblige us by positioning the handle in line with the limb-tips and these do not suffer from twist; some won't.

If, however, the handle of a badly bent piece of yew is firmly wedged into the stock (or, to use the old term, tiller) of a crossbow, this tendency of bow handle, tips, and centre of the drawn string all to lie on a plane, can be resisted, and if the limb-tips bend upwards, the line of flight of the arrow will run clear of the bow. We can live with a state of affairs where this does not obtain provided we restrict ourselves to the shooting of arrows, but our special interest is in shooting a bullet, and here we must be more careful. The head of an arrow lies, at full draw, to the side of a bow, and provided the arrow is stiff enough not to break on being shot, the rest of the arrow will follow the head past the side of the bow. This presents well-known, well-documented and well-filmed problems about spine (the whippiness) of the arrow shaft, which do not concern us at all. Shooting a bullet means we absolutely must ensure that the centre of the bow does not lie on a plane with the limb-tips and the centre of the drawn string. For a stonebow we deliberately select a billet wherein the centre is offset from the limb-tips. There has to be clearance for the flight of the bullet. Fortunately we can find plenty of pieces of yew where the centre is offset from the limb-tips. Longbow makers are constantly having to chuck them out. I hold a personal theory that this is a possible origin of the crossbow: it allows the longbow-maker to use more of his wood.

The crossbow-maker, therefore, can use wood which is of no use to the longbow-maker, and indeed may prefer such wood. But a warning is necessary. For the purpose of bullet-crossbow making a sideways cant to a bow is a Good Thing, but if this is accompanied by an otherwise desirable backwards cant – what bowyers call reflex – the bow will often twist its string backwards on being braced, and render itself perfectly useless. Therefore we seek out wood which has a deflex as well as a sideways cant, and as this is of no value for any other purpose whatever, we seize upon it with glee [Fig. 3.2]

To be of any practical as opposed to merely experimental use, a crossbow must be physically small. A long bow and a long stock is an encumbrance among the hedgerows. A small bow can only be drawn a short distance, and since energy derives from the distance drawn multiplied by the weight drawn, it follows that a short bow must have a high draw weight.

Unfortunately a high draw weight requires a stout bow, and a stout bow is physically heavy. I built such a bow: it was 51 inches between the nocks, had a draw length of 14 inches and a draw weight of 196 pounds. In theory it should have been equal in

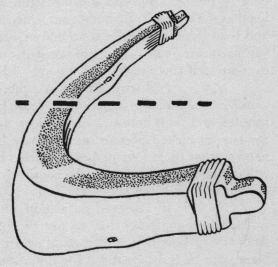

3.2 Yew bow for a crossbow with both sideways cant and deflex

performance to a bow of 98 pounds and 28 inches draw. But having a mass of exactly 2 pounds, its recoil from full draw was slow, and in order to shoot efficiently it needed a very heavy projectile, and in order to survive it needed a very heavy string, weighing 340 grains. It shot a 3¾-ounce arrow at 125 fps (a sort of aerial club), and a 2½-ounce arrow at 145 fps, and requiring as it did a bending lever to span the string, I did not use it much. A good cricketer, we read, can throw a 5½-ounce ball at 132 fps. The armies of antiquity had slingers, who were presumably more efficient, but we know not how much more efficient. Today's researchers have not attained the degree of skill requisite to sling a stone through an electronic chronograph, and the Biblical slingers of Benjamin's army who did have this skill did not have the electronic chronograph. As they were perfectly able to discomfit their enemies, I note (uncomfortably) that possession of a chronograph is not essential. I like my chronographs.

Are higher velocities possible? A much smaller bow, with a 10-inch draw, a 65-pound draw weight, and a string weighing 60 grains shot an arrow weighing 150 grains at 150fps and one of 49 grains at 206 fps [Fig. 3.3]. Such high velocity – for yew – suggests a low bow mass, and having a length between the nocks of only 25 inches, a width at the centre of 1 inch, and a midlimb thickness of ⅝-inch, such is the case. But high velocities are achieved by dramatically reducing bullet weight, and unfortunately physics being what it is, this results in dramatic reductions in efficiency. Either a lot of energy is removed from the bow by a heavy bullet, or a little energy is removed from it by a light bullet; the remaining energy remains in the bow, and if too much of it remains in the bow, the bow will break with a loud bang. So reducing the bullet weight to get a high velocity endangers a yew bow: it seems, from current experience, that somewhere around the 200 fps mark is as high as you can go.

For the mathematically-minded, in 1947 Klopsteg, Hickman and Nagler published *Archery, the Technical Side* in which they went into the physics of bows and arrows in some detail, and for all practical purposes they noted that one-third of the string weight may be considered as arrow weight, and that the velocity is inversely related to the cube root of the arrow weight. The figures just given above for the small yew bow bear this out:

$$170 \div 69 = 2.464$$
$$\sqrt[3]{2.464} = 1.35$$
$$1.35 \times 150 \text{ fps} = 203 \text{ fps}$$

One third of the string weight is 20 grains, so the arrows may in each case be regarded as 150 + 20 = 170 grains, and 49 + 20 = 69 grains. 170 divided by 69 is 2.464. The cube root of 2.464 is 1.35. 150 fps times 1.35 is 203 fps. This isn't quite the measured 206 fps of the lighter arrow, but it is a pretty good approximation.

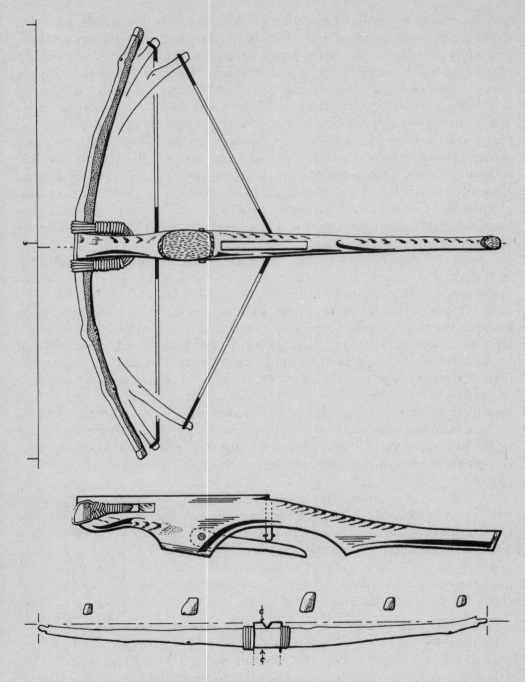

3.3 Top and centre: *All-wood crossbow*
Bottom: *Yew bow, 25 inches long*

Let us concern ourselves with each aspect of this in order. First we need our piece of yew. Making a bow has been described in such detail in so many books that any discussion here is to some extent a repetition, and to attempt to deal with it in as little space as I have available is to court failure, so I shall confine myself to that which is the concern of the crossbow-maker, and indeed more specifically to the maker of wooden stone-bows.

The crossbowman can use pieces of yew far shorter than can the longbow-maker, and since long pieces of good yew are very much rarer than short pieces of good yew, we will later kick ourselves if we use anything other than the poorest of wood, for nobody on earth who ever made a bow was satisfied with that first one. Do not be deceived into thinking this puts us at a disadvantage, either in the making or later in the shooting. With short wood, there is less woodwork to be done, and the tips of a short bow, equally strong and equally bent, recoil at a speed proportional to the inverse square of the limb length – that is, a bow half as long will recoil four times as quickly.

With poor wood, it doesn't matter too much if the bow breaks on the tiller, and in fact we want to be taking our wood so close to the limits of its performance that this must happen from time to time; my descriptions of yew breaking with a loud bang are reported with considerable personal authority. But we are not unduly concerned, although nowadays we do take such precautions as experience determines necessary (eye protection is always wise, however troublesome it may be) and accept that the risk adds a little zest to the proceedings. I so much enjoy making little yew bows, and so little enjoy making their strings, that I would rather build the bow to the string than the other way round. To every bowyer who raises an eyebrow, I merely repeat the old adage, 'each to his own'.

A good start is a section of bough about two to three feet long and about two inches in diameter. Ideally a length is chosen without any knots, and the crossbowman intending to make a small bullet-bow can find a good number of suitable pieces. Ideally, too, the wood is freshly cut from the tree; if so, take the bark off immediately with a blunt knife-blade made from the shinbone of a cow; this will prevent too much damage to the sapwood underneath. I once tried old, dead wood which, I reasoned, was nicely seasoned in situ. It didn't work, for though hard it was brittle. Woods other than yew can be used, of course, though the success will depend on how they are made – I have found laburnum, which the French call *bois d'arc* (wood of the bow) to be excellent, and both ash and elm work perfectly if wide and thin enough. I have successfully made leaf-spring crossbows from wide sections of bamboo, and because each leaf is hardly stressed they can be shot with very light arrows without endangering the strength of the bow wood. But bamboo does not come with a sideways cant, and I have fought shy of a bullet-bow of this material.

The great advantage of fresh wood is its ease of working. It is wet, soft and tough. When cut to roughed-out dimensions, it seasons very quickly; in as little as a fortnight in a warm, dry house. I have frequently been rash enough to make the bow there, then and fresh from the tree, and have watched long weathering checks appear, but alarming as they seem I haven't broken a bow with them in it yet. This does not mean I won't, for they are undoubtedly localised weaknesses, and with repeated bending they will get worse and finally give way. If a yew billet is left it in its roughed-out state for a month, the checks appear less frequently or not at all.

If the branch is already seasoned, we take the bark off very carefully with a draw knife, and try not to damage the surface of the white sapwood that lies underneath, for this surface will be the back of our bow, and will take the tension of the bow at full draw. The heartwood will take the compression and although it be flat, we will refer to it as the belly of the bow. Using the raw outside of the tree – minus bark – vastly simplifies the workload, and I try to pretend that thick sapwood such as is often found is of little disadvantage. It may be true, because crossbows are held at full draw for as much as half a minute before being shot, unlike handbows, and wood held at full strain needs as much help as it can get. Certainly this is the view of the distinguished English bowyer Chris Boyton, who preserved the thick sapwood in the yew crossbows he built for the Royal Armouries. But where the bow-back is too curved in cross-section – 'crowned' the Americans call it – or where the sapwood is too thick for there to be a heartwood belly, I will cut the back of a flatbow down until it has a flat surface, allowing only that the layers of sapwood are fairly parallel with the length of the bow, which means that their fibres are largely intact. Flat crossbow laths are wide and a wide bow-back is less imperilled by damaged rings of sapwood than a narrow back may be.

If – as is always the case so I don't know why I say 'if' – I'm using a short section of a bough, I cut each end of the section neatly with a saw, and examine it carefully. There will be a discrete layer of white sapwood, and a centre section of lustrous red-brown heartwood. Very rarely indeed does the pith run down the centre of the sapwood in a bough; generally it runs close to the top of the bough as it has grown out of the tree, and there, too, will the sapwood be at its thinnest. It is not entirely true to say that we must split the bough, though this is easily the quickest method of obtaining our bow blank. For short lengths, the grain won't usually twist (all grain twists to some extent) out of the side of the bow, and for the short lengths we need, a little twist in the bow hardly matters.

Splitting short logs is quite easy even if the wood is dry. The secret is to ensure the split bisects the section of the limb, so that neither half-bough is stronger than the other. I like to split along the pith, and this deter-

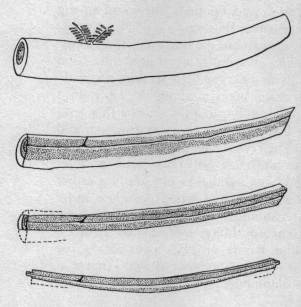

3.4 *Bough to bowstave*

mines exactly where the split must be, since there is only one line which bisects the bough and passes through the pith at the same time [Fig. 3.4]. Horizontally-growing boughs tend to have a pear-shaped cross-section with the thickest sapwood on the under-surface (i.e. nearest the ground), and a preponderance of pins from which grow leaves, on the upper surface, (i.e. nearest the light source). On splitting the limb in two, the bowyer must contend either with extremely thick sapwood or an enormous number of knots; or if the split is made vertically through the cross-section of the bough, a combination of both problems. The ideal bowstave is long, unblemished, even and has a flat layer of white sapwood of about a quarter-of-an-inch in thickness. Fat chance. Yew is normally short, or bent, or of twisted grain, or knotty, or having a thick layer of sapwood. The art of the bowyer is to accommodate the defects as best he can, and learning the art is done by trial and many errors, each of which reveals itself with a loud bang. But making a short bow for a crossbow is not as difficult as I once imagined. The Norwegian whaling crossbows had a bow little more sophisticated than a split balk of timber about an inch thick and about two inches wide for the entire bow's length. Any problems of stress concentrations at the middle of the bow were crudely dealt with by arranging a draw length of a quarter of the bow length. That such an approach can produce a workable bend may be demonstrated by swinging a large weight from the living branch of a living yew tree. In my enthusiasm for experiment, swinging on such a branch, I once found that a diameter of two inches will support a mass of 150 pounds with a deflection reminiscent of that expected from the tip of a crossbow lath. On that particular occasion it was disconcerting to find the vicar and the verger watching my antics with interest from the church porch – I was not known as the most pious of parishioners in the village.

The Americans have shown us that we don't actually need sapwood for a yew bow, though I have handled a heartwood-only yew flatbow made by Roy King (the bowyer to the Mary Rose Trust), and dated 1985 – before the Americans published their works on bowmaking. It was stamped

'45# @ 26"', though when I examined it, it drew 50 pounds, the wood having dried a little more and become stiffer since it was finished.

When the bough is split we rough out the bow to its final shape – viewed, that is, from the target. Yew, like all woods, is stronger in tension than in compression, and yew longbows, with a curved belly section, generally show some chrysalling, or small compression creases, along the belly. In a curved section chrysals are self-limiting in width but in a flat section they tend to spread across the whole width of the bow and lead to its destruction, and there isn't much you can do about it. Their characteristic diamond shape, instantly recognisable even to someone who has only ever read of their existence, is due to the fibres of the wood lying parallel to one another rather like pieces of string glued together; as each fibre of wood detaches under compression, it piles up on the next one's shoulder, and the shoulder in turn gives way to the extra stress it's having to accept. I have several such flatbows, and I am vastly proud that the chrysalling has taken place over almost the entire surface of the belly, showing that it is the rogue piece of wood that is at fault, and not my skill in tillering. If this diamond-shaped chrysalling appears, we abandon the piece of wood.

I like a width at the centre of about an inch and a bit – I have one bow, split from the rim of a completely hollow tree that came down in a gale, which is three feet long, two inches wide in the centre, and perfectly flat. But it is a rare piece. Most are much narrower than this. If a piece of wood is perfect but for a single knot, then we 'raise' the knot, which means leaving a little extra thickness around it, and since it strengthens the locality according to the square of the thickness, it should protect the area against disaster. How much to leave? Roy King's raised knots are slight, and gently merge with the bow limb, preventing stress concentrations which are the big danger with stiff sections of a bow limb.

The width of the bow tapers from the centre to the nocks. The nocks cut into the sides – not the belly, and not the back – and I smooth them with a small round file such as can be found in the woods where lumbermen carelessly discard those they use for sharpening their chainsaws.

The physicist tells us to taper the width to zero, but then there isn't anything to hold the loops of the bowstring. Yew, particularly, is prone to splitting, but binding linen thread round the shoulders of the bow-nock, and soaking it liberally in glue, protects against this misfortune even if it adds little to the beauty of the weapon. If the limb is 5/8-inch wide at the tips, a stump 1/4-inch wide is enough for the string to sit in a nock. Longer bows may need narrower stumps lest too much speed-robbing weight is attached to the limb-tips, but crossbows are very short and short bows have a rapid rate of recoil.

Then the bow is tillered, the heart of the craft of bowmaking.

A straight bow can be mounted on a wall tiller, and with a strong and rather too long string, progressively bent. Assorted pulleys, mounted below the holding point of the bow on the wall, allow the maker to view it as the string is drawn, and bow-making is nothing more complicated than scraping until it is thinner any bit of bow which appears too stiff. To make a longbow I resort to some kind of bending gauge, but crossbow laths are short enough to be done by even the most unskilled eye. If the crossbow lath has some side-set to it, it will twist on a wall tiller, so it has to be fixed firmly in the stock of the crossbow before being bent. I use G-clamps, but pad them against the bow with soft pine to prevent damage.

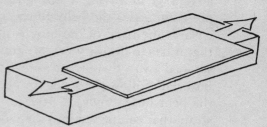

3.5 Removing the burr from a cabinet scraper on the oilstone.

Some bowmaking books speak of 'training the wood' to bend. Paul Comstock, rather more precisely, has explained that what happens in a bent piece of wood is the wood-cells of the belly of the bow, under compression, begin sequentially to collapse until a stable state is reached. If the tillering is too rapid, this steady period of cell collapse doesn't happen until the bow is already in use, and then what happens is what has occurred all too frequently, especially to elm bows built by me – a concentration of wood cells have collapsed in one zone of a limb, and I am left with a 'hinge' in the limb, which is impossible to repair. Even scraping the rest of the bow thinner and accepting a reduced draw weight doesn't work, perhaps because of cell collapse deep in the limb at the hinge. Wood is stronger in tension than in compression, and if there is a thin point compression collapse always occurs.

3.6 Squaring the edge of a cabinet scraper.

So Comstock showed that, when once a bow is bending, there is a great

3.7 Raising the new burr on a cabinet scraper.

advantage in leaving it strung for a day before proceeding with the work. This pre-compresses the belly fibres, and reveals strong and weak patches; it also ensures the back of the bow is up to the task of containing all the stretching that it has to do. As work progresses, and the most compressed belly fibres are scraped away, there is advantage in again leaving the bow strung for a day. The bow will 'follow the string' or become permanently deflexed in the direction of the bent bow. Bowyers strive to avoid this because it reduces the amount of strain that can be fed into the wood as the arrow is drawn. But if the option is a broken or a hinged bow, a little deflex is a Good Thing.

As for tools, anything will do. Our forebears used flint. I was given a beautiful cooper's drawknife, with convex blade, and have learnt its characteristics so well that I use it for scraping as well as everything else. A rasp and a cabinet scraper are good, and provided the latter is sharp, it is a beautiful tool to use. A cabinet scraper is a rectangle of thin steel. To sharpen it, first rub it flat on an oilstone to take off any burr [Fig. 3.5]. Next hold it perpendicular to the oilstone, using a block of wood as a guide, and rub each edge until that too is square [Fig. 3.6]. Clamp the scraper in a vice, and with a hardened steel tool – I use an old file, ground smooth for the purpose – rub this edge hard a dozen times as if deliberately trying to ruin the edge of a penknife blade [Fig. 3.7]. This creates a tiny and very sharp burr. The cabinet scraper is held with both hands, fingers and thumbs bending it to a curved section, and rubbed along the bow with the burr lightly biting into the surface of the wood. Sharpening it is difficult to describe and yet in one simple demonstration from a woodworker, you will learn all you need to know of it.

I try to bring the belly of the bow to a perfectly flat surface, but I always start with a very slightly curved surface [Fig. 3.8]. It is much easier to reduce the thickness that way – easier to take off the top of the 'hill' as it were, along the length of the bow. The aim is to ensure that the thickness tapers very slightly from centre to nocks,

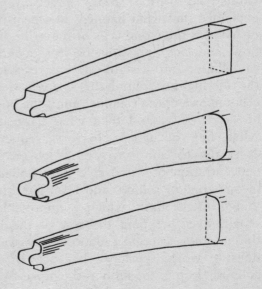

3.8 Bowstave to bow. The flatbow is always formed by reducing a rounded section.

always and constantly getting thinner. All sorts of gauges can be used, but finger and thumb, run down the length with bow-limb pinched lightly between them, reveal instantly any localised thickenings or thin patches. Thickenings are not too dangerous, but any local thin patch absolutely requires the bow-maker to thin the sections on either side to restore the constant taper. Neglect this and the bow will fail at the thin section, because the bits at either side feed the bow's curvature into the weakness – a stress concentration. But every wooden bow has uneven strength along its limbs and some variation is inevitable. Fortunately wood is a fibrous material, and therefore forgiving of minor mistakes. It will not snap across a scratch, as plate glass will. If it does break, so what? We simply make another bow. The first bow we ever make, scraping nervously and testing constantly, will take about eight hours to tiller. The twentieth bow will take about half an hour. Truly, there is no substitute for experience, though it may be reassuring to mention that with care, there is no reason why that first bow should not work very well. My first is still shooting perfectly. But of course, there are two safeguards one learns – first, don't shoot a wooden bow on a frosty winter's night because the wood goes brittle with the cold and breaks with a loud bang; and second, if a bow hasn't been shot for a while, leave it strung overnight to re-compress the belly fibres before shooting it. The belly wood may have expanded over time, and if the bow is strung up and shot straight away this may over-stress the back fibres so that the bow breaks.

As with all bowmaking the power depends on combining a long draw length with a high draw weight. Of these, a long draw length is by far the most important, because it allows a longer period of time for energy to be transferred from bow to bullet.

A good weight to aspire to is around 100 pounds at around 14 inches of draw length. I aim for this, become terrified of breakage at 80, and accept 75 which after a time drops to 70, where it settles. Occasional bits of yew give higher draw weights. Equally, they often break.

The physicists, who enjoy nothing more than speculating about bowery, have given us a body of knowledge to suggest when a bow actually will break. Yew will safely withstand a strain of 1%, but so will most other materials for that matter. In fact Roy King's bow proved that heartwood alone will stand a strain of 1% (being more curious than reverent, I measured it), but to exceed this, sapwood on the back seems to be necessary. To measure the strain directly, tape one end of a piece of paper to the back of the bow, and mark on the wood the other end. Then brace the bow and pull it to full draw, and smooth the piece of paper along the back of the bow and mark the end again. Using an A4 strip of paper, which is 297 millimetres long, it will be seen that there is a gap between the two marks, and if the gap is 2.97 millimetres (I can measure to an accuracy of about a quarter of a millimetre, so 3 millimetres is about right) then the wood is strained by 1%. If the gap is 4 millimetres the strain is around 1.33%.

Unfortunately this crude method measures only the overall strain, which means that a thick piece of wood at the centre of the bow may be bending very little while the much thinner tips of the bow are bending far more. My favourite yew bullet-bow has withstood an overall strain of 1.55%, but before I backed it with vellum – which backing may otherwise be thought to explain its performance – it took a higher strain still. Indeed, this bow which is 29½ inches between the nocks, was given an initial bracing height of 1¾ inches, and drew 98 pounds at 14 inches, so with a mid-limb thickness of 15 millimetres at the crown the strain here could well have been approaching 2%. Even I grew scared at this point, and since backing it with vellum (vellum is calfskin, and a covering can be carefully glued to the back of the bow with casein glue; the theory is that this protects individual wood fibres from splitting away from the back, thus preventing rupture) I have not drawn it beyond 13 inches, where its draw weight settled at 70 pounds.

The relationship of strain to draw length is a mathematical one. The radius of curvature of a bow is equal to the thickness of the bow, divided by twice the strain. If the thickness of wood is half an inch, at 1% strain the bow will describe part of a circle whose radius is 25 inches. The complication is that the thickness at the crown of the limb is more

$$\frac{\text{thickness}}{\text{strain} \times 2} = \text{radius of curvature}$$

than half an inch, and only at the edges is it a half-inch. Further, the curve of the bow at full draw is almost never the arc of a circle. It is thought that a crowned limb, whether the crown is on the back of the bow or the belly, allows the less strained fibres at either side of the crown to support those more highly strained in the middle. The mechanics of this defy imagination, but the fact that yew bows regularly exceed the limits of strain which the theoreticians dictate, shows that either such support is going on or that the theories are all wrong. But yew is a natural material and the grain is of unknown complexity, and theories dreamt up in the absence of hard data are rarely dependable.

Another method of deciding a draw length is to think of a number which relates arrow length to bow length. Tim Baker's finding that the fastest 28-inch arrow comes (in a straight bow) from a 66 or 67-inch bow, suggests that this number is 2⅜. If the crossbow's draw length is to be 12 inches, we multiply this by 2⅜ and the distance between the nocks should therefore be 28½ inches, so every effort at the tiller should be devoted to ensuring that the yew lath of this length is as thick as it possibly can be without breaking. Naturally this point can never be arrived at, because either the wood will survive, in which case the thought will be ever-present that it was made too thin, or the wood will suddenly break with a loud bang in which case an air of regret will accompany the realisation that it should have been a bit thinner.

Therefore the best guidelines I can offer based on experience rather than theory are that a 28½-inch flatbow, 1⅜ inches wide at the centre, a whisker over half-an-inch thick at midlimb, ought to have a draw weight of somewhere between 60 and 80 pounds at 12 inches draw length. A wider bow can be correspondingly heavier, or it can aspire to the same weight, in which case it will probably be more durable. A longer bow will also be more durable, but will not shoot as quickly. A shorter bow will not shoot more quickly either, and may well be less durable. In hot dry climates, or in bitterly cold weather, the wood will be more brittle and the bow will need to be longer to survive.

Next, we fix the bow in the tiller. This is not like the tiller used to develop the curve of a longbow. This is the tiller, or stock, of the crossbow itself, as it will finally appear.

Elm is a good wood for a tiller, being very hard to split. I have a stonebow which simply presses into a transverse slot cut in the top of an elm tiller, the yew wood protected, and squared, by thin slips of hard leather glued in place on the centre of the bow. The bow is lifted out, still strung, for transport. Otherwise, and certainly for a first attempt, it is as well to cut a hole through the tiller which fits, as far as possible, the centre section of the bow.

The minimum width (as viewed by the shooter) for the tiller seems to be about three quarters of an inch, and the maximum about two inches, though it has to be said that wide tillers make it especially difficult to get a good fit of the bow in the hole. I have found the easiest way to do this – since yew bows are never uniform in section about their centre – is to cut a piece of cardboard, and in it cut a hole to the approximate size of the centre of the bow, and to drop this down the bow limb: it is easy to see where more hole needs to be made to get the card to slide all the way down to the middle, and there to sit tightly. The card is then used as a template on the tiller itself.

For a bullet to fly freely we need clearance between the string and the top surface of the tiller. If the bow is canted to the top edge, well and good: otherwise it will need to be braced, and then held in the hole in the tiller at such an angle that the string is free of the tiller. Additionally, of course, there will be two strings separated by pillars, so this clearance needs to be sufficient to admit half the width of our proposed bullet to fly past the tiller unscathed, plus a bit for vibration. Therefore, tie a piece of thread between the nocks and check that this pleasant state of affairs exists before much work is done on the tiller. Ancient stonebows commonly have a downward curve where the string flies free, usually unnecessarily exaggerated; but free flight is essential to the intrinsic accuracy of the weapon. A heavy bullet has too much momentum to get knocked off course over 25 yards by air molecules, but it can very easily get knocked a whisker off course by skimming bits of crossbow tiller. Bearing in mind Dr Flewett's shooting, it can be seen that the free-flying bullet-crossbow is more accurate than many air rifles at their suitably limited, and equivalent, ranges.

The hole itself is cut with a chisel. I have tried an electric router, but for a good fit I have always had to finish the hole with hand chisels. It is sensible to remove the bulk of the wood with a drill, or brace and bit. The chisel I like is a quarter of an inch wide, and very sharp: even so, final fitting of bow to hole takes an hour or two. It need not, of course, for as soon as the bow breaks I will have to glue little pieces of leather or wood into the hole to pad it for the centre section of the replacement bow, and yew is not so kind as always to grow in identical sections. No matter: I like making holes with my chisel. It puts me in spiritual touch with my forebears. No mediæval craftsman had an electric router.

The bow lath is now introduced to its resting-place, and small wedges can be driven gently into the hole to hold it in place. I like to make these of bamboo, about two inches long and a quarter of an inch wide, feathering to nothing in their thickness, something very easily done on a bench grinder. Ashwood, or dry sapwood of oak, which is softer than heart of oak, is perhaps more European. An advantage of wedging is that the bow can be squared in the tiller; that is, the string made perfectly perpendicular to the top view of the line of flight. The sensible craftsman also lashes the bow in place with stout cord, of which nylon is readily available. An ugly, but easier alternative, is a long thin strip of rubber cut from a bicycle wheel's inner tube. If this is used in tension as a binding, its capacity to hold the bow immovably in the tiller is phenomenal, and if the last wrapping is tucked into itself so it can be pulled free as one undoes a bootlace, the bow can be swiftly removed should swift removal suddenly be required, as occasionally happens where bullet-crossbows are concerned.

Next we worry about the release mechanism [Fig. 3.9]. The levers of the trigger mechanism I make from cow bone. The simple revolving nut – a cylinder with rebates for the bowstring, arrow and sear – is proven by

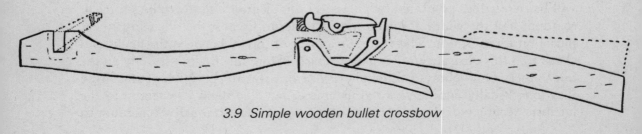

3.9 Simple wooden bullet crossbow

generations of makers, and since the bowstring has a loop at its centre and does not shoot an arrow there is no need to cut an arrow slot in the nut like those we see in museum crossbows. Bone is an adequate material, though we read that the stump of red deer antler is both the traditional material for crossbow nuts and six times as strong as ordinary bone. I incline to scepticism on the latter claim because no suggestion was offered as to how one might go about measuring this strength. Nevertheless I do equip my crossbows with a nut turned from the stump of the antler of a red deer simply because I happ'd by chance on a deer farm in Scotland, and the skulls of those shot were thrown into a ditch by the side of a track. The antlers had been hacksawed off, but I took away twenty or thirty male skulls, to my wife's disgust, and set about them with a hammer. It is astonishingly difficult to smash the top of a deer's skull with a hammer; the skull is a good deal bouncier than anyone without prior experience can anticipate. Anyway, when suitably smashed I cut away all the unnecessary bits of skull with a machete and now have a bag with a great many of these stumps of antler. As large a circle as the material admits is wise, but the thickness of the disc from which the nut is formed, is decided by the width of the bullet to be shot. Half an inch will shoot a half-ounce ball. The nut is best turned on a lathe, but a fair job can be done with care and little more than a file [Fig. 3.10]. We are apt to set too much store on machinery.

It is, incidentally, extremely difficult to find any British antler stumps big enough to give as large a diameter and as great a width as those described by Mr. Credland. But deer grow larger in America and New Zealand and may have grown larger in mediæval Europe. A cord through a central hole will prevent the loss of the nut in a coppice frequented by pheasants some dark, windy winter's night.

The nut sits in a hollow cut in the top of the tiller, perhaps reinforced at the front with a block of hardwood. A little ingenuity will work out a way of communicating movement of some kind of trigger to some kind of intermediate lever which will release this nut.

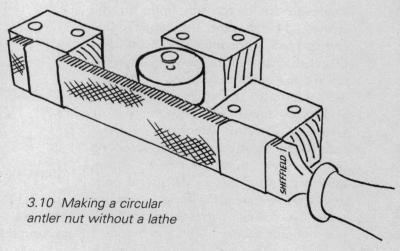

3.10 Making a circular antler nut without a lathe

Conventionally, the trigger of a crossbow acts on a shelf cut into the nut from below, frequently reinforced with a small wedge of steel. Cunning calculation of the respective lengths of the intermediate lever can reduce the pull on the trigger, and it is worth mentioning that the actual pull on the claw of the nut is determined by measuring the vertical distance between the place the string is hooked on the nut, and the foremost point at which the nut rests on wood when it is under tension. The nut, when stationary, does not itself know it is to rotate, and while holding the bowstring it merely thinks of itself as a static lever. Therefore when the bow is spanned, the nut behaves as if it is a lever pivoted on the foremost edge, where it bears against the recess in the tiller. The leverage is that of the vertical distance between the string and the pivoting edge, divided by the distance from this pivoting edge to the sear. This second distance is irrespective of direction, and one day it occurred to me to double the distance by retaining the nut at the back, and from above. Thus the distance between the pivot and the sear was doubled, which halved the pressure on the sear. Moreover, the theory turned out to work in practice, and with the additional reduction of the secondary trigger lever, it gave a very pleasant trigger pull. If, therefore, the claw of the nut is cut quite deeply so that the string is sitting barely above the nut's centre, there will be much less force required at the nut's perimeter to stop it rotating. By extension, the most advantageous place to hold the nut and prevent this rotation until the trigger is pulled is at the rear, because this is the greatest distance from the point of pivot, which is naturally at the front of the nut [Fig. 3.11].

I therefore like to cut a single groove in the nut both for the string and for the sear. A secondary bone lever presses, from above and behind, on this shelf, and the trigger is arranged to release this secondary lever. Dispensing as it does with the groove for the sear, and with fewer rebates, the nut is stronger. Careful attention to these details can greatly reduce the stress on both the nut and the trigger release mechanism, and allows the use of bone as a trigger material without it coming under very much stress, or suffering concomitant wear.

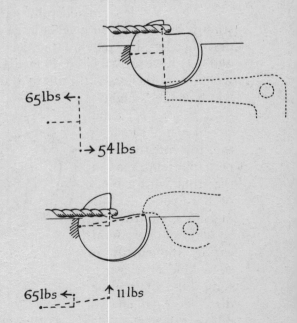

3.11 *Sear pressure on the crossbow nut can be reduced with careful geometry.*

One problem may present itself by use of the nut release, especially if the groove for the string is cut behind the vertical centre. This position will exaggerate the upward flick of the string loop at the moment of release. It is a small movement but can be quite significant because of the speed at which everything subsequently takes place. The gyrations of the string are fairly dynamic, and if the string releases the bullet when it is rotating too sharply either backwards or forwards, the bullet will receive a tiny flick either up or down just as it flies free of the bow, which can easily be enough to ruin all accuracy, and if one is remarkably unfortunate, it can plunge the bullet into the forepart of the bow. I have found it prudent when first shooting any kind of bullet-crossbow to attach a thread to the trigger, and to conceal myself behind a stout wooden board with a tiny hole drilled in it through which this thread may be pulled. A number of bullets buried half-an-inch deep in this board bear testimony to its value. My wisdom has frequently been painfully acquired.

If in any doubt, a release mechanism can be devised which allows equal movement of two jaws, as if a pair of pliers was abruptly opened. Target crossbowmen in recent years have used the mechanical string-releases favoured by many compound bow shooters, mounting them in home-made crossbow stocks.

The string occupies some time to make. We are spoilt today for there is in existence a material called Fastflight®, which is strong and light-weight. Most authors recommend a single skein, wound about many times to give adequate thickness. This must be very soundly bound at the loops to prevent slipping at the bow-nock. It certainly works for light draw weights such as 70 pounds, but for heavier bow weights, it may be better to make two separate strings of identical length but half the thickness, off-setting them by the thickness of the end loop (see Chapter 2). The pillars separating the string sit about a third of the way from the bow-nock to the pouch; too close to the pouch and they have to be accelerated too far, which uses energy, and also prevents easy closing of the pouch about the bullet as the string is drawn back. They need to be light in weight and can be made of nothing more than a tiny stick, though almost everyone makes a meal of them by turning them on a lathe out of cow-bone, the common substitute for ivory. If the pillars holding the bowstrings apart are longer than the diameter of the bullet plus double the thickness of the pouch material, then the bullet is more freely and more consistently released. I have a strong suspicion that the ultimate failure of my glass-fibre experimental bow was due to there being too small a gap between the two strings – the bullet having to flick its way free from the pouch, rather than being smoothly released. An inch between the strings is enough for a half-ounce ball, itself a whisker over half an inch in diameter.

The pouch these days is best made of a thin strip of nylon

webbing, very stoutly sewn with waxed dental floss, because on release the pouch takes a hammering, and poor sewing shows up as rapid disintegration.

The question has to be addressed as to why we use Fastflight. Sir Ralph did not, and who are we to gainsay him? I used Dacron in my first yew bullet-crossbow, and it weighed 19.82 grams (about ¾ ounce), mostly concentrated in the thick central pouch and the heavy loops. I was unimpressed with its performance as a stonebow, it being far less credible a weapon than the wrist catapult. Shooting it:

Dacron string:		
220-grain ball	127 - 138 fps	8.6 foot-pounds
140-grain ball	127 - 143 fps	5.8 foot-pounds

With a single string, however, I had found this bow shot a light arrow very quickly, something I had put down to the absence of friction, there being no arrow-channel, just a gap in the tiller between bow and nut. But when finally I considered that there may be something in the opinions of a vast array of knowledgeable bowyers (that string weight, especially concentrated at the nocking-point, absorbs kinetic energy as surely as if it were attached to the arrow), I took some Fastflight® and made a light-weight double string, using ten strands, with the separating pillars as close to the nocks as I could get them.

For the pouch I used a narrow piece of nylon webbing, and for the loops I used only four strands of Fastflight®, reasoning that they would need no more strength than the final draw-weight. This string weighed a third of the Dacron string, just 6.81 grams. Immediately it transformed the performance; it still didn't seem to want to throw a half-ounce ball with any great conviction, but a .451-calibre ball, weighing about a third of an ounce, fairly flew – indeed its kinetic energy doubled:

Fastflight string:		
.527 ball	167 - 169 fps	13.78 foot-pounds
.451 ball	197 - 200 fps	12 foot-pounds

The tiller of the stonebow prevents me shooting larger diameter balls than .527-inch, but with the lighter weight of ball there is the happy marriage of efficiency and velocity.

Any sights at all can be made, but the use of a peep-sight will allow the full potential accuracy to be harnessed. We very quickly learn that the foresight needs to be mounted sufficiently clear of the flight of the bullet so as not to be struck by it, and a safe position can be found readily by fixing pillars to the front of the bow so that stretching between them a piece of paper, or silver paper, or best of all rice paper (the bullet will smash a discrete hole through rice paper, which is made of starch and not fibres) reveals the line of flight. Then we position the back-sight and shoot into a square of paper pinned to a hanging blanket at a very short range – three yards to start with – and adjust the back-sight to match the hole in the paper. Adjusting the foresight is a mistake. Especially, adjusting the foresight downwards is a mistake. One may end up making a new foresight, or if the foresight was stoutly made, one may end up trying to grow a new eye. The bullet-bows of old had grooved pillars at the sides with the foresight affixed to a thin cord stretched between them, perhaps to avoid this misfortune. They also had a strong steel plate pierced by a small hole as the rear-sight, and this too would have afforded some armour to at least the shooting eye in the event of a rebound. But our forebears died young, and perhaps did not attach much importance to what I consider essential facial features such as my eyeballs.

An interesting optical effect is found in a rear peep-sight with a small aperture, the pinhole camera effect.

A camera works by the lens focusing that which is in front of the camera onto the photographic plate. Some parts are out of focus, and appear so on the photograph. A more ancient camera was formed by having no lens, just a tiny pinhole through which light reached the photographic plate. Since the light so doing was very dim, such photographs needed a very long exposure – minutes rather than fractions of a second. The great virtue was that both foreground and background were simultaneously in focus, the light from any point reaching the photographic plate in a single line because it had to travel through the point defined by the pinhole. As such, pinhole cameras do not suffer from spherical aberration, a standard fault in even very good refracting cameras.

If the rear aperture is a pinhole, then both foresight and target appear to be in focus simultaneously.

Unfortunately, a pinhole lets in so little light that the target is unlikely to be well-enough defined for clear aim to be taken. But pretty much the same effect, and with a marked increase in accuracy, can be found by making the rear sight hole a millimetre and a half in diameter. In an experiment, making the rearsight of a bigger aperture resulted in a poorer grouping because the target was less well focused. Yet making it smaller than a millimetre also resulted in a poorer grouping because the eye does not then receive enough light to define the target. The results shown were shot at 13 yards with a 6-millimetre foresight aperture.

Foresight aperture	Rearsight aperture	Group
6 mm	5 mm	30 mm
6 mm	2 mm	13.5 mm
6 mm	1 mm	8 mm
6 mm	0.5 mm	17 mm

No other sighting arrangement apart from the telescopic sight will allow the target to appear in focus at the same time as the foresight; and telescopes on any bow are a horrid anachronism. As has frequently been observed by riflemen, the chief advantage of the telescopic sight is to be able to see where to aim the rifle when the target is, for understandable reasons, trying to conceal itself. But shooting at silhouettes, such as certain long-tailed birds present in the bare branches on midwinter nights, can as easily be done with peep sights as with a telescope.

CHAPTER 4

Catapults

As the crossbow is the most over-rated weapon in existence, so the catapult is the most under-rated. That it is so under-rated is because other weapons are more glamorous and no-one has thought it worthwhile to discuss what seems to be so humble a thing. The evidence suggests that the rubber manufacturers have done their homework, but those who assemble catapults for retail are in as much ignorance as everyone else, relying on hunches and empirical guesswork rather than even the most rudimentary, let alone systematic, examination. It has led to the foolish use of rubber too heavy for the missile; my brother-in-law (an aficionado) noticed decades ago that the 3/16-inch square-section catapult rubber seemed to shoot faster than the 4/16-inch rubber, and he adopted the lighter material accordingly. He was right to do so, and would have been were he more than a gardener. I mention, in parentheses, that he uses a shotgun to dispatch rabbits in the cabbage patch, but finds the catapult, kept hanging by the kitchen door, effective in encouraging the neighbourhood cats to find alternative toileting arrangements. On receipt of a missile he reports that, like Dr Lambie's yelping cur, a cat can suddenly understand why it should vacate his newly-dug flower-beds.

As a weapon the catapult seems so simple a device that it ought, in Prof. Sir O. G. Sutton's phrase, to 'be relegated to the category of solved problems', so it is disconcerting to find upon close examination that it is really rather complicated. Despite the attentions of some of the most inventive weapon designers of the past century, its virtues and vices have yet to be fully understood. Consider this: among my catapults are two, identical in every respect other than the fact that one uses latex tubes of 12 millimetres diameter and has a draw weight of 28 pounds, and the other with tubes of 8 millimetres tapering down to 5 millimetres at the pouch gives a draw weight of 17 pounds. All the tubes have a 2-millimetre wall thickness. The big tubes are much the strongest, and we would expect them to shoot much the fastest. The findings belie all expectations.

The 28-pound draw weight shoots a half-ounce bullet at 163 fps.
The 17-pound draw weight shoots a half-ounce bullet at 166 fps.

How *ever* can a lighter draw weight shoot a heavy bullet faster? Take another of my catapults, again identical to the first two but for 9-millimetre tube diameters giving it a draw weight of 22 pounds. It has just obligingly shot me a half-ounce bullet at 182 fps.

Results like this will cause a scientist to doubt the rigour of the experiment – there must have been a flaw. Perhaps in shooting technique? – surely shooting a catapult cannot be a very accurate business. But there was no flaw at all. These are not only accurate figures, but they stand up to close scrutiny when we come to tease them apart.

We might ask how it is that the catapult exists at all if it is so imperfect, and perhaps the answer lies in the Darwinian model, that despite working with less efficiency than it could, the fact that it works, and the fact that there is little evolutionary pressure for it to work better, has precluded further developments. Were some government to ban all rifles, airguns and bows, the catapult would develop rather quickly in that country, and the government would probably have cause to regret its ban, because the catapult is capable of a prodigious performance, delivering up to 25 foot-pounds of energy to its target, with a short-range accuracy every bit equal to that of the hand-bow. Moreover the catapult is simple and there is merit in simplicity. For centuries the military in England foreswore crossbows in favour of longbows, and then rifles in favour of smoothbore muskets, the latter in each case having the great merit of simplicity. Even in recent times, the Hawker Hurricane, which is generally considered an inferior aircraft to the Spitfire, had a simpler and more robust airframe, and in the Battle of Britain in the early part of World War II the Hurricane accounted for roughly twice as many German aircraft as were shot down by Spitfires.

Rubber, derived from the sap of a tree, is a wonderful substance; it has great advantages to those of us wicked enough to wish to wing small missiles through the air, but pleasingly it also has a number of profound disadvantages which prevent us becoming complacent.

Principal among the advantages is the fact that rubber is both light in weight and strong for its volume, which makes the catapult an ideal thing to stash away on a country ramble. As Richard Jefferies wrote:

'Even in summer the old squire generally had his double-barrel with him – perhaps he might come across a weasel, or a stoat, or a crow. That was his excuse; but, in fact, without a gun the woods lost half their meaning to him'.

A walk without purpose is dull. A double-barrel is too often conspicuous, but a walk with a catapult in the pocket at least conveys to the walker the impression of participating in the world rather than being but an observer.

Among the disadvantages is that, as a naturally harvested material, rubber is far from uniform. My brother, an engineer who works extensively with rubber, tells me that despite tennis ball companies buying rubber exclusively from the same plantation to have control over their source material, different batches of rubber have different characteristics and necessitate the spending of a seven-figure sum on enormous, heavy, powerful homogenising machinery to mix the harvested latex. Yet even with absolute control over the manufacturing process, no two batches of rubber emerge with exactly the same bounce characteristics. Quoting him:

Natural latex is a long chain molecule, in its natural state dispersed in water. Dissolving it in petrol breaks down the chains, so you lose the property that makes it useful. Also, it is unstable with time once dried out. Which is why vulcanising was first used, and still is. You will find that the natural latex is vulcanised, too. Most rubber compounds need other properties so the latex is dried out, and then mashed in a big heavy mixer to break down the long chains. Then, or simultaneously, it is blended with the various additives (fillers, reinforcing agents, etc.). Next it is mashed up again with sulphur and accelerators and extruded to a form of consistent shape or size. As it is a thermoset, it is pretty difficult to injection mould, so generally it is compression moulded from individual blanks.

The unvulcanised blended rubber can be dissolved and poured; however, you need to remove all the solvent before vulcanising it. The vulcanising process is irreversible. It forms the long chains required for the properties associated with rubber.

Natural latex has a relatively short life. It degrades with heating and sunlight. Heating occurs often from stretching and relaxing (hysteresis loss) which is why the rubber bands from model aeroplanes don't last very long.

Latex racing bicycle inner tubes are good for cycling as they have less hysteresis loss. However, not only are they more porous, but they suffer the degradation from heating I mentioned above. Butyl rubber is used for inner tubes normally, for its heat and porosity properties. Whatever is used is selected on a basis of various properties. There are literally hundreds, maybe thousands of commonly-used rubber compounds made from natural rubber (among the cheapest polymers available) as well as wholly synthetic compounds.

He concludes with a characteristic understatement:

'The chemistry can be quite complicated, too'.

Take one of my catapults, that with the 9-millimetre diameter tubes. After a time – somewhere between 60 and 500 shots – the tubes start to show signs of fracture, usually at the pouch. Then they have to be replaced. So, measuring results of different tubes:

Tube dia.	Pull weight	Bullet weight	Velocity range	Average velocity
9 mm	22 lbs	1/2 oz	175 - 195 fps	182 fps
9 mm	22 lbs	1/2 oz	193 - 199 fps	198 fps
9 mm	22 lbs	1/2 oz	174 - 179 fps	177 fps

Every experiment therefore needs to be tempered with the caveat that among catapults, as among wooden bows, no two will give identical results. Trends can be described, but accurate prediction is impossible. This is important, for exploring the catapult's innermost workings is best done through a series of experiments.

How do we define the catapult? Ignoring Roman artillery, it can be defined as a weapon using rubber as the material that combines storage of energy, and the primary transmission of energy to a projectile. The name is by no means fixed; in Australia when I was an infant it was called a Shanghai for reasons my father never explained, and it still is; and in northern America it is called a slingshot. To the Englishman the catapult is a Y-shaped forked stick: rubber is attached to the tip of each fork, and the branch from which both tines originally sprang is held in the left hand [Fig. 4.1].

The projectile – among boys invariably a pebble – is pulled back in some kind of improvised pouch in the right hand, the whole device being shot instinctively [Fig. 4.2]. A more recent development (at least thirty years old and originating I know not whence but mine was from Canada), is the addition of a wrist brace to the base of the handle part of the forked stick [Fig. 4.3]. This

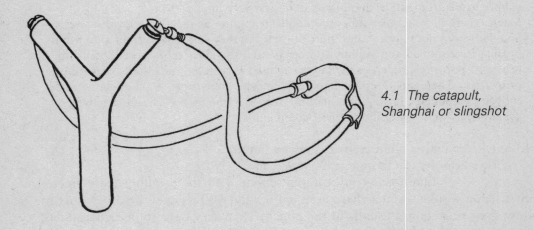

4.1 *The catapult, Shanghai or slingshot*

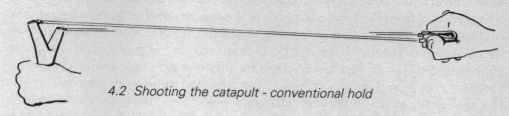

4.2 Shooting the catapult - conventional hold

transfers most of the force required to hold the forked stick upright from the left hand to the left forearm, and enables both a heavier draw weight to be used, and a steadier aim to be taken, making the catapult a thing to be taken seriously. The wrist brace commonly folds back upon the handle for the convenience of sticking it in a pocket. Why in the vast wastes of Canada one might wish to carry a concealed slingshot I truly do not know.

With this working definition, the first crossbow I ever built as a boy was a catapult insofar as it had no bow, just an inflexible flat of wood with a piece of catapult rubber where the bow and string should have been. Had I known it, this was an echo of Richard Hodges' weapons of the 1840s. Mine was a dismal failure because the rubber hopped over the release mechanism – a simple peg which protruded from the stock and was pulled downwards by the trigger – and missed the back of the arrow.

Hodges' weapons were more successful in that two ended up in the Tower Armoury, but that they did not entirely supersede all other pot-hunting weapons is not solely the consequence of the development of the smallbore rifle.

Hodges had experimented with, and patented, a series of weapons whose projectiles were propelled by what he called 'purchases'. A purchase was a latex tube of about a foot in length and about 3/4-inch in diameter, having end fastenings.

Were it not an anachronism to say it, the Hodges weapons resemble the rubber-powered fishing speargun now popular among recreational

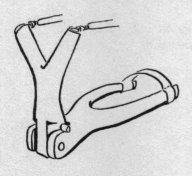

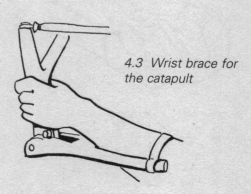

4.3 Wrist brace for the catapult

Scuba divers, differing only in that the rubber purchases were individually stretched, and from the breech forward to the muzzle, to charge the weapon. The rubber-powered speargun is sometimes called the arbalete to distinguish it from spearguns powered by a spring, by compressed air, or very occasionally by gunpowder, and as all varieties are built for different prey species the dimensions vary. Of the three I have examined, the first had rubber 'purchases', to use Hodges' term, of 15 millimetres diameter and 11 inches long. (The scientist weeps at such mixed measurements, but we blithely ignore him.) Two are fitted, linked by a twisted steel rope of 2 millimetres diameter and 35 millimetres long. The spring-steel harpoon is ¼ inch diameter and rather more than three feet long. The draw length is 36½ inches.

The second has a draw length of 49½ inches, a harpoon a foot longer, and uses four purchases. The third is the same as the second, but uses two purchases each of 19 millimetres diameter.

All the rubber used in all three spearguns is solid. The forward mounting is a moulding, tucking the middle of a long single piece of rubber out of the way under the nose of the body of the speargun so that each free end of rubber points back towards the trigger mechanism [Fig. 4.4]. The loss of energy through both creep and the cooling effect of the seawater is enormous, but the range of the harpoons is limited by the distance prey fish can be seen, and is normally 2-5 metres. E. E. Papagrigorakis states that even a pistol bullet will travel no more than 2 metres underwater.

Richard Hodges' weapons were shaped rather like the musket of his time, with the barrel slotted along its sides. A missile was introduced into the barrel in front of a 'follower', and to the sides of the follower, outside the barrel, were stretched the rubber purchases from the muzzle. A further development was the abandoning of the barrel, and a stretcher being placed at the muzzle, rather like an elongated bullet-shooting crossbow [Fig. 4.5]. Some of them still

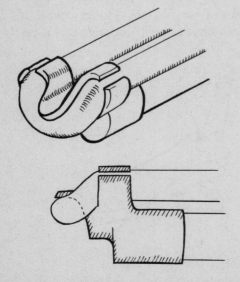

4.4 *Front mounting for rubber tubes in a speargun*

exist outside museums, and at least one has been restored to working order.

The musket idea is fairly self-explanatory, but the crossbow idea, using a lateral stretcher at the front of the weapon, is a more intelligent approach. Energy among those who shoot is measured in foot-pounds. Joules, of which there are .734 in a foot-pound, are more widely appreciated among scientists, but I shall stick to that which is already relevant to anyone possessed of an acquaintance with shooting literature. Albeit oversimplified, the energy available to shoot an arrow from a bow is equal to half the number of feet you pull back the arrow, multiplied by the number of pounds of your final draw weight.

$$\frac{\text{draw (feet)}}{2} \text{ x final draw weight (lbs)} = \text{energy available}$$

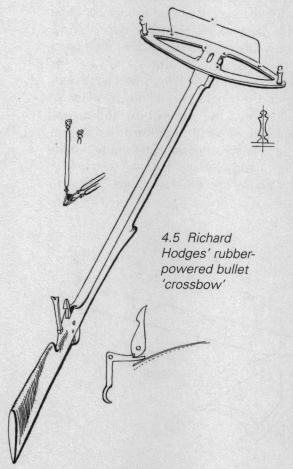

4.5 *Richard Hodges' rubber-powered bullet 'crossbow'*

If for the first foot of the draw of one of Hodges' weapons the rubber is slack, it cannot be doing any work. Suppose the 'barrel' were six feet long, and the rubber tubes at either side of the barrel were a foot long. The tubes would be working for only five feet. Now suppose the tubes were held taut on a two-foot stretcher at the front of the six-foot barrel. If we were to pull them precisely six feet again, Pythagoras tells us that the rubber tubes would make up a six-foot hypotenuse of a triangle, and with the stretcher at the muzzle of the device acting as the shortest side of that triangle, the barrel length would be five feet eleven inches. Therefore by the simple addition of using the lateral stretcher we would have lost one inch of total draw, and gained twelve inches of working draw. Overall gain: almost a sixth as much draw length, and hence, it seems, a lot more power.

Theories being of little value until tested by experiment, I built a very wide catapult, wide enough to hold the rubber tubes taut and like the string of an undrawn crossbow, at right angles to the line of fire [Fig. 4.6]. I was vexed to find I could no longer grip the bullet in its pouch with finger and thumb; to pull strongly backwards, an initial firm hold on the ball (or pebble, or marble – I use a musket-ball) must be possible, and with the rubber tubes not only pulling forwards but now also sideways, they so unsettled the grip that the pouch could not be pulled back to the full distance that I draw a catapult, and the ball involuntarily sprang from the grip at about 26 inches of draw, indenting the door-panel of a pinewood sideboard in front of which I was rash enough to attempt the draw. Thus is my house. Small hemispherical impact sites on all sorts of pieces of furniture, ranging from antique dining chairs to the garage door. Sacrifices to science.

Thus became apparent the logic of Hodges using a fixed weapon, a sort of crossbow-catapult rather than the floating draw of a hand catapult. I therefore clamped my wide catapult to the front of a plank of wood, and to the back I clamped a crossbow release mechanism. Given that the rubber tubes were seven inches long, and that Hodges had asserted that rubber could be stretched by six times its own length, the distance between the two was 42 inches. It was, of course, necessary to attach a thin cord to the back of the pouch to hook onto the release mechanism, but this was not difficult.

The device ensured that the effective draw length was increased. I pull the pouch of a catapult to just behind my right ear, a full draw of 39 inches; a good deal more than the 28-inch draw I use with a bow and arrow. Expecting therefore some improvement in velocity I was greatly surprised to find that as a consequence of all this labour, the velocity of my ball was now diminished by fully a quarter. Clearly some other factor, unsuspected, was at work.

During the Second World War, the Special Operations Executive

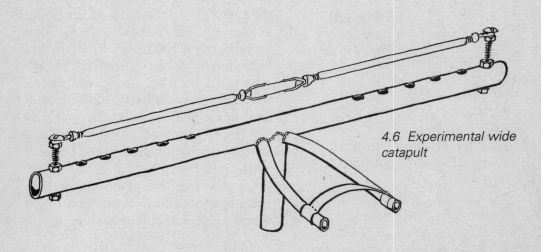

4.6 *Experimental wide catapult*

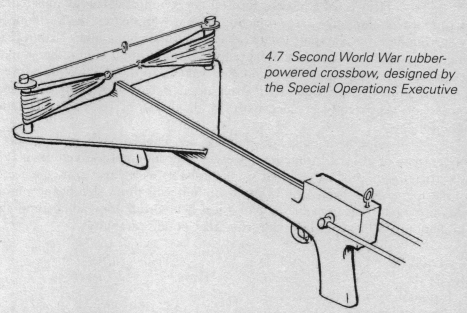

4.7 Second World War rubber-powered crossbow, designed by the Special Operations Executive

developed several shortened versions of what in essence was Hodges' design [Fig. 4.7], and from their manual we have figures describing the performance of these weapons. Their purpose was to shoot, silently, assorted missiles ranging from darts to explosive charges. The 'draw weights' were staggeringly high – upwards of 400 pounds – but the velocities of their projectiles were never more than 200 fps. The response was unenthusiastic from the soldiers to whom they were issued, very few being made and even these remaining unused on active service.

An experiment: take a large rubber band, hook it on a spring scale, and pull it until you feel there is no stretch left in it whatsoever. It will be anything from four to seven times as long as it originally was. Hold it there for 15 seconds, and watch the weight on the spring scale creep downwards. Repeating the experiment just now, a ³/₈-inch wide rubber band, 3¹/₂ inches long, had a pull of eight pounds at 23 inches, which after 15 seconds had crept down to seven pounds.

A second experiment: take the large rubber band and suddenly stretch it hard. Immediately hold the taut rubber to your lips. It feels hot, but cools down in about five seconds. This is not a new discovery; we are aware of the necessity of checking car tyre pressures when the tyres are cold, and deduce therefore that the flexing of tyre rubber by the car's rolling along generates a good deal of heat.

A third experiment: take the same rubber band, suddenly stretch it hard, then immediately relax it, and hold the floppy rubber firmly to the lips. It does not feel hot.

Heat is, of course, a form of energy and the energy must come from somewhere, and any energy which is used in warming up the air immediately surrounding our catapult isn't available to shoot our bullet. I confess to having been surprised by this discovery, which illustrates that I am rather stupid. An engineer friend to whom I mentioned it was not in the slightest bit moved, and simply reminded me that when a teaspoon is bent repeatedly the metal becomes hot. Apparently engineers are in the habit of repeatedly bending teaspoons.

Now as it happens, amongst my piano ornaments I possess a chronograph – or at least I sometimes possess a chronograph; sometimes it is in the electrician's shop being repaired – and probably as a direct consequence of this loss of energy to heat, I find that a catapult will shoot significantly more quickly if the release is immediate, than if it is held at full draw and careful aim taken. Shooting a 1/2-ounce lead ball from a 22-pound catapult:

Method	No. of shots	Velocity (fps) Range	Average
Instantaneous draw and release	7	174-195	182
1-second pause at full draw for aiming	5	175-177	176
3-second pause at full draw for careful aiming	5	166-172	168

The highest velocities are achieved by a 'snatch' release, pulling rapidly to full draw and instantly letting go. The same conclusion has been reached among archery flight shooters, who hold that even a second's pause between reaching full draw and releasing the arrow is deleterious to a long shot. Unfortunately these snatch shots are highly erratic – no disadvantage among flight shooters, of course – but a second's hold at full draw, while sacrificing 6 fps, buys both consistency and the opportunity to take reasonable aim. This is therefore the technique I favour. Three seconds' careful aim leads to a further 8 fps drop in velocity, and probably ought to be avoided. My Hodges 42-inch draw device, with its mechanical release mechanism and spreader, took 20 seconds from the moment of stretching to the moment of aimed release through the chronograph, time for an enormous loss of heat energy to the air. All Hodges' weapons must have suffered this loss, and all the Special Operations Executive weapons must have suffered it too, which accounts for their very poor efficiency.

In fact there may be a more complicated mechanism than this going on, with a degree of temporary creep in the rubber, but I have not thought of a way to investigate this and have to rely on the word of my brother the engineer, who told me that rubber heats as it stretches and begins to crystallize as it cools. After cooling, there is some residual stretch. If warmed, it should return to its unstretched form.

Certainly heat has a marked effect on velocity. I took my 22-pound catapult and kept it in the refrigerator for half an hour, and then shot ten half-ounce bullets through the chronograph, watching them get faster as the rubber warmed up.

Then I put the catapult in the back of the car for half an hour where, it being a sunny summer day, the rubber became fairly hot, before obtaining another ten readings with half-ounce bullets; compare the figures.

VELOCITIES IN FPS	
After refrigeration	*After heating*
148	181
161	186
164	184
171	179
174	177
173	182
171	179
173	172
171	167
172	183

Engineers talk of creep as the permanent distortion of something under prolonged load. Attaching a spring-scale to my catapult, I pulled it to 39 inches, at which it drew 22 pounds, and over a 15-second period I watched as the draw reduced to 20 pounds. It was not a permanent loss; after a short pause, I drew it again to 39 inches and again it registered 22 pounds pull. That this creep exists, and exists with a vengeance at higher stretches, is very certain.

We might, from this discovery, conclude that a better approach would be to abandon rubber, and replace it with more dependable steel coil-springs. However, Professor J. E. Gordon pointed out a great advantage of rubber.

A friend who was taught by Gordon recalls (whether accurately or not) that one lecture was enlivened by the professor asking a student to hold up a piece of plate armour, and from time to time he would shoot an arrow at him from a longbow. Unfortunately from the point of view of associative memory, he could not remember anything else about the lecture. Gordon did, however, write two of the most brilliant and accessible books on materials for engineers, *The New Science of Strong Materials*, and *Structures, or why you don't fall through the floor*. From these books we all borrow shamelessly; they are brilliantly written and always entertaining. He notes that a characteristic of rubber is its peculiar force-draw curve and points out, as we have all observed, that a rubber balloon is hard to blow up at first, but much easier to blow up when once it has a body of air in it. Leaving aside the added complexity of the diameter of a pressure vessel, this observation is true of all rubber, yet it is an observation which seems to have escaped the manufacturers of catapults, though not the suppliers of their rubber.

Steel obeys Hooke's law. If I stretch a steel spring six inches and the pull is six pounds, I can predict that a further six inches of stretch will increase this pull to 12 pounds and yet a further six inches of pull will take it up to 18 pounds. This, of course, is the principle behind the spring scale for weighing things like the large salmon I have never managed to catch.

Rubber does not obey Hooke's law, and a spring scale can't be made out of rubber. Suppose I got a piece of rubber and attaching a six- pound weight found it, like the steel spring, stretching by six inches. Another six pounds would stretch it to about 18 inches, not the 12 inches Hooke suggests. Adding small weights would make the rubber stretch further to surprisingly long distances, until suddenly it would seem that it had hit a wall, and large extra weights added to the rubber would only add tiny amounts of stretch, and all of a sudden, the rubber would snap.

Exactly this happens when we prepare force-draw curves for a catapult. Not least because of the temporary creep, these are difficult to obtain with any accuracy, the best makeshift being to speak weight readings into a tape recorder as the pouch is drawn back with a spring scale.

Natural rubber comes in a great many forms. The original catapults which appeared about a hundred years ago were powered by latex, but it deteriorates quite rapidly when exposed to sunlight, and before long much more heavily-vulcanised rubber, usually in square section, came to be used. But this has the huge disadvantage that it will only stretch to about two and a half times its own length, and it does not shoot very quickly at all. In the days before the electronic chronograph, longevity was valued over missile velocity. The trend today has been reversed, and catapults produced commercially are all powered with latex tubing. It still deteriorates rapidly in sunlight so we all keep our catapults in a dark bag or closed drawer. The simplest and most practical test to see if a sample of rubber will shoot quickly is to see by how much it will stretch – rubber bands stretching to four times their length won't shoot a paper pellet as fast as those that stretch to six times their length.

As Hodges pointed out, latex can be stretched to six times its relaxed length, just beyond which it 'hits the wall' and ceases to stretch very much; at some point slightly beyond this, it breaks. Since the distance I can hold my outstretched arm, and draw my other hand to my ear, is 39 inches, it seems logical to allow six and a half inches of free, relaxed rubber on either side of the pouch of a catapult. This would appear to be making all the rubber work to its limit, so that there is as little slack as possible, and every available inch of draw is doing work; work which will eventually emerge as bullet-velocity.

It is not the best system because the final few inches tend to 'stack', which is to say the draw weight goes up far more per inch at the end of the draw. Because the bullet in its pouch is held by the pinch of finger and thumb, an intrinsically weak hold, it tends to snatch itself free and release the ball before you yourself are ready to release it, which is catastrophic for accuracy. Catastrophic too for velocity, which depends far more on draw length than on any other factor. This point is always worth reiterating – the launch velocity of a bullet is the result of it being accelerated by the rubber. Acceleration is the gaining of speed over a short period of time, and the longer the time we give it to gain speed, the more speed will be gained. So the further the bullet can be pulled back, the more time it will have to accelerate and the higher its launch velocity will be.

The implication of our force-draw curve is that in the first few inches of draw, we do a great deal of useful work. I have a catapult with big, stout latex tubes, 12-millimete outside diameter, 8-millimetre bore. The total slack in the system is 12 inches, which means of course that for the first 12 inches of draw I am not putting any energy into the rubber, and my bullet is not going to derive any energy for that distance. But stretched just over six inches, the pull is already 16 pounds, and I now only need to add four pounds of pull to take the draw back a further six and a bit inches. Another four pounds gives me a further six and a bit inches of draw, and a further four pounds gives me a total of 39 inches of draw. So although my final draw weight is only 28 pounds, well over half of that has been achieved in the first six inches of stretch. Although the very first 12 inches of draw are slack, and therefore useless, the pleasant sensation of a smooth draw at the most difficult portion, behind my ear, compensates for these first useless 12 inches.

Commercial manufacturers similarly provide long latex tubes, and there is usually to be found on either side of a central pouch about 7 1/4 inches of rubber which can be stretched, and an additional inch which is immovably clamped to the catapult frame. The fact that so much of the work is done so early on in the draw means that no significant disadvantage is suffered, and there is the dual advantage of both a pleasant draw, and the rubber not being stretched to its breaking limit.

The tubing most commonly found has a bore of 5 millimetres and a wall diameter of 2 millimetres, giving it an outside diameter of 9 millimetres. Slack for the first 9 3/4 inches – the fixing to the catapult frame at one end, and the length of the pouch at the other accounting for the extra to the 7 1/4 free inches of rubber – the pull is as shown.

It has a total energy input of about 29 foot-pounds.

This force-draw curve [Fig. 4.8] is

Weight (lbs)	Pull (inches)
0	9 3/4
10	17
15	26 1/2
20	32 1/4
23-22-21-20	39

characteristic of all rubber
and to archers is reminiscent
of a well-designed recurve
bow. It means we are putting
a lot of energy into the
system early on in the draw.
Were we unwise enough to
replace the rubber with
helical steel springs, we
would expect the measure-
ments to follow Hooke's law
almost perfectly, and instead
of us reaching half the pull
within the first quarter of the

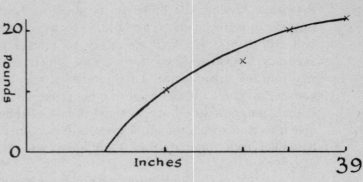

4.8 Force draw curve for rubber-powered catapult

draw, we should not achieve this until we had stretched the springs by fully half
the total stretch. We are therefore storing a good deal more energy by using
rubber than we would if we were to use spring-steel.

Rubber is very light. The energy we put into drawing the bullet
back must not only propel the bullet; it must also propel the pouch, and it must
propel the equivalent of half the weight of the rubber which is doing the work
of recoil. Rubber being light, and steel being heavy, a rubber-powered weapon
should recoil more quickly than a steel-powered weapon.

This leads us on to our next important consideration. When I
first started experimenting with catapults, knowing that energy can neither be
created nor destroyed I measured the draw weight of the 12-millimetre latex
tubes and was gratified when I saw that this was 28 pounds, a significant gain.
The 22-pound version had shot a 20-bore ball at around 163 fps. Energy is not
something that can be destroyed, so without going to the trouble of making a
force-draw curve for this new weapon I persuaded myself to hope that the
velocity of the ball powered by 28 pounds would now go up to perhaps 184 fps,
which would mean that the extra energy of the draw was going directly into
bullet velocity.

Result? 176 fps. Well of course I was disappointed, but there was
a certain satisfaction to be had in being faced with a physical impossibility which
needed to be thought through. In passing, I once read that someone had found
that for the English longbow, a clothyard draw length was 'biomechanically
impossible' which sounds so wonderfully scientific that it has to go unques-
tioned. Korean and Japanese and Chinese archers, to name a few, were
uninhibited by biomechanical impossibilities and have been seen to shoot such
draw lengths, so this does rather make us wary of accepting anything couched
in pseudo-scientific language. When an experiment disproves a theory, it is

possible that the experiment is faulty but it is also possible that the theory is faulty.

Energy cannot be created, nor destroyed, but I was wrong to imagine that my catapult shared my immediate concerns about ejecting the bullet with higher velocity. The catapult is in fact a completely neutral system, and has no desires in any direction.

After a pause for reflection I recalled that the energy supplied by me, in drawing back the pouch, had to perform several tasks only one of which was the bullet's flight. The energy had also to return the leather pouch, and it had further to return the two rubber tubes, even though they themselves, in recoiling, were releasing the energy I had stored in the system. On recovery, the catapult accelerates:

weight of the projectile
+ weight of the leather pouch
+ weight of the fixings to the latex tubes
+ half of the weight of the latex tubes.

I took the catapults apart, and weighed everything.

	22-pound catapult	*28-pound catapult*
Latex tubes bore	5 millimetres	8 millimetres
Latex tubes wall thickness	2 millimetres	2 millimetres
Component weights:		
Projectile	352 grains	352 grains
Pouch	54 grains	54 grains
Fixings	15 grains	23 grains
7 1/4-inch tubes	112 grains	
6 1/8-inch tubes		147 grains
Totals	533 grains	576 grains
Of which projectile weight is	66%	61%

This means, simply, that of the extra energy I had supplied, only 61% of it could possibly emerge as bullet velocity, the remainder being used in accelerating all of the rest of the gubbins, the pouch, fixings and half the weight of the tubes. So this was precisely the result I got – I had achieved 176 fps and the sums now told me I should have achieved 176.8 fps. Almost too precisely, in fact, for one learns over time to be very suspicious of results this accurate.

A first rational conclusion – and indeed the obvious one, if the process of thought were to come more easily to me – is to shoot from a heavier catapult proportionately heavier bullets. We are not yet at the terminal velocity of recoiling rubber, but there is more to be gained from putting more energy into the projectile by increasing its mass, than looking for small increases in velocity. The heavier the ball, the greater the proportion of the available energy that must go into it, and the more efficient the shooting. For of course putting more energy into the system means just that – putting more energy into the system. It does not follow that the extra energy will emerge as bullet velocity. It does, perhaps, follow that the extra energy will be shared out between bullet, pouch, fixings and half-tubes-weight, and all of these together will perhaps travel a little faster, but the only bit which we measure in our chronograph, and of course the only bit of value to us, is the velocity of the ball. All the rest has to be accelerated or the ball itself will not fly; yet that is unharvestable energy. Necessary use of energy, yet unharvestable.

If we put a heavier ball in the pouch, we will still put the same amount of energy into the draw, since the projectile weight has nothing to do with the draw weight. On release, the heavier ball means that the total mass being accelerated will slow things up a little – it must. What interests us is how that energy is now shared out. The total energy used up by the gubbins – that is, by the tubes, pouch and fixings – will actually be slightly less, because these things have not changed their weight, and yet are being accelerated more slowly. Therefore there is more energy available to accelerate the ball, and although the ball itself will not be flying quite so quickly, it does follow that it will have more energy.

This we can prove in practice. Kinetic energy is half the mass, times the square of the velocity. Knowing the mass and the velocity, we can calculate the energy.

$$\text{kinetic energy} = \frac{\text{mass}}{2} \times \text{velocity}^2$$

If we shoot light-weight bullets and measure their velocity, and heavier bullets and measure their velocity, and draw ourselves some pretty graphs they will show both that heavier bullets give lower velocities (which instinctively we expect) and that these same heavier bullets, travelling more slowly, give higher energies (which perhaps we hadn't expected at all).

The results I obtained using 22-pound draw latex tubes shooting different balls are shown in the top part of the table opposite.

To see if this pattern was duplicated by a second set of tubes, immediately afterwards I shot another series, the results of which are shown in the second part of the table. The new tubes were fitted and then stretched to their full extent twice before shooting commenced to eliminate any artificially high initial figures.

There are three rather important caveats, however, which although to a scientist will sound like excuses (a scientist works on the basis that any experiment accurately described can be repeated) are in fact nothing of the kind.

Ball material: Ball weight (grains):	Steel 54 gr.	Marble 86 gr.	Steel 87 gr.	Lead 140 gr.	Lead 220 gr.	Marble 299 gr.	Lead 351 gr.	Lead 371 gr.
Velocities (fps):	233	235	236	190	202	186	178	170
	234	239	240	206	200	184	180	169
	238	230	238	217	203	182	182	173
	241	234	224	215	202	190	179	174
	240	235	233	223	197	185	178	173
Velocities with new tubes:				216	197		162	172
				216	198		172	172
				219	199		167	157
				188	197		179	167
				218	198		166	168
					193			
					198			
					193			
					198			

First, as the experience of the tennis ball manufacturer predicts, different latex tubing of identical measurements does not always give identical results. I found on a single day's shooting that a set of tubes would give consistent results but when these broke and were replaced with an identical-looking set of tubes, strikingly different results were obtained. The fastest results were from a set of tubes which lasted only sixty shots before they broke.

Second, we have already seen that holding a catapult at full draw for even a few seconds allows heat to be lost from the rubber, and energy lost as heat is energy which is no longer available to the bullet. In hot weather, the bullets will fly faster than in cold.

Third, different target archers obtain dramatically different results from identical bows and arrows. John Holden describes six archers achieving velocities ranging from 159 fps to 194 fps using the same bow and the same arrow. We have to assume that different catapult users would achieve a similar disparity of results even if they had identical bullets and catapults.

We can, however, know the maximum velocity at which a ball might fly regardless of the shooter; we need the force-draw curve (simply, the accumulation of measurements of how many pounds the weapon pulls at each inch of draw) which tells us how much energy we have put into the system, and we need to know the weight of bullet, tubes, fixings and pouch. The energy coming out of the system cannot exceed that going into the system, and is likely to be less than this. John Holden makes the point that regardless of the skill of individual target archers, a survey of their equipment showed that 85% were so ill-tuned as to have an adverse effect on their scores, something which we need to bear in mind with our catapults. It is to be hoped that future researchers will publish further points which we should address.

Again, unfortunately, a caveat. Obtaining an accurate force-draw curve even from a bow, which suffers nothing like the creep of rubber, is far from the easy task it sounds, as any archer who has tried it knows. With my 28-pound catapult only two measurements were easy: that it had a pull of no pounds whatsoever at 12 inches, and that this had increased to 28 pounds at 39 inches draw. By means of a series of G-clamps, pulley-wheels, planks of accurately inch-marked wood and a spring scale, and by recording the figures into a tape recorder, I managed the figures shown on the right.

After noting the creep at the end of the draw, a quick glance at these figures shows that they are unlikely to be accurate, and in fact archery manufacturers use a machine to obtain more reliable figures for bows. It would be easy to massage the numbers and publish those which seem more likely, but this does not encourage anyone who might be unable to arrive at perfect increments; a better approach is to draw a graph and allow the smoothness of the line to indicate the readings that are probably accurate.

An alternative to drawing a graph is simply to use these figures as obtained to derive the total energy input. This can be done with reasonable accuracy simply by adding together the difference between consecutive readings for each inch of draw, and dividing the whole by twelve to convert inch-pounds into foot-pounds.

Summing all the figures in the last table, then, we arrive at a total of just over 500 inch-pounds of energy, allowing for the creep at the end of the draw, which translates to 42 foot-pounds of energy.

Being minded to trust experiment more than sums, I took a 16$\frac{1}{2}$-bore lead ball and shot it ten times through my electronic chronograph. Coincidentally, the resulting average of 146.6 fps, is exactly a 100 mph, giving 20$\frac{1}{2}$ foot-pounds of energy.

But as we have seen, this only represents the bit of energy coming out of the system as bullet

Draw (inches)	Pull (pounds)
12	0
13	2
14	6
15	8
16	10
17	11
18	13
19	14
20	15
21	16
22	17
23	18
24	18$\frac{1}{2}$
25	19$\frac{1}{2}$
26	20$\frac{1}{2}$
27	21
28	22
29	23
30	23$\frac{1}{2}$
31	24
32	25
33	25$\frac{1}{2}$
34	26
35	27
36	27$\frac{1}{2}$
37	28
38	28$\frac{1}{2}$ - 28
39	29 - 28

16$\frac{1}{2}$-bore lead ball (readings in fps)	
145	146
151	141
149	147
148	146
150	143
Average = 146.6 fps	

velocity. We also need to consider the pouch, which weighs 54 grains, the fixings which hold the pouch to the rubber tubes, which together weigh 23 grains, and half the weight of both latex tubes, each of which weighs 210 grains.

Therefore we actually have a total of 711 grains travelling forwards, and reaching a velocity of 146.6 fps, and this figure represents an energy output of 34 foot-pounds. Somewhere along the way we have lost eight foot-pounds of energy; this always seems to happen in any energy transfer system and the best the scientists can offer by way of explanation is the word 'entropy' which they will have us believe indicates that all energy tends to end up as heat lost to the environment. The hand holding the catapult is jerked forwards, perhaps some is lost as heat from the latex tubes during the draw, and perhaps some is lost as sound energy, catapults being not quite as silent as we might sometimes wish.

Then to consider what might happen with a lighter bullet. What about a .527-calibre ball? This weighs half an ounce.

In theory, we have 34 foot-pounds of energy coming out of the system. The total accelerating mass becomes 219 grains (the projectile) plus 54 grains (the pouch) plus 23 grains (the fixings) plus 210 grains (the half-weight of both tubes) which is a total of 506 grains. 506 grains possessing 34 foot-pounds of energy should mean that the final velocity is 174 fps (15 foot-pounds) and we should therefore see the half ounce bullet emerging at this velocity.

Weight of	grains
Projectile	219
Pouch	54
Fixings	23
Tubes÷2	210
Total	506

I shot a half-ounce bullet five times through the chronograph, which gave me an average of 165 fps, an energy of 13 foot-pounds. One mutters darkly the excuse that losing 2 foot-pounds is certainly within what I might aspire to in terms of experimental error, and perhaps I should not have forgotten that with my 16½-bore ball I had somewhere lost 8 foot-pounds of energy, so it is quite possible – indeed likely – that there is some other minor energy loss which I can only speculate about. There is, of course, always the uncomfortable possibility that my maths has gone astray.

28-pound catapult
½-ounce bullet
(readings in fps)
167
164
162
167
165
Average 165 fps
(13 foot-pounds)

The theme, however, quite clearly (and quite accurately, notwithstanding experimental or any other wayward error) emerges that a far greater efficiency is achieved by using heavy bullets, and that if we want bullets to possess energy we are well advised to invest in bullet-mass rather than to hope for bullet-velocity, because reducing the weight of the bullet simply means more of the available energy is being used to accelerate the rubber tubes and pouch and fixings, and none of this can emerge as bullet-energy.

This is an important lesson, since the ammunition recommended by commercial catapult manufacturers tends to be steel ball-bearings of about .38 calibre, or 3/8-inch. These do not weigh very much: 54 grains. Performing all the above calculations, the most we can expect them to do, even if we have none of the losses we actually measured, is 215 fps, and a ball-bearing weighing only 54 grains travelling at 215 fps possesses only 5 1/2 foot-pounds of energy. In the event, five shots gave the readings shown. It has to be said, however, that the ball, being so small, slipped out of the fingers for the last two shots and I didn't feel confident that they represented 39 inches of draw length. Averaging the preceding three, however, we still arrive at a velocity of only 192.6 fps, or 4 1/2 foot-pounds of energy.

There is, of course, another and quite unexpected complication. The commercial catapults are not sold with these big, heavy latex tubes, but with smaller, lighter tubes, giving a draw weight of only 22 pounds at 36 inches, and having much less physical mass.

Taking my 22-pound catapult, I shot the same 54-grain steel ball five times – an average of 212 fps, which translates to 5 1/2 foot-pounds.* Quite unexpectedly, I have put less energy in – pulling only 22 pounds at 39 inches – and got more energy out.

Explanation? The pouch still weighs 54 grains, but the fixings weigh only 15 grains and the half-tubes weight is now only 112 grains. Total mass being accelerated is therefore 54 + 54 + 15 + 112 = 235 grains, and to get 235 grains going at 212 fps requires only 23 1/2 foot-pounds, a good deal less than that of the big catapult, and certainly well within the amount of energy we might expect to put into this light-weight, 22-pound draw catapult.

The conclusions so far are astonishingly perverse in that they all go against commonsense. First, a heavy-weight ball may fly more slowly than a light-weight ball, but it will have more energy. Second, for a light-weight ball, a weak catapult gives a higher velocity output than a strong catapult.

Inevitably, then, we begin to wonder if there is not an optimum

28-pound catapult
54-grain bullet
(readings in fps)
190
196
192
(181)
(184)
Average 192.6 fps
(4 1/2 foot-pounds)

22-pound catapult
54-grain bullet
(readings in fps)
210
209
213
216
211
Average 212 fps
(5 1/2 foot-pounds)

Weight of	grains
Projectile	54
Pouch	54
Fixings	15
Tubes ÷ 2	112
Total	235

*Notice that these latex tubes, identical in dimensions to the former ones but obviously from a different batch of latex, were no longer producing 240 fps with these ball-bearings.

bullet-weight for each catapult; a weight of bullet which produces the highest possible energy output. Very clearly now we can see that the converse is true; for a given weight of bullet, there is an optimum catapult, where either a more powerful, or a more feeble, set of latex tubes will give a poorer result.

I took my 22-pound catapult and from it shot a 424-grain ball ten times. There was a spread of velocities ranging from 134 fps to 154 fps, with an average of 146 fps, an energy of 20 foot-pounds.

Next I shot a 377-grain ball ten times from it. This gave a spread of velocities ranging from 151 to 162 fps, the average being 158 fps – an increase not unexpected. But this translates to an energy of 21 foot-pounds, a gain on the heavier ball. So we're right: for any catapult, somewhere there lurks an optimum bullet weight, where a heavier or lighter ball gives a lower muzzle energy. Thus I am foolish shooting 424-grain bullets from my 28-pound catapult, since I can achieve the same energy, with less consumption of lead, and a higher velocity of bullet, using bullets weighing 377 grains from the lighter, easier-to-handle 22-pound catapult.

What if we go the other way? I took three rubber bands and looped them together as we used to at school, then made a paper pellet and rather than looking for an exposed hand or ankle of a colleague upon which to discharge this implement, I shot it through the chronograph. Result: 264 fps, with the pellet weighing 11 grains, an energy of 1.7 foot-pounds, and something which perhaps now explains the extraordinarily invigorating sting on being the victim of such a missile on a torpid Friday afternoon. The rubber bands had a draw weight of around 10 or 11 pounds at between 22 and 26 inches of draw, something rather difficult to measure accurately because, being drawn to the absolute limit of rubber's elasticity, they had a tendency to break.

Curiously enough, I still possess the Webley Mark 1 air pistol with which I was taught to shoot when a child. Its 7-grain pellet flies at 330 fps, and develops 1.69 foot-pounds of energy. My father drummed it into us that we were handling a 'real' gun and, beautifully made as those old Webleys were, we believed him. We learnt to have a subconscious care of the muzzle of the gun, such that it was always pointing at the ground and never at another person, yet my father turned out to have been rather wiser than we credited. Perhaps he knew full well that the air pistol was a fairly safe thing for children to use to learn about gun safety. Our rubber bands and paper pellets are just as dangerous.

The corollary was to examine the very light-weight latex tubes, which are 8 millimetres in diameter, with a 4-millimetre bore, and taper down to 5 millimetres with a 1-millimetre bore. Since the strength of a piece of rubber depends solely on its cross-sectional area, and the 22-pound tubes have a cross-section of 44 square millimetres, it follows that at full stretch, 2 square

New tubes 39-inch draws (pull in pounds)	
1st	18
2nd	17
3rd	16
4th	16
5th	17
6th	16½
(20-second break)	
7th	17
8th	16
9th	16½
(20-second break)	
10th	17
11th	16½
12th	16½
(20-second break)	
13th	17
14th	16
15th	16½

New tubes 54-grain ball (velocity in fps)
228
232
-
243
239
242
236
242
232
-
235
234
Max/min variation 7%

millimetres of cross-section will give 1 pound of draw weight. The light-weight tubes have a cross-section of 37.7 square millimetres, so we can predict that they should give us a draw weight of 18.85 pounds. That they are tapered should not affect this result, because the mechanism of pull is such that the thinnest portion will stretch until it 'hits the wall', whereupon the thicker portion will stretch. Therefore the final draw weight will be that of the largest working cross-section.

I took some tubes brand new from their wrapping, fitted them to a catapult and pulled them out to 39 inches. The loss of energy through temporary creep was quite noticeable, and it may be as well to give the exact figures to create an accurate idea of how much innate variation there can be when a catapult is used. I drew 15 times, with 20-second breaks after the 6th, 9th and 12th draws.

We cannot, therefore, be much surprised to find that in a range of 12 shots with these tubes and the recommended ball-bearing ammunition, weighing 54 grains, the velocity varied by 7%. Nor can it be predicted when the velocity is likely to be highest. (The blanks in the table are when the chronograph failed to register.)

Further to emphasise the difficulty of making predictions with an organic substance grown as sap inside trees, it seemed logical that these light latex tubes should show very clearly the phenomenon that there is an optimum bullet weight, and that a heavier bullet will give a reduction in energy output. It proved not to be so, though there was a levelling-off with the heaviest bullet I had available. The challenge is to decide where to make the trade-off between bullet velocity and bullet energy, for though 15.86 foot-pounds is better than 12.26 foot-pounds, 199 fps is a lot better than 127 fps.

Bullet weight (grains)	*Velocity (fps)*	*Energy (foot-pounds)*
54	236.3	6.76
87	219.2	9.28
140	198.6	12.26
220	166.0	13.46
353	139.0	15.15
444	126.8	15.86

However there is a further complication, were there not enough already. We know from the work of Paul E. Klopsteg that the speed of an arrow is, roughly speaking, inversely proportional to the cube root of its mass. A first glance at these figures seems to show that this does not hold true for catapults. The cube root of 54 grains is 3.78, and the cube root of 87 grains is 4.43. If we divide these cube roots by one another, we see that the 54-grain ball should be going at 1.17 times the velocity of the 87-grain ball, which should be 257 fps, but the chronograph shows that it is only going a whisker over 236 fps.

The latex tubes do not know that this is what is supposed to happen. The latex tubes have no idea what it is that they're accelerating, so they accelerate the pouch and the bullet together, at the same speed, just as if the two combined were the missile.

I took this catapult and removed the pouch, and found it weighed 91 grains. If the cube root rule holds true, then I have to re-calculate, adding 91 grains to the mass of the bullet in each case. So I have to find the cube root of 178 (87 + 91) grains, and divide it by the cube root of 145 (84 + 91) grains, which is 1.07.

$$\frac{\sqrt[3]{87}}{\sqrt[3]{54}} = \frac{4.43}{3.78} = 1.17$$

$$1.17 \times 219.2 = 257 \text{ fps}$$

$$\frac{\sqrt[3]{(87 + 91)}}{\sqrt[3]{(54 + 91)}} = \frac{5.63}{5.25} = 1.07$$

$$1.07 \times 219.2 = 234.5$$

Our prediction then becomes 234.5 fps, and as it actually shot at 236.3 fps, that's well within the experimental errors we might expect. It follows, then, that an exceedingly good plan is to lighten the pouch. Hunting about in the sideboard drawer I found – as one does – several odd bits of nylon webbing straps from which one might make a catapult pouch, and carefully weighing sections on a chemical balance it became apparent that some are much lighter, (hence better) than others [Fig. 4.9]. Sewing 2-millimetre diameter nylon cord loops to the ends of a ³⁄₄-inch width of light nylon webbing, I made a pouch weighing only 28 grains [Fig. 4.10]. This meant, in theory, that I had lightened the load by 63 grains; a considerable amount, especially at the lighter bullet weights.

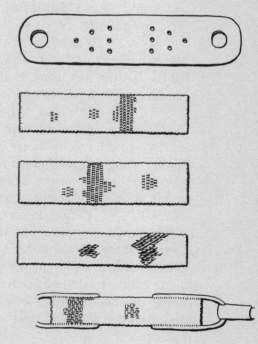

4.9 *Pouch materials*

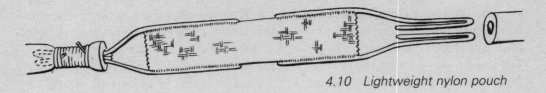

4.10   Lightweight nylon pouch

I then predicted that the very light 54-grain ball would fly at the cube root of 145 (54 + 91) divided by the cube root of 82 (54 + 28), which is 1.21, times as fast. I took five shots: 258, 276, 276, 278, 276 = average of 273 fps (9 foot-pounds). Not quite as quick as predicted, but if the terminal velocity of a piece of stretched latex is around the 270 fps mark suggested by the paper pellet experiment, then we're not likely to get much faster whatever we do.

$$\frac{\sqrt[3]{(54 + 91)}}{\sqrt[3]{(54 + 28)}} = \frac{5.25}{4.35} = 1.$$

$$1.21 \times 236.3 \text{ fps} = 285.7 \text{ f}$$

The 140-grain ball ought to give a closer reading to the prediction. Dancing around a calculator, it should be 1.11 times as fast, or 221 fps. Again, five shots: 218, 219, 219, 217, 217 = average of 218 fps.

$$\frac{\sqrt[3]{(140 + 91)}}{\sqrt[3]{(140 + 28)}} = \frac{6.14}{5.52} = 1$$

$$1.11 \times 198.6 \text{ fps} = 221 \text{ fps}$$

Finally, the 220-grain ball at 1.08 times as fast, should go at 179 fps. Five shots measured: 185, 194, 193, 195, 186 = average of 191 fps.

Well this was a pleasant surprise, of course, but when I checked the weights I found it was a slightly lighter-than-usual bullet, weighing 211 grains, accounting for the difference.

$$\frac{\sqrt[3]{(220 + 91)}}{\sqrt[3]{(220 + 28)}} = \frac{6.78}{6.28} = 1$$

$$1.08 \times 166 \text{ fps} = 179 \text{ fps}$$

This fact led me to think again about developing a more efficient catapult, and studying carefully all the results of my experiments, it occurred to me that a logical development might be to attach short, heavy rubber tubes to the catapult itself, and to the heavy rubber, attach lightweight tubes going to an exceedingly light pouch [Fig. 4.11].

The force-draw curve of rubber being what it is, the lightweight rubber would stretch rapidly to the point where it hit the wall, whereupon the heavier rubber would stretch, and in this way extra energy would be stored without adding weight at the velocity-expensive pouch end. This is in contrast to one commercially-made catapult, which uses heavy plastic split rods to attach rubber to pouch, adding weight at the worst possible place – its pouch had a total mass of 106 grains, where the .38 steel balls sold for it are half that weight [Fig. 4.12].

I therefore took a wooden catapult of my own make and fitted

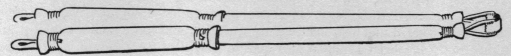

4.11 Stepped latex tubes

it with stepped latex tubing. The construction of this catapult was actually slightly more complex than its appearance suggests, and deserves a detailed description. I took the forking branch from an ash-tree bough which had been given to me as firewood – ash logs burn well, as the old poem tells us – and cut from it the classic Y shape of the catapult frame. The diameter of the bough was about three inches; the final diameter of each of the three parts was around an inch, a little thicker in the handle to make it comfortable, and slightly oval in the two prongs, with the longer axis pointing forwards to ensure maximum strength in the plane of stress.

At the base of the handle is pivoted, on a holly peg 8 millimetres in diameter, a wrist brace with a total length of 7½ inches. This comprises a fork of oak with at its distal end a parallel gap of 4½ inches length, and three inches width. The two arms are connected by a one-inch wide piece of nylon webbing just long enough not to hold the arms of the brace in tension except at the moment of the shot. The webbing is looped round each arm, and tightly sewn with dental floss, which has the advantage of being pre-waxed. The whole of the wrist brace swings forwards out of the way for storage, and as it comes round below and behind the handle, it bears against a stout beechwood peg half an inch in diameter. There is no particular merit in my choice of a variety of woods – they merely happen to be scraps I found in the waste bin of my workshop. A better choice is elm throughout; elm is both light in weight, and very difficult to split. The brace itself is particularly likely to split, and the oaken one has repeatedly been glued together at this point.

The length of each of the upper arms is three inches, and the distance between the centres of their tips is 4¼ inches. I have found that I can

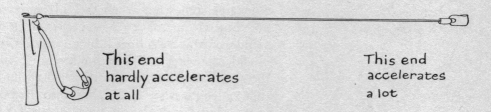

This end
hardly accelerates
at all

This end
accelerates
a lot

4.12 Importance of pouch fixings weight

shoot more accurately if the arms of a catapult have this gap, than if they are closer together, though experiments really need to be done here by many catapult owners to see if there is a universal optimum for accuracy. (Archers are reasonably agreed that a straight, lightly set longbow is more accurate than any other, but it has been a long-argued question.) Drilled from the top and along the length of each arm is a hole 5 millimetres in diameter, and this is tapped to a 6-millimetre metric thread to a depth of an inch and a half. Into each arm is screwed a 6-millimetre roofing bolt, with a 14-millimetre domed head [Fig. 4.13].

At first it might be thought inadequate to use a metal-work thread along the grain of a piece of wood, but of course the strain is imposed sideways on the tip of the bolt, and the thread merely serves to retain the bolts at the tip of each arm.

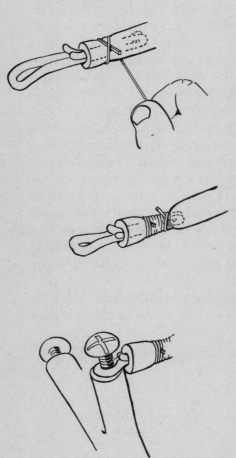

A length of 7½ inches of nylon cord, having a diameter of 4 millimetres, is then twice folded and four thicknesses of the cord are poked an inch and a half deep into a piece of latex tubing 12 millimetres in outside diameter, 8 millimetres in bore, so that a nylon cord loop protrudes from the end of the latex tubing. I have found it necessary to make a tool comprising a wooden handle housing an oval nail whose head has been filed off and slightly vee-formed, to poke the cord into the bore of the rubber tubing; it needs to be a pretty tight fit. Ordinary rubber bands are then tightly looped round and round on the outside of the latex tubing so that it is compressed onto the nylon cord, and the loop is placed around the shank of the roofing bolt which is then screwed tightly into the arm of the catapult. The latex tubing is three inches long; it elongates somewhat when the rubber bands are bound in place. A second piece of standard catapult rubber tubing, 9-millimetre outside diameter and 5-millimetre bore, with the pouch attached to the other end, is cut so that its length is six inches, and into the bore is introduced a single fold of nylon cord, two inches long, such that within it is a 'solid'

4.13 *End fixings for latex tubes*

length an inch long. This inch is then poked into the inside of the large diameter latex tubing, an easier activity to describe than to perform, and is once again heavily bound with two or three ordinary rubber bands.

A word of warning – although one does not want to make these bindings too heavy (since weight in the middle of the propelling rubber carries a velocity penalty), for safety's sake it does not do to cut corners. If, at full draw, anything comes astray, the best one can hope for is being struck in the cheek, rather than in the eye, by the rubber. Since we are dealing with more energy than is obtained from the muzzle of an average air rifle, the pain and shock of this happening can be imagined, and if it can't, I can testify that a bruise to the cheek will be on show for over a week before it fades. Catapult makers take the precaution on their packaging of warning their customers to wear eye protection and though I doubt if anyone complies, it is actually sound advice. Doubtless the warnings are only there to protect against the makers being sued, but they are nonetheless valid for all that.

It is worth mentioning that while catapult latex tubing can be bought from any gunshop or fishing shop, I needed to go to a specialist rubber supplier to order the larger diameter latex tubing, and was then compelled to buy ten metres of it. The cost little differs from that of commercial catapult tubes, which must therefore be regarded as something of a bargain.

The whole of this process is repeated for the other side, and one ends up with a catapult with heavy latex tubing at the wooden end and light latex tubing at the pouch end. Three inches plus six inches minus an inch of overlap should not equal nine inches (which the rubber actually measures), but for the elongation caused by the bindings.

The most common method of attachment of the tube to the leather pouch of commercial catapult tubing is to make a hole at each end of the pouch, and the rubber tube is introduced through this hole. A very small hole, about 2 millimetres in diameter, is punched in one wall of the rubber tubing, about an inch from its end. The remainder of the tubing is then drawn through this hole, and it emerges from the bore of the stump an inch further on. This is a hugely stupid idea, and demonstrates that the designers have failed to understand Griffith on crack propagation. The colossal disadvantage of this form of attachment is that the unstretched length will in time cut into the stretched tubing which reduces dramatically in diameter as the draw is made, and impacts against this cut end at great speed on every shot. Latex tubes almost always break at this point of weakness. As Gordon so unexpectedly says, taut rubber is a brittle material, and once a crack starts, it is likely to propagate. It only takes a pin-prick to burst a balloon.

A better plan, especially if a light-weight nylon webbing pouch is used, is to insert the nylon into the ends of the tubing and lash it in place with rubber bands. As the mass of the non-working portion of rubber is about 14 grains, and as two ordinary rubber bands, 2½ inches long (that is, each with a total length of rubber of 5 inches) with a 1-millimetre square cross-section, together weigh 8 grains, and if whipped on tightly are enough to secure the tubing to the pouch, a very significant weight saving is possible, resulting in higher velocities. Moreover this method of attachment is much less prone to fracture than using the rubber looped back through a hole in itself.

I have tried a variety of other methods of attaching pouch to latex, but always there has been a weight penalty, revealed in every case by the chronograph. Gordon makes the point that in any tension member, the end fixing is likely to be the weak point, and catapults are in this respect no different from any other tension member. It is preferable for the rubber to break at the pouch end, since it will then recoil towards the hand, not the face. Fortunately the cracking of the rubber is visible before it actually does break, and provided the rubber is securely attached to the catapult handle, a routine inspection of the ends of the rubber every ten shots or so will give a warning. I have found rubber lasting as few as sixty shots and as many as five hundred shots, so it isn't possible to predict with any accuracy the life of rubber; and besides, no two people will have the same draw length. There is a tendency for the fracture at the pouch to occur on one side only, and a close inspection of technique usually reveals that the wrist-braced catapult is not held perfectly square to the draw; commonly one side is stretched further than the other. This unevenness can be corrected by judicious lengthening of one of the nylon cords, though oddly enough, accurate shooting seems to depend more on practice than on reverence for fine detail in the weapon. My only experience of an inherently inaccurate catapult was a commercially-made one in which the arms were a good deal closer together than my preferred 4¼ inches, and the advantage of the narrower weapon (being able to stick it in the pocket) is outweighed by the disadvantage – being unable to hit anything with it.

The draw weight of the stepped latex tubing, when I fitted it, crept up a mere two pounds to 24 pounds, but it managed to shoot a 16½-bore ball, weighing 424 grains, at 160 fps, or almost 25 foot-pounds; five times as much energy as the commercially-sold catapults with their commercially-recom-mended ammunition. If commercial makers choose to apply themselves to improvements in catapult design, the two areas most immediately productive will be found to be redesigning the end fixings, and tapering the tubing so that it is thick at the catapult end and thin at the pouch end. This tapered tubing is still made by the American Proline latex company but demand for it was so slight that it became very hard to find after only a short time – a great shame since with the right ammunition and pouch it developed half as much energy again as the standard heavier tubes normally sold for catapults. The power of choosing heavier bullets lies in the hands of the shooter.

Worthy of surprisingly serious study is the Johnny Popper, an interesting and either dubious or commendable example, depending on one's viewpoint, of Lateral Thinking in the Modern Child. It is the name given to something that was a vogue in Scottish schools some time ago; the shooting of dried peas from rubber condoms. The mouth (if that is not too insensitive a word to use in the context) of the condom was drawn over the neck of a soft drinks bottle, from which the base had been removed. The dried pea was dropped into the sac of the condom, and using the remainder of the bottle as a tubular handle, the pea was drawn back and shot through the bottle opening. With no pouch weight, speeds of 270 fps have been claimed. I tried it with an 8-grain chick pea, but only managed a maximum of 252 fps. Twenty shots were possible before the condom started to split, but an attempt to shoot a 140-grain lead ball failed, the sac breaking free round the bullet because the tensile strength was unable to overcome the bullet's inertia. The condom in question was two inches wide when flattened and had seven inches of free rubber when mounted on the bottle. It represents a curious demonstration of the quality of stretchiness of the rubber used in condom manufacture. One resists, with some effort, further comment on the need for such a quality in that particular product. A finger, an inch wide and two inches long, from a latex examination glove, similarly mounted, achieved 231 fps. Both of these provide further evidence that the terminal velocity of rubber lies in the region of 270 fps. As a school plaything it was highly inappropriate because at such a speed, and in dense crowds of children, the danger of a burst eyeball was all too real.

This indicates one final, but vital, aspect of the catapult. The chief merit of latex tubing is its convenience. It does not get tangled up. That is all. The only relevant features or requirements of the rubber propellant are length, cross-sectional area, and a capability of being stretched ideally to six times its own length. Lacking latex tubing, we could use bunches of condoms or bunches of latex gloves. In fact, because of its tapered shape the condom may represent an effective source of power. Naturally each requires careful washing to remove such pharmaceutical additives as in this context are redundant, and naturally it requires very careful drying afterwards to remove water droplets which add mass and thereby reduce velocity. An eight-inch condom with half an inch pinched at each end will stretch to 45 inches, and it weighs 26 grains. A latex examination glove is nine inches long, weighs 113 grains, and will also stretch to 45 inches. Whether one can persuade a urologist to hand over a couple of catheters is not for me to say, but they will be found to be of 5-millimetre outside diameter and 2-millimetre bore and a most convenient 16 inches length; I deem it prudent neither to reveal my source nor the results, since it is questionable whether something manufactured to enhance health should be used to reduce it. But there is always the ubiquitous rubber band, and even in East Timor, far from the Western industrial complex, we read of boys with plaited rubber bands shooting birds with catapults.

What of shooting techniques?

My interest in the catapult stems from meeting an elderly poacher who demonstrated that it is an effective weapon if commanded by the necessary skill, by putting a succession of shots into a Coke can someone had considerately thrown into the hedge. Inspired, I bought a bullet-mould, made a bagful of bullets and set about ordering the local rabbit population according to my beliefs. As a matter of observation, a .451-calibre lead ball travelling at around 200 fps will go through a rabbit but without penetrating the skin on the far side, so you get the bullet back, and it gives a very clean kill. I soon found that the degree of success is directly related to taking the weapon seriously. It was tempting to take casual shots at wildly long range, which neither afforded the encouragement of success nor the conservation of ammunition. It is far more successful to go through the painful steps of silent stalking to the very close range that is the only guarantee of a close grouping; no more than the 20 yards that as an archer I knew gave the greatest chance of success. However, my dentist who grew up on a South African farm tells me the local boys carried a catapult with them at all times and they could, and did, hit absolutely anything nearby using only pebbles as ammunition. But he said that they were so practised, and so highly attuned to the requirements of the weapon, that they were constantly but effortlessly on the look-out for the ideal pebble and where he saw only the veld, they would spot any likely spherical stone from yards away and pop it into a pocket for later use.

There is a need for many more experiments. At first sight we had thought of the catapult as simple – we now find it not to be so. It seems highly unlikely that these few investigations, conducted with apparatus no more sophisticated than a ruler, a spring-scale, a grain scale, and a chronograph, in a laboratory comprising my hall and my garage, can be the last word in a field but little understood. Nevertheless, we have something which is capable of giving velocities equal to those of the flight of an arrow from a longbow, with a bullet having the mass of a target arrow, and the challenge of learning to shoot it with the raw skill an instinctive archer would recognise, rather than the meticulous use of highly-refined sighting arrangements which might make a rifleman lean towards the use of the more precise bullet-crossbow.

CHAPTER 5

The hand stonebow

The handbow normally shoots an arrow, for which there are good reasons. The head of an arrow commonly lies in front of the handle of the bow, and barring the accident of over-drawing the string, the tail of the arrow flies round the side of the bow on release. The target archer spends a great deal of money on an arrow, seeking uniformity in weight, in bendiness (the 'spine' of an arrow), and in fletching. Uniformity is more difficult to accomplish in the primal jungle and a phenomenon of the primitive archer is the length of his arrows. Ethnologists in Papua New Guinea, South America and Timor remark constantly on it. Among hunting peoples the arrows are often longer than the bow and are derided by the westerner because a long arrow is heavy and therefore slower than it could be. But where most of the arrow lies ahead of the bow at full draw, the rear has little choice but to follow on after release, and these arrows are accurate enough to hit a pig at twenty paces. The 28-inch hollow alloy target arrow is a beautiful sight glistening through 100 metres of clear still summer air, and the target archer would not dream of a seven-foot bamboo arrow with ten-inch fletchings – but then in Timor bows and arrows are not playthings to be shot on mown lawns by archers dressed in white flannels.

A disadvantage of the long arrow is that it is time-consuming to make, and therefore expensive, and if it misses the pig it may end up in some underbrush and never be seen again. The reward of a whole pig makes the gamble worthwhile, but if the hunter is simply after small birds there is much to be said for shooting a cheap and disposable missile instead. Bows have been used for shooting bullets as well as for shooting arrows in Europe and Arabia, and they are said still to be so used in India and Africa today. The bullets are rarely metal because metal is expensive; the Indian rolls a ball out of clay and vegetable oil and puts it in the sun – the oil, it seems, prevents the bullet from cracking as it dries. Stones too are shot, and may be expected to have no more accuracy than stones shot from a catapult. It is this that Sir Anthony Aguecheek called for in *Twelfth Night*: 'O, for a stonebow, to hit him in the eye!'. Perhaps he refers to the light, pellet-shooting crossbow, but this is not the place for semantics.

As the performance of the steel English bullet-crossbow can be matched with a yew crossbow, thanks to modern string materials, so too can the hand stonebow.

That sentence needs to be read with some care. The emphasis is on the modern string, not the modern bow. The English bullet-crossbow had a heavy draw weight with a very heavy string, and we know that the mass of the string has a bearing on the speed of the bullet. The bowyers of old convinced themselves that a high draw weight and a short draw length gave an efficient bow. They do not. Final velocity is entirely dependent on acceleration; a bow accelerates the missile from a standstill, and the longer the time it has to accelerate, the faster will the final velocity be.

This is really rather important as it has implications for draw length. Increasing the draw weight of a bow leads to a very small increase in the speed of an arrow, though it can have a direct effect on shooting a heavier arrow at the same velocity.

In theory, halving the length of the bow will make the limb-tips fly forwards four times as fast. The logical approach seems to be, therefore, to focus on shortening the limbs, but this has rather a big disadvantage in that eventually the string slips off the nocks. Worse, the triangle comprising both limb-tips and the nock of the arrow at full draw – or in our case the bullet at full draw – becomes too acute, and we lose the advantage of long bows, which is that a small movement of the limb-tips results in a big movement of the arrow's nock. It was exactly this principle by which air cadets once used to launch gliders. A non-commissioned officer arranged, usually with a good deal of shouting, two lines of air cadets with a rope between them as if they were to indulge in a tug o' war. The glider was hooked in the middle of the rope. The two teams of cadets marched away from the nose of the glider, and at a signal ran directly apart from one another, as if they were the limb-tips of a bow and the glider was the arrow. It worked – after a fashion.

However, too short a bow will set a definite limit on the draw length, and Galileo teaches us that the taller the tower of Pisa (Chapter 1, page 13), the greater the time for acceleration. Consider what would happen were the tower twice as high – assuming it did not fall down, which being somewhere around 16 feet out of true it probably would. Instead of 179 feet, it would be 358 feet high. A bit of physics reveals that the time available for the bullet to accelerate is now 4.7 seconds, which means that instead of a final velocity of 107 fps, the bullet will hit the ground at 152 fps. Note that this isn't double the speed, but it is double the energy.

Now there are all sorts of complications which mean that such a desirable state of affairs doesn't obtain in our weaponry, but this principle is sound: increasing the draw length increases the time available to accelerate our bullet, and the general rule is that this will have a great effect on increasing its launch velocity. In fact we find it impossible to achieve the 'other things being equal' bit that so delights the theoretician, but nevertheless increasing the draw length is invariably a better strategy than increasing the draw weight.

Above all, then, we concentrate on increasing our draw length. The easiest way to do this is to dispense with the cross bit of the crossbow, the tiller, and make a handbow instead.

Many today are sceptical of wood as a material for bows, but this is a reflection of the success of the advertising industry rather than a consideration of the desiderata of spring-making. For that is all a bow is – a spring. Wood is an ideal material for bows as it is an ideal material for aeroplanes, and while this may conjure up the biplanes of the First World War, we should remind ourselves that the most successful fighting aircraft of the Second World War, the de Havilland Mosquito, was made out of wood, and the inherent light weight allowed it to out-perform all other aircraft until the advent of the jet engine. Glass-fibre has only one bonus to the bowmaking industry; it does not break readily, and the industrial bow supplier can offer a guarantee, and further can reduce the skill levels required of his workforce. But on a personal level it was the failure, many years ago, of a glass-fibre bow that led me to concentrate on making wooden bows. I had a beautiful short 'Classic Hunter' bow explode on me after only a few hundred shots, the wooden core fracturing in shear along the glue-line, and though I sent it to him to examine, the owner of the shop with a large retailer's reputation to lose refused to replace it under his warranty because he could not credit that such a failure could have occurred without the bow having been abused. He, and indirectly I, were both victims of a misplaced faith in glass-fibre, a faith sustained more in the mind than in the material world. I found it quicker to make a wooden bow than to pursue him through the courts, and a good deal more fulfilling.

Wood is one of the miracles of the natural world, and having evolved over billions of years to do a certain job, which is to say to hold leaves up in the sunlight where they can photosynthesise food and survive there year in, year out, in storms and winds from every direction and in every condition, it is very good at it.

Not all trees live in the same places, and the bowyer seeks out the tree which experience has taught is the most suitable. Most woods will make a bow; it is the writings of most notably Baker, Comstock and Hamm, that have drawn the attention of the world to the simple fact that a weaker wood will work efficiently if the bow is made very thin. Two thin bits side-by-side equals one thicker, narrower bit, and so we have the flatbow, which is wide and thin.

The special nature of the bow as a spring lies in the fact that we want it to recoil as quickly as possible, and to store as much energy as possible.

For a rapid recoil, two things are desirable – first that it should be short, and second that it should weigh little. Fortunately they go together. Halve the length of a bow, and it will recoil four times as quickly, a fact demonstrable every time a schoolboy twangs a ruler on the lid of a desk. But the tip of the ruler is mostly made up of dead weight, and removing dead weight will greatly reduce the amount of energy consumed by the tips of the bow when they flip forwards on release. A logical move is to make the bow limbs taper to a point, and in fact that is what is done. You have to examine the six-foot yew longbows of the Mary Rose, which had tips thinner than my little finger though they drew 150 pounds and had a handle thicker than plump bicycle tubing, to see how much you can taper bow limbs.

Unfortunately a short light bow is made of very little material, and in order to store energy, one has to have some stuff to store it in. The more stuff, the more energy can be stored. Life is ever a compromise, and the bowmaker seeks the point at which a lot of energy can be stored without the bow becoming too clumsy.

The nature of wood needs to be considered under a microscope, when it is at once apparent that it is composed of cells. Bend a bow, and the cells on the back will be stretched and the cells on the belly will be compressed. Up the middle of the bow lies a sheet of material at the neutral plane of bending, where the cells will neither be compressed nor stretched.

The wooden crossbows of old, and indeed a good many of the wooden crossbows of today, where they still exist in Africa and have not been replaced by the AK47 assault rifle with its dainty little cartridges, are made of very thick material in the belief that thick wood is strong. Alas, thick wood cannot bend very far, and these crossbows have very short draw lengths.

Brief consideration of the fact that the cells on the back of a bow stretch, while those on the belly compress, reveals why thick wood is entirely the wrong approach to the problem. The closer to the neutral plane of bending, the less the wood cells distort. If the bow were made of just a single layer of cells there would be no compression or tension of cells at all, just distortion as all the energy was stored within the cell walls alone. Such a bow would be infinitely flexible, but there would be very little material in which energy could be stored. A woodshaving, as many people have remarked, is thin and can be curled on itself, but it doesn't have the spring to return itself to a straight line.

If a thick beam of yew has a rope attached to its ends, as was the case with the Norwegian whale-shooting crossbow of the late 1890s, then very little of the yew is being compressed and very little stretched, compared with the total mass of yew being bent. Most of the wood is sitting in between back and belly, contributing nothing but distance between the two, and adding a large amount of useless mass to the spring. (I built one, to find out; see Chapter 3, page 39).

Therefore what the bowyer seeks is a bow where there is comparatively little wood so that as much as possible lies along the back and the belly, and as little as possible lies around the neutral plane of bending. So this dictates the flatbow design.

Archers – well, English archers – are predisposed to the longbow, and the longbow is made of yew, and yew is a surprisingly strong and surprisingly light wood. If we accept that English archers pulled an arrow 28 inches, not wishing to divert ourselves around the controversy of the clothyard shaft, then the bowyer's intention was to make a light bow which would allow the string to be pulled back 28 inches. Bowyers, and I speak as one, are as lazy as they can be, and the easiest way to scrape a bow into a taper is to make its section as round as possible, lots like a broomstick and as little as possible like a ruler. A round bow may not have quite so much surface area under tension and under compression, but it also has not quite so much surface area requiring very accurate and controlled scraping, and it is always quicker and easier to make a round-sectioned bow than a flat-sectioned bow. Yew being light, there isn't very much weight penalty in a thick bow; and yew being strong, it will accept quite high stresses – you can compress the belly a lot and stretch the back a lot and the bow will not break – so it can be made thick. A thick, narrow bow will usually have less mass than a thin, wide bow of the same draw weight. Other woods are less forgiving of thickness than yew, and they have to be made into wide, thin bows or they fail. Bowyers commonly divide all bow designs into these two main groups – longbows and flatbows, and though there are a great many long bows which are flatbows, and also a great many short bows which have a round and not a flat cross-section, it is still a division having some modest value to the taxonomist.

When we built a crossbow we saw that the flatbow will bend a long way to use up all the available compression and tension of the cells along the back and belly, giving us a long draw. Moreover, flatbows are easily shaped to a point at either end, and as – if short – they are easily made, nothing inhibits our taking them to the limits of their performance.

A handbow is a little different, because a handbow needs more length, and the embryonic bowyer has only to make one full-size six-foot flatbow to discover that there is a great deal more careful wood-thinning in making a long flatbow than there is in making a long round-bow. Most long bows tend to be round in cross-section. One of the most interesting early flatbow designs, the Holmgaard, was in fact a short flatbow with long stiff round-section tips to it, and it is quite possible (and I believe quite likely) that this design evolved to accommodate the laziness of the bowyer. I have made such bows; the skill of the bowyer compensates for the saving of work. It is a high-risk design, because there is a tendency for the wood fibres to spiral up the tree when it is growing and this tends to give all wooden bows what Jim Hamm has aptly called 'propeller-twist'. In itself this isn't usually too harmful, but deep narrow bow-ends emerging from a twisted limb have a tendency to twist sideways themselves, whereupon one does not have a short flatbow with stiff ends, but a long flatbow with a kink in the middle of the limb and the ends badly out of tiller [Fig. 5.1].

The handbow differs from the crossbow in there being a definite limit to how far the arrow may be pulled. Asiatic archery shooting techniques admit of a draw well beyond the ear. How accurate this may be I cannot say because I have not tried it, and what constraints it imposes on other aspects – draw weights, perhaps – again I cannot say because there exist records of Chinese recurved bows of great draw weight and very long draw. It is unsatisfactory to have to admit of ignorance of the reasons behind a problem, but it is a good deal better than propagating supposition as if it were fact. Most limitations on bowyery have been imposed by craftsmen believing that they knew why certain things were just so, and it has taken the brilliance of people like Hamm and Comstock and Baker to overcome what they have shown to be prejudicial ignorance.

Living within the limits of our knowledge, if we accept that a handbow admits of a limited draw length – 28 inches for the Western hold – then bow design is geared to that one limitation.

Dutch elm disease first hit England in the 1940s, and within 45 years 17 million had died and almost all the mature elms had gone. It changed the landscape of the country within a generation. Many of the roots survived the disease and sent up suckers. Elms always were likely to send up suckers, and conse-

5.1 The Holmgaard bow: view from the back; view from the side of how it is supposed to bend; view of how, all too often, it does bend.

quently were widely planted as hedgerow trees. The young shoots seem to be protected from the disease, but a recurrence of the attack occurs after a couple of decades. A very large number of healthy saplings are found on the outskirts of London, but when they reach a diameter of about eight inches, once again they die of the disease.

As clusters of saplings they grow tall and straight and without too many branches – ideal bow material. If, from the thinnings of a clump of saplings, we find ourselves offered a straight-trunked example of slightly flattened section about three inches wide and two inches thick – and this happens more often than you might imagine, or did when I lived in England – we do not eschew it. The English seem to have a deep dislike of guns but for some unknowable, paradoxical reason it pays to let everyone know you are a bowyer, if you live there. We carefully de-bark it on the spot with a penknife to create what might become a bow-back, and melt some candle wax onto each end of the seven-foot log with a blowtorch. The wax will prevent any checking, to which elm is especially prone as it dries. (A check, in woodworkers' parlance, is a split along the grain of the wood.) Should small branches sprout out from the trunk, we do not worry unduly because elm is very difficult to break, and all that is needed is a little swelling of the wood there to safeguard it against localised bending. We do not even need to worry about the grain, with elm, as we would have to for yew.

Elm is noted for its rapid rate of drying. With a thin sapling, liberties can be taken, and the log can be sawn lengthways immediately. It will be seen that both pieces take an immediate three-inch backset. I had thought this was due to the rapid drying, until I read Gordon who showed that the centre of a tree-trunk, the core or sapwood, is under compression and if a tree is cut in half lengthways, the compressed inner is allowed to expand. It is this that gives the future bow its backset.

The particular choice of elm as a bow-wood for a stonebow lies in the fact that it is so abominably difficult to split. You can only really split it when it is still wet, but sawing it at any time is successful. Very thin sections dry – which is all seasoning is – very quickly, but the handle section in an embryonic stonebow must, absolutely must, be left thick and wide for a long period so that it does not warp as it dries. The reason is this. We are about to make a sideways curve in the handle, so that the pressure-point of the hand, at the base of the thumb, lies below a large window sliced out of what bowyers call the riser. This missing section is essential to a successful stonebow. We do not have an arrow to lie alongside the bow, and bullets do not flex in flight past the handle as do arrows.

The necessity for this abrupt curve immediately above the handle is because of the plane of forces which we encountered in making a bullet-crossbow. As a bow is drawn, the tension of the bow-string and the bending strains in the bow-wood, combine so that all four contact points – the point where the hand is holding the bow, the point where the fingers are holding the back of the arrow, and the two limb-tips, lie on a perfectly flat plane. It takes only a small amount of force to pull the string a little to one side, and it is this that makes it possible to have a canted bow in a bullet-shooting crossbow. But the crossbow has a rigid stock, or tiller; and it will be found, if you have the bravery to try the experiment, that the human arm and hand are very far from rigid and no sooner do you let go of the bullet in a hand-held bullet-bow, than the bow jumps round sideways and the bullet crashes into the bow-wood. It is a fact that a great many people in antiquity and in India and Africa today manage to teach themselves to counter this movement by a simultaneous twist of the bow, and they manage successfully and even accurately to shoot bullets from a straight bow, but I have not. Therefore, in this instance, I shall stick to my dogma and advocate the cut-away, centreshot bow for a stonebow.

We leave the limbs untouched with the original surface of the wood, just below the bark, as the back of the bow. It will be wobbly and wiggly and probably a bit twisted, but it does not matter. And, following the discoveries of Comstock, Baker and Hamm, we make the bow limbs two inches wide for most of their length, tapering to as close to a point as we dare during the final third of the limb length. I take mine to $3/8$ inch wide at the nocks.

How long? I like elm bows of around six foot. Baker and Comstock have shown that the optimum length is about 67 inches, but the extra length is good insurance. The limbs taper in thickness from about $5/8$ inch down to $3/8$ inch. One does not measure these things accurately because the wandering nature of wood's uneven grain prevents it, and because different trees grow with different density. All we can do is give approximate measurements, and the final measurement is arrived at in the making.

As all bowyers know, the initial cutting to shape of a bow, laborious as it may be, is as nothing compared with the importance of tillering. The newly roughed-out bow is placed on a tiller – mine is bolted to the workshop wall – and the string is fitted loosely at first and given a short pull [Fig. 5.2].

With any reflex, the bow is usually determined not to bend, but to flip over so that the back takes the tension. This problem can be solved by attaching square 'sides' to the tiller to jam the handle of the bow and stop it rotating. Once the bow bends a little, it can be seen if there are any stiff spots in the bow limb, and also if one limb is markedly stiffer than the other. Tillering is nothing more than scraping the thickness off wherever the limb is stiff. Every book on bow-making tells us so, and every book is right, but there is no substitute for making a bow yet devised that can persuade the newcomer that it

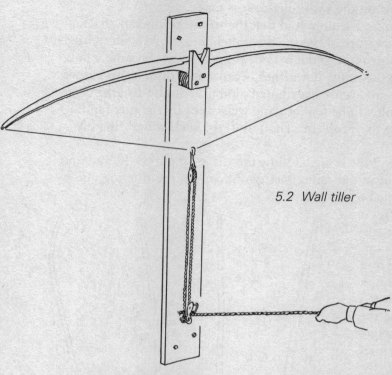

5.2 *Wall tiller*

is so simple. But that really is all there is to it. If one limb is stiffer than the other, scrape the stiff limb. If one bit of a limb seems too stiff, scrape it thinner. And at all times, leave the bending bits alone. Use a rasp if you're impatient: the work will go quicker and the chance of the bow ending up too light will be increased, but it will add valuable experience and the next one you make will be better.

Being of natural stock, we have to accept that the side profile of the wooden bow is not straight. Baker suggests drawing parallel lines on the side of a bow, and tillering the lines, not the wood, to a desired curve. I have a dial bendmeter such as Dr. Elmer described in the 1950s, but I do not use it because it is almost impossible to place the outer two datum pins on exactly the same place of a particular section of limb, and very slight differences in aligning the bendmeter along the limb mean that the central moving pin can be displaced not by the bending of the limb, but rather by the camber of the limb back. Drawing parallel lines on the side of a bow is never easy, and especially difficult if the sides are themselves uneven, but it is worth persevering for it allows the use of an extremely simple device to replace the bendmeter. This is a short piece of straight softwood with a 6-millimetre hole drilled through it. A quarter-inch dowel will jam tightly in this hole, but can be pushed in or out to give a set protrusion. The ends of the softwood stick are put alongside the straight lines, and the tip of the dowel made to extend as far as the 'straight' ruled lines, when the bow is bent. This makes it comparatively simple to identify which parts of the limb are the stiffest, and they can progressively be scraped down.

Any 'propeller twist' to the limbs disguises the fact if one edge of a limb – the edge with the parallel lines ruled on it – is bending perfectly and the other edge of the same part of the limb may be either too stiff or too bendy. The bow needs frequent reversals on the wall-tiller as it is made.

      With elm bows, I seldom find that the strains of the bow-back at full draw match the even curvature of the ruled parallel lines. Bows with twisted limbs have a reputation for breaking and it may be that this is not because a bow limb must not twist during the draw, but rather because it is difficult to ensure that the strains of bending are evenly distributed along the limb's length. Over time, the bend of a bow-limb will be fed into any weak spot by the surrounding stiffer wood, compounding the problem. The failure of such a limb is only a matter of time.

      We can expect the bow to follow the string after a while, and one of mine with three inches of initial reflex lost two inches in the tillering and a further inch during subsequent shooting, but it has quite a pleasant draw with no perceptible stack. Reflex, for the non-bowyers among us, is where a bow bends towards the target before it has its string fitted [Fig. 5.3]. Stack, again for the non-archer, is the horrid feeling when a bow-string becomes very hard to pull during the final bit of the draw. Both topics are gone into in great detail by books on bowmaking.

      Failing all the above, there is no reason not to make a glass-fibre stonebow. Such limbs as we are likely to find, discarded and therefore suitable for experiments, are going to be recurved ones since that is what the target archer shoots. The hunting archer these days generally shoots a compound bow, and though I have an idle dream of a compound bullet-bow (Chapter 11, Fig. 11.1), it is a lot of work to make and my experience is it will not get used enough to

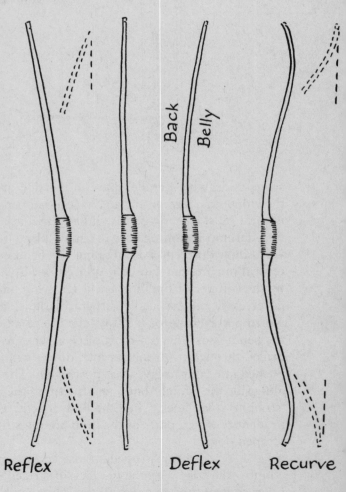

Reflex   Deflex   Recurve

5.3 Nomenclature of wooden bows

make this a sensible investment.

The recurved bow needs to have the string very precisely aligned with the tips and with no twist at all, or on shooting the string will shed itself from the limb nocks. This is exciting to watch, and relatively safe too, because it happens after most of the available energy has gone into launching the arrow. You do not, however, much want it to happen to a stonebow, and it is more likely so to occur because the string is wider. Wider? The string needs to be a double string with a pouch between to hold the bullets. Unlike the bullet-crossbow, only one pillar is needed because the string is so much longer; whether there is any advantage in two pillars I do not know, never having become proficient enough to have developed sufficient accuracy to find out.

Solid, single-piece glass-fibre bows are more risky. I fitted a double string to a straight, cheap fibreglass flatbow and shot a lead bullet using a twisting motion to ensure that the bullet flew past the bow. The twisting motion was not quite twisty enough and the lead bullet flew into the bow and then back into my face, which was offputting.

Astonishingly, however, I went on to build a wooden, fully centreshot handle for a pair of glass-fibre recurved target limbs [Fig. 5.4]. To ensure everything was square, I used a short flat plank of beech, and at each end

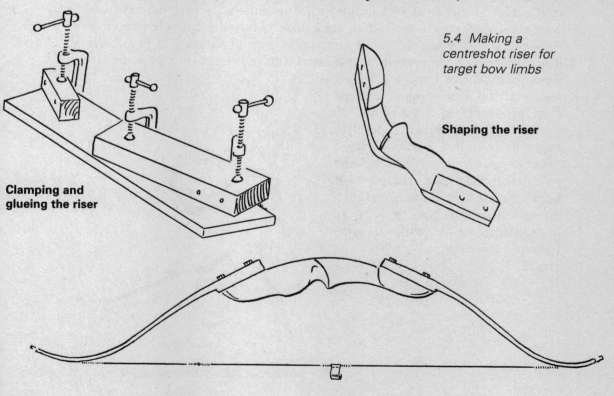

Clamping and glueing the riser

5.4 *Making a centreshot riser for target bow limbs*

Shaping the riser

epoxied another, squared block at enough of an angle to eliminate most of the recurvature of the limb-tips. This expediency reduced the risk of the string coming off the bow on discharge.

Another block was epoxied to the middle of the beech plank as the handle, and everything surplus cut away. What I ended up with was a chunky but strong riser – the middle, unflexing part of a bow which incorporates both the handle and the limb-mounting points – with a large, clear sight window above it. I had a pair of Yamaha YTDII 44# limbs and fitting a double string, with a wooden separating pillar 1¼ inches long, found I could get it to throw a 22- gram (20-bore) lead ball at 199 fps, but I had to hold the pouch with the ball between finger and thumb, and the string, additionally, with another finger to get sufficient purchase on it for it not to slip before full draw [Fig. 5.5]. This is like the Morse Secondary Release: viz., the bullet held 'twixt index finger and thumb, while the third finger plucks the string. I tried a one-ounce bullet, fondly thinking greater mass would give greater efficiency. Whether through the slight increase in diameter of the ball (though it was so slight that I doubt it could have had this effect) or through the slight sideways twist imparted by the string slipping off the third finger, the bullet bounced off the inside edge of my centreshot handle and there followed a whining sound followed by a distinctive clonk, as it hit the fence of an unidentified neighbour. In haste all experiments were thereupon concluded and all equipment removed indoors. Examining the riser afterwards, when it became clear nobody else had heard, I found a large lead-mark where the pressure button would have been, had it been an arrow-shooting bow, and I was left with a feeling that I should have made it even more centre-shot than I did.

Whether practice might be rewarded with accuracy, I cannot, alas, say. I believe the potential is there, but this too must fall to the lot of some future experimenter to explore and, it is to be hoped, elucidate the matter in some book yet unwritten.

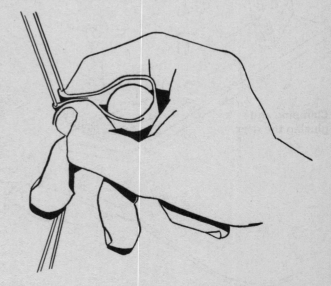

5.5 *Morse Secondary Release applied to a bullet-bow*

CHAPTER 6

Blowpipes

Were ever war to become obsolete – a vain hope – there would still be merit in a gun that may be had for the making, a gun capable of providing provender for the table. The great problem with firearms is the enormous cost of ammunition. Cost is, of course, relative; three-quarters of all the world's rifle cartridges fired each year are .22, most of them the .22 Long Rifle, and where I now live one may buy 50 for US$3. One may also buy 20 AK47 rounds, the 7.62mm x 39mm, for $3. But 20 of the high velocity 7mm mountain rifle rounds cost $40. And although 500 .22 air rifle pellets might cost $3, if one is in the middle of East Timor where $3 might be almost a month's income, then this is very expensive indeed.

Airguns can use bullets, but they can also use darts and indeed the very first airguns almost certainly did. The advantage of the dart is that it can contain its own means of stabilization, whereas the bullet must be stabilized by a spin imparted to it by the barrel. Hence, of course, the rifle. A dart can be shot from a smooth barrel and if well-designed will stabilize itself in flight, as is known to all archers. As this is the method used in the blowpipe, it is a logical move to use it also in the low-pressure airgun. All that we need to know is that to be stable in flight, the rear end of a dart needs to have a high aerodynamic drag, and the front has to have a low aerodynamic drag. There is an advantage in the front of a dart having a greater mass, and although the blowpipe dart usually doesn't have a weighted nose, best accuracy is obtained by combining these features; a heavy nose with low drag, and a light tail with high drag.

Air, unlike gunpowder, is cheap, and we have all had a fascination with air as a propulsive medium ever since Latin lessons necessitated the use of a pea- shooter to alleviate the declension of such things that, were we not minded to so alleviate, we would now be able to remember. Thus school-teachers deceive themselves as to their function. My revered Latin teacher fondly believed that I was among a crowd of young souls anxious to acquire a classical education, whereas I regarded Latin as a forty-minute period three times a week to indulge in clandestine physics, and it has to be said that the physics has amused me throughout my life while I have rarely found myself disadvantaged by the want of an ability to chat to a Roman soldier.

The pea-shooter was a plastic blowpipe a foot long which on one startling occasion sent a dried pea through the lightbulb in my bedroom, leaving a small entry hole, a large exit hole and shards of frosted glass all over the bedding. I still remember the shock of the exploit, and I am still astonished at the force this must have exhibited. As a juvenile I thought the mouthpiece essential; it was not and later I found great delight in forming tiny cones of paper and Blutack, at the tip of which a dressmaker's pin was embedded. At a range of 20 feet with a two-foot-long piece of laboratory glass tubing these would fetch down a balloon at Christmas time, to the consternation of the secretaries who deplored such idleness, though it did not prevent their taking slightly longer over a cup of coffee than their piety implied.

A rebirth of the interest came about when I bumped into an old friend in England. He had been to Borneo and returned with what he told me was a Proscribed Weapon, which is to say a Sumpitan or blowpipe made by one of the Penan tribesmen. According to the Statute Book possession of a blowpipe, like a machine-gun, has been forbidden by the UK Home Secretary, who must be more than unusually optimistic. It's hard to ban what is nothing more than a tube. Perhaps the worry was over the poisoned darts. My friend had darts, but the tribesmen would neither part with poisoned ones nor with the information required to make the poison, so perhaps the Home Secretary's anxiety was misplaced. Misplaced or not, my friend took the London Underground home from the airport pretending, he told me, that it was not a blowpipe but rather a curtain rod. Exactly how you pretend something is a curtain rod I do not know. I have travelled the Underground with all manner of objects, and never once been questioned as to whether they were or were not curtain rods. Nor have I ever noted the typical behaviour of a curtain-rod-carrier. Anyway, the blowpipe itself did look a little like a curtain rod, provided the curtain rod was one of those shaped like a six-foot tapered mahogany blowpipe.

Typical of those already described, this specimen was called a 'kelaput' by its maker, and weighing 965 grams was 1842 millimetres in length, made of a mahogany-coloured dense hardwood – maybe from the jagang tree – one longitudinal half of which appeared to be of a lighter colour than the other, perhaps as a consequence of being prepared partly from sapwood. It was bought directly from a Penan tribesman in the Baram district of north east Sarawak, Borneo. It is not certain that any significance should be attached to the possible use of sapwood.

The bore, as is normal, adopts a curve along the length. It is reported that during the boring process the wood is deliberately bent, and usually claimed that the weight of the spear-head which is attached to the muzzle of the blowpipe to allow a coup-de-grace, straightens the bore in use. This is probably wrong. My friend who had observed blowpipes in use said that they are commonly used vertically to shoot at monkeys aloft in the tree canopy, and in these circumstances the spearhead cannot have any straightening effect.

The spear-head that came with this blowpipe [Fig. 6.1], a plain leaf-shaped steel blade 44 millimetres across at its widest and no more than 3 millimetres thick, with a total length (including a 100-millimetre-long rectangular-sectioned shank), of 220 millimetres, had a weight of exactly 100 grams. The binding was missing, but an experimental lashing of a rubber strip cut from a tyre inner-tube showed that even when held horizontally, there was no straightening in practice. There was a flattening and slight grooving at the muzzle of the weapon which, forming a convenient site for the spear-head was probably a deliberate feature. That this was placed diagonally to the inclination of the curvature casts further doubt on the assumption that the spear-head's weight had a part to play. Nevertheless, the bore exhibited so marked a curve that, viewed from one side at the breech, the hole at the muzzle actually disappeared from sight, though from the opposite side of the bore the muzzle was entirely visible [Fig. 6.2]. Regardless of the actual effect of the mass of the spearhead, my friend told me that the spearhead itself was always aligned in the same way for shooting and it is possible that the original users believed that straightening ensued from this mass. I would propose an alternative theory; that because the tip of the dart rests upon the base of the bore and is therefore initially pointing downwards, the curve of the bore could be imagined to straighten the flight of the dart as it leaves the muzzle.

There can be little doubt that

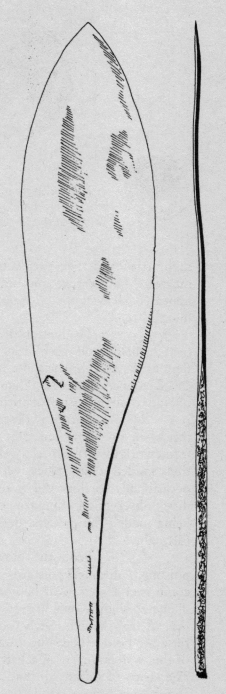

6.1 *Spearhead of Penan Blowpipe*

6.2 *Looking straight down the muzzle (left) and mouthpiece (right) of the Penan Blowpipe.*

this curvature, for whatever reason, is indeed deliberately induced, because from the outside no similar curve could be detected, and indeed the hole at the breech was displaced 1.5 millimetres from the centre of the wooden pole. Yet this must remain in doubt, since the eccentricity of barrel wall thickness at the muzzle was not in the same plane as that at the breech. The outside diameter was 36 - 37 millimetres at the breech, slightly oval, tapering rapidly to 32 millimetres over the first 63 millimetres and then evenly tapering to approximately 20 millimetres at the muzzle. Many cracks and apparently accidental longitudinal gouged grooves appeared all over the weapon, as well as a groove 60 millimetres long at the muzzle.

The bore itself, smooth but not polished, was slightly oval; more oval at the muzzle where it measured from 10.8 to 11.4 millimetres in diameter than at the breech where the variation in diameter was 10.7 - 10.8 millimetres. Of an engineer's comment that this might suggest it was bored muzzle-first, I was unable to obtain either confirmation or contradiction.

Boring is described in the literature as being accomplished by means of an elongated iron chisel operated entirely by hand, yet set in a framework up a tree directly above the wood blank, so that the drilling which is thus guided takes place vertically. An assistant tips water into the bore occasionally to float the wood chips out. The details were confirmed by the direct observation of my friend – lucky fellow – who had watched the blowpipe being made. The process, he said, takes from six to ten hours, spread over a fortnight.

With the blowpipe came a quiver ('tehloh') of darts; none poisoned, although poison is an essential aspect of their use. The quiver itself comprised a section of bamboo 282mm in length and 63 - 70mm in outside diameter, slightly oval in section, having a node of the bamboo as its base [Fig. 6.3]. A leaf-shaped, notched extension to the bottom allowed for a binding of rattan to hold in place the lower part of a large clasp for carriage. The upper end of this was bound with a belt of woven rattan to the upper part of the quiver. The strips of rattan still had the remnants of nodes of the plant present, and could have been formed from thin strips of bamboo; something we couldn't judge without expert botanical examination. This clasp had some decorative carving on one side only, and the whole was of a fine-grained wood, perhaps a rosewood. The quiver had a cap, also of bamboo and having a similar ovality, perhaps of the same piece of bamboo. It too was closed at one end by a node, and being somewhat tapered inside, and the upper 90mm of the quiver being tapered from the outside and then painted with a matt back, an almost air-tight seal could be obtained with the closed quiver having a total length of approximately 360mm, not including the lower projection or the clasp.

Within the quiver were 28 darts and, impaled one upon another on a separate bamboo needle, 15 truncated conical pith sealers. Two other implements were inside the quiver. One, carved from a single sliver of bamboo 11 millimetres wide and up to 4 millimetres thick, had at one end a curious free-vibrating prong contained within the sliver, and an equally curious dragon-like carving at the other end. This, my friend thought, had a musical use, working on the same principle as a Jew's harp [Fig. 6.4].

The second implement was of

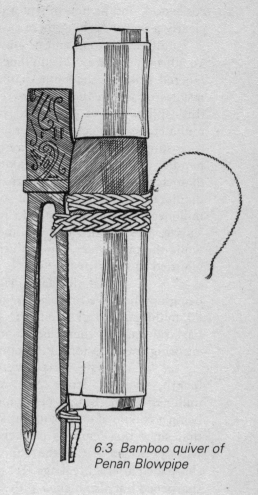

6.3 *Bamboo quiver of Penan Blowpipe*

6.4 *The Jew's harp*

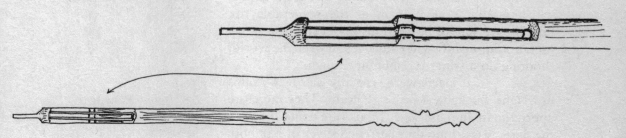

rosewood, and having in situ a pith sealer, was very clearly a jig for making them easily [Fig. 6.5]. It was 272 millimetres long and of circular section, having an abrupt cutaway 21 millimetres long leaving a tapered spike of the same diameter as the bamboo needles of which the darts were composed. Behind this spike was a swelling, starting from 11.4 millimetres diameter, and thereby acting as a gauge to ensure a tight fit in the bore of the blowpipe, the handle expanding to a maximum 13-millimetre diameter and tapering to the rear to 5 millimetres in diameter, terminating in a cylindrical knob 9 millimetres in diameter and 13 millimetres in length. This is pressed into the abdomen to hold it steady while the pith sealer is put on the spike and swiftly whittled to uniform shape.

Of the darts, eight were barbed by being notched five times at irregular distances, up to 80 millimetres back from the forward point. The barbing makes them break off in the wound, ensuring transmission of the poison to the prey.

The darts were not of uniform length, varying from 258 millimetres to 310 millimetres, the longer being more common. There being a couple of darts with broken tips, it is possible that since the Penan is unlikely to do his practice with poisoned darts, the shortest was simply re-sharpened after a breakage. Yet this one was not only sharpened but also nicked at the tip, though with just three notches 5.5 millimetres apart, the foremost being 13 millimetres back from the tip. One might question whether darts for practice would be nicked, which would weaken them at the vulnerable tip. Equally, we should be cautious about the over-inter-pretation of insufficient evidence; all over the world, shooting on a whim is common enough.

Darts were typically of 21-26 grains in weight, the lightest being 19 grains They therefore approximate in mass to a .25 air rifle pellet. Each of the darts was a long thin barrelled sliver of bamboo, superficially resembling a knitting needle. They were

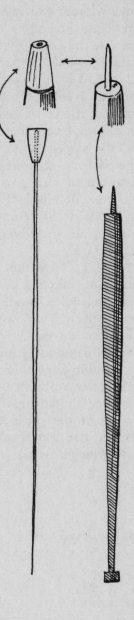

6.5 *Penan Blowpipe dart, and hardwood jig for carving its pith sealer.*

a surprisingly consistent 2.8 millimetres thick at the centre and 2.5 millimetres thick at the rear, where there was also an abrupt conical sharpening of 4 millimetres, and they all tapered to a point along the foremost 100 millimetres. The rearmost 20 millimetres entirely penetrated a very light-weight soft piece of plant pith, tapering from around 11.4 millimetres at the back to 9 millimetres at the front, acting both to seal the bore against the breath and to put drag on the back of the projectile in flight to stabilise it. The piths were not all that regular, but the material was so soft that some damage had occurred, and the tool for their uniform manufacture suggests that originally they were much more consistent.

My chronograph would not measure the velocity of these darts, since their length, taper, and narrowness meant that often the rearmost chronograph sensor was not tripped until the dart was part-way through the machine. So I made a series of small bamboo pellets having paper skirts to seal them against the bore, and shot these through the chronograph at six- inches' range to get an idea of the velocity. Initially, an even exhalation produced velocities of 124-145 fps (average 131 fps) with a pellet weighing 12 grains, but using a more sharp exhalation, best described as a spit-blow, this was increased to 148-163 fps (average 158 fps). An 8-grain pellet could be blown sharply at from 183-203 fps (average 193 fps). A 20-grain pellet ranged from 150-173 fps (average 160 fps) and a 19-grain pellet managed a single reading of 174 fps, being lost in the attempt.

These velocities, of course, are by a Westerner having no experience in using the weapon, and I am no trumpet player. It is likely, therefore, that the indigenous owners are capable of producing higher performances.

Exhalation method	Pellet weight (grains)	Velocity (in fps)		
		Min.	Max.	Average
Sharp	8	183	203	193
Even	12	124	145	131
Sharp	12	148	163	158
Sharp	19	-	-	174
Sharp	20	150	173	160

Yet of course both archers and airgun users are acquainted with the fact that a heavy projectile tends towards greater efficiency than a light one. The Laws of Physics are difficult to evade, and doubling a velocity requires four times as much input energy, or probably a bit more given the reduced efficiency seen in weapons shooting a light-weight projectile. Doubling the mass of a projectile and retaining the velocity requires us only to supply double the energy, but increasing the mass of a projectile usually gives greater efficiency, and therefore maintaining velocity with a heavier missile may require less than double the input energy. We can reasonably speculate that our velocities with the 8-grain pellet might be matched by the more powerfully-chested Penan with his original

26-grain dart.

Given that a 26-grain dart travelling at 200 fps gives a kinetic energy of about two foot-pounds, it is clear that the use of poison with these weapons is something of a necessity; indeed, we might turn that statement around and suggest that the use of poison requires a projectile having considerable powers of penetration yet so little kinetic energy as not to pass straight through the body of the intended victim. In both respects, the blowpipe dart is ideal. My friend said penetration was three inches in flesh, and although I was unable to check owing to an understandable reluctance on his part to expose his leg to me, the darts went this deep into expanded polystyrene.

The effect of poisons is best attained by a deep injection of the substance into the bloodstream, and the notching seen on some darts indicates the deliberate policy of weakening the tip to ensure it remains in any wound without being torn out by a monkey progressing through the twigs and branches of the tree canopy. I was gloatingly told – he had seen the weapon in use and I had not – that a monkey would drop from a tree about a minute after being hit, the poison apparently acting to stop the heart muscle. What steps were taken to prevent the heart muscle of the hunter stopping on eating the dead monkey, I cannot say. I believe that the poison acts in the bloodstream but not via the stomach, which suggests a courageous approach by the pharmaceutical industry of the tropical rainforest. An ancient and widely-quoted tract has a sixteenth-century Spaniard telling us to use the sap of the Euphorbia family of plants as a crossbow-bolt poison, but I never tried this and, not being required by starvation to feed myself by hunting monkeys, had no inclination so to do even though it was a common enough weed in England – found in the garden the last time I bothered to look.

The use of the bow offers far greater kinetic energy to the projectile and may obviate the need for poison, yet within the still air of the forest, shooting through small gaps in the foliage where the movement of the limbs of a bow may be hindered by twigs or branches, the Penan capitalised on the potential accuracy of the blowpipe. With this weapon Blackmore states that 'Borneo head hunters put six out of ten into a potato at a distance of 50 paces'. We were unable to replicate this, but at an accurately-measured ten metres managed a five-shot grouping of 175 millimetres using five randomly-selected darts, and with no practice whatsoever. An archer will appreciate how long it would take a beginner to achieve so close a grouping as this with a bow and arrow, yet on his travels my friend had noticed in a Penan encampment perhaps as many as two hundred darts radiating from several small fires where the poison was drying on their tips. This indicated the possibility that a successful shot might by no means be guaranteed, and that the users also relied on the silence of the weapon to give a number of shots at the same target.

It is to be hoped that the poison was subject to rapid deterioration since otherwise the forest floor must offer the hazard of a random distribution of lost poisoned darts. Despite diligent enquiries, the Penan would not divulge the contents of their poison ('tahjum'), preparing it in secret and refraining from selling poisoned darts to the curious young Westerner. Despite inducing paralysis, the poison was said to have a different mechanism of action from the curare used to poison projectile heads in South America.

We can tentatively conclude that an intelligent use of an accurate dart possessing very little kinetic energy but deep penetration, and involving a sophisticated grasp of practical pharmacology, gives the Penan a specialised alternative to the bow as his primary hunting tool, adapted both to his prey and to his environment.

Now the observant reader will notice that the above description is a little like a paper in a scientific journal, and indeed some years ago I did submit it to the Society of Archer-Antiquaries, but they declined to publish it even though the weapon was a six-foot cylinder of wood made by a primitive people in the jungle, on the not-unreasonable ground that it wasn't a bow.

I did try to argue that the darts were a little like arrows, but they were unconvinced – and after a while, so was I. For it occurred to me that it would be an interesting exercise to see if this self-same weapon would perhaps shoot a bullet. When my wife was clearing out her belongings to make way for a new sofa I had salvaged a medical peak-flow meter, and I found that if I blew hard, I could manage 680 litres per minute, while if I used a spit-blow such as described above, the flow rate went off the scale and therefore must exceed 880 litres per minute.

If the blow-pipe has a bore of 11 millimetres and a length of six feet, it contains 0.1738 litres of air. To blow a pellet through it at 200 fps, I am moving 0.1738 litres over six feet in 0.03 seconds which works out at 347.6 litres of air per minute. In theory, then, and in the unlikely event of my having got all the maths right, I ought to be able to shoot a pellet at 880 divided by 347.6 times 200, which is 506 fps, provided the pellet is light enough.

$$\frac{880}{347.6 \times 200} = 506 \text{ fps}$$

Since he doesn't make regular trips to Borneo, my friend declined my request to experiment further with his blowpipe, which had by now resumed its dignified role as a wall decoration in his living-room. I therefore began to think back to laboratory glass tubing. The local plumbing merchant did not have any glass tubing but did supply me with a two-metre length of copper pipe, 15 millimetres in diameter, with a nominal bore of 13.6 millimetres. I took a .451-calibre lead ball, wrapped it in tissue, and blew it through the pipe. It flew so slowly through the chronograph that it did not give a reading, which means it must have been travelling at less than 100 fps. There the matter rested for some years.

CHAPTER 7

Low-pressure airguns: the theory

Building a bow is usually safe. Building a crossbow is usually legal. Building an airgun is always dangerous and often illegal.

Many countries have passed laws on what one might have in the way of an airgun. The laws of governments can be – and all too often are – disobeyed. You will or you won't obey your local legal code regardless of anything I might say, but the laws of physics are not to be contradicted and if we break one of these we will find, with compressed air, that severe punishment is ordained and there is never any appeal. So pay heed to any and all warnings of danger. Compressed air is very dangerous indeed. To paraphrase one website, there is a line between building yourself an airgun and building yourself an unexpected hand grenade. It is as well not to make it a fine line.

Bicycles are progressively easier to pedal as the tyres are pumped harder, so there is an incentive to pump them as hard as possible. The law of diminishing returns sets in at about 90 pounds per square inch (psi) so though you may pump the tyres harder, the bike doesn't thereafter get easier to pedal. Pump the tyre too hard, and the law of diminishing returns sets in rather rapidly, as the air pressure overcomes the strength of the tyre itself, and the inner tube pushes the tyre off the rim. When this happens there is a moment's grace as the exposed inner tube swells to a point where it can balloon out, and then because the pressure of air is spectacularly above the strength of the inner tube, there is the most enormously loud bang as it explodes.

Replacing such a tube after such an explosion, I found myself wondering if it might be possible to replace my lungs with a short length of bicycle inner tube and compress some air into it with a bicycle pump. I tried this out by tying one end of the inner tube to seal it, but of course pumping it up and releasing the other end simply allowed the air to escape with that cheery noise which the world around causes merriment and laughter.

This leads to the important distinction of the two functions of air as a propulsive agent. In the blowpipe, the air is simply the medium through which force is transmitted to the projectile. The air is doing no work: the lungs are doing the work. Similarly, attaching a balloon or any other rubber container to the breech of the blowpipe, does not involve the air except as a mechanical harness, in the same way that hydraulic fluid only acts to conduct movement through a series of tubes from a pump which does the work, to a mechanism where work is wanted. In tying one end of an inner tube and using it as a balloon it is the power of the rubber that is doing the work, not the power of the air.

The second and quite different function of air, and that which distinguishes the blowpipe from the airgun, is when the air is compressed and therefore acts like a spring. Work is done to the air by the pump beforehand, and on release, it is the springiness of the air that provides the power. The vessel containing the air, unlike the human lungs in a blowpipe, does no work at all other than preventing expansion. When this distinction finally penetrated the turbid depths of my consciousness it became clear that the rubber inner-tube would hold some pressure of air only if there was a bicycle tyre wrapped around its outside. Various complications were averted by my taking two pieces of car seat-belt webbing and sewing them into a tube four inches in circumference (seat-belts being two inches wide).

A standard engineering formula tells us that for a pressurised vessel, if we double the pressure, we double the stress in the walls. If we halve the diameter of the pressure vessel, however, we halve the stress in the walls [Fig. 7.1]. The bicycle tyre is a pressurized cylinder, and – regarding it as a long tube – it is more likely that the circumference will swell, not the length. Again, engineering formulæ tell us that the stress round the circumference of a tube is double that along the length [Fig. 7.2]. Pressures higher than 100 psi are possible if the tyre is of very small section, and racing tyres go as high as 160 psi with a diameter of under an inch. But 160 psi is very

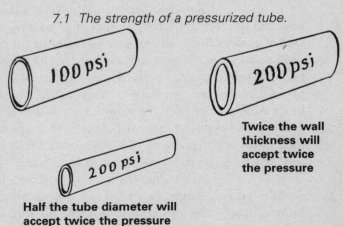

7.1 *The strength of a pressurized tube.*

Twice the wall thickness will accept twice the pressure

Half the tube diameter will accept twice the pressure

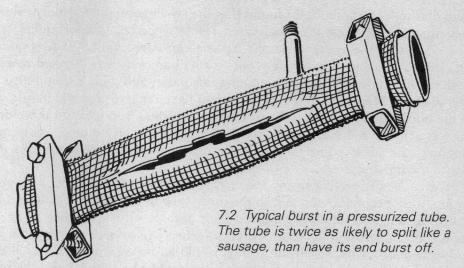

7.2 *Typical burst in a pressurized tube.
The tube is twice as likely to split like a
sausage, than have its end burst off.*

dangerous. Though we all know that high-explosives kill us by means of compressing air, until we have actually suffered the effects we are apt to dismiss air, through its invisibility, as an overstated danger.

One adventurous evening I took a two-litre plastic carbonated drinks bottle and drilled an 11-millimetre hole in the lid. Then I cut a Schrader valve together with an inch disc of rubber from an inner-tube. Popping the one through t'other, I screwed the lid down and pumped the bottle up to 70 psi. It was still at this pressure 12 hours later, so temptation, as it often does, overcame caution. Donning ear defenders and goggles once more, I took a smaller plastic bottle with a diameter of half the larger one, and pumped this to 180 psi. This did not tell me what the burst pressure might be, but as we know that the strength of a pressurized cylindrical vessel is inversely proportional to its radius, I reverted to the larger one and determined to find the burst pressure. Naturally I popped it outside the garage door, with me and the pump on the inside, and commenced pumping.

At 130 psi, there was no further increase in pressure despite more pumping. Puzzled, I thought I ought to have a little look to see how it was getting on.

I opened the door. It seemed that the top end was beginning to bulge. To save myself the trouble of thinking why it was bulging I went to release the pressure, and bent to take the pump connection off the Schrader valve. As I touched the bottle, there was the most enormously loud bang and my hand felt rather as if someone had just hit it hard with a big lump of wood. Chastened, I leapt in the air and subsequently trembled for ten minutes. Half the bottle remained, somewhat crumpled, attached to the pump; the other half I found ten yards away. A few drops of blood formed on finger and thumb from plastic-lacerations, and I found that the swelling on my forefinger started to abate about an hour and a half later. The bruising lasted a fortnight.

The energy released can be calculated as 2,900 foot-pounds which is rather a lot. Fortunately only a small amount was directed towards my hand or I daresay I should be typing this paragraph with a stump near my elbow. Had I been at all intelligent I would have realised that the plastic wall of the bottle (diameter 3⁷/₈ inches) starts to stretch at 130 psi, and therefore it cannot achieve a higher pressure, but only a larger volume, with more pumping. At some point thereafter the stretched plastic becomes too thin. Hence the bursting.

Reverting to my meditation on means to construct a big-bore airgun, a first thought was to lash the inner-tube to a gate valve taken from a gas oven, but this gate valve was so tight and slow to open that all the air hissed out, rather than burst out as it does when you over-charge your bicycle. Suddenly it struck me that if the air tube could be closed with an external gate, a bar of iron clamping it from the outside, it would be a simple matter to hinge one end and instantaneously release the other. All tremulous, I nailed a rod of iron to a block of wood, and made a trigger [Fig. 7.3]. One end of the webbing tube was sewn up, a rubber band was bound very tightly round one end of the inner-tube to seal it, the open end was lashed to a two-metre length of copper pipe, and I poked a .451-calibre lead ball wrapped in tissue, down from the muzzle with a length of dowel acting as a ram-rod. I pumped three times on the bicycle pump, and hit the trigger. Hah! Instant gratification. The ball hurtled out of the end of the copper pipe into a hanging blanket with all the force of a catapult. Thus was born the simplest airgun I could devise.

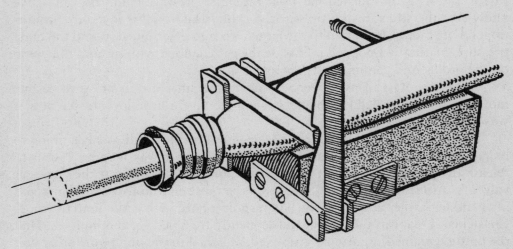

7.3 Simple trigger shows the principle of the low-pressure airgun.

If the seat-belt webbing is two inches wide, such a sausage of air, sealed at one end, has a diameter of 1.27 inches and if it has a length of 9½ inches, gives a volume of about 12 cubic inches. Pumped to 100 psi, this contains 12 times 100 inch-pounds of energy, times roughly two, or 200 foot-pounds of energy. Why times roughly two? Because we actually multiply it by Log_e of the number of

> @ 100 psi:
> $2 \, (12\text{in}^3 \times 100 \text{ in-lbs}) = 200 \text{ ft-lbs}$

atmospheres squeezed into the reservoir, and there are seven atmospheres in 100 psi, and $\text{Log}_e \, 7$ is roughly 2. The reason we do this is not as complicated as mathematicians would like us to believe when they invented frightening terms like Log_e, but rather because the air is acting like a spring. Log_e is a mathematician's way of talking about gently adding more and more energy by the expedient of squeezing the air a bit harder. Numerate archers likewise talk about force-draw curves. If we didn't add this bit to the equation, then 100 psi in 12 cubic inches would have the same potential energy as 50 psi in 24 cubic inches, and clearly in the bigger air reservoir where the air isn't compressed so much, there is less squeezing of the air molecules to be released into our bullet.

Do not imagine, however, that such a reservoir of air will make a ball fly through the air with 200 foot-pounds of energy. The transfer of potential energy stored in compressed air to kinetic energy of a bullet is necessarily inefficient. By the dependable method of experiment I have learnt that the efficiency of energy transfer is rarely more than 20%.

One lesson is useful to the experimenter: that of writing everything down. I find from my notebook that my first success was on the 22nd January, but the inner-tube kept bursting within the webbing tube. Nevertheless a .451 ball had a velocity of 326 fps recorded for posterity. That first day I also discovered that a half-ounce lead ball fitted almost perfectly down the copper pipe and it achieved 168 fps at 5 bar (70 psi). On 23rd January there was a trial clamping the webbing and inner-tube together from the outside with a couple of strips of rubber wrapped round two pieces of angle-iron. Obviously this didn't work, because on 25th January I seem to have been busy sealing the end with tight nuts and bolts using the same pieces of angle-iron through which had been drilled fresh holes. The mechanism would be refined later, but the principle was established. The air-bag was soon pumped to higher pressures – 7 bar (100 psi) – and the copper pipe, which is flexible, lashed to a length of angle-iron as a stiffener, and I was shooting a 4⅝-inch group at ten yards.

Why mention the notebook? In my case to demonstrate how haphazard the process of discovery can be. Only later would I come to examine all the figures carefully and discover, for example, that a barrel four times as long yielded twice the muzzle energy, or that double the pressure gave double the energy. I had long been aware of the antique full-bore airgun, but being deeply stupid it never crossed my mind to consider how this worked. Why the dates? Only to show how swiftly we learn when we try an idea out in real life. With a simple home-made mechanism and the entertainment of a chronograph and idle evening hours of trial and error, I laid out to my entire satisfaction the basic principles of very-low-pressure big-bore airguns. The heartless reader will note that I am very easily pleased.

Had I been more alert I imagine I could have found something similar in the literature, for it doubtless exists; almost any invention at all will be found to have been invented independently elsewhere. Certainly there are some delightful, if not downright dangerous, things to be found in these times of global communication on the Internet – under, for example, a search for 'spudgun'.

I was left, however, with the principles, which are an intrinsically interesting lesson in physics. What, then, are these basic principles?

First is the valve. When I lived in England I had the great good fortune to know Tony Holmshaw, who in his workshop took small underpowered two-stroke East German motorbikes and converted them into ferocious racing beasts with such success as to win national championships with them. I remember watching him opening the valve of a cylinder to such an extent that he had to leave a tongue, a sort of aluminium uvula, hanging down to prevent the piston falling out of the exhaust port. An airgun also requires a valve and as those who tune race-winning motorcycle engines will tell us, the smoother and the more direct the airflow through a valve, the more efficient it will be. Air does not like to be disturbed in its progress from one place to another; when it is disturbed, it exacts a penalty.

When we consider antique airguns we find they usually had a straight-line valve and used a pressure of about 500 psi, though Reilly (who made such guns and published a pamphlet claiming such a pressure in the 1850s), tells us that no pressure gauge had been made that was accurate above 375 psi. Some historians say 'well over 1,000 psi' but coyly do not go into how such a pressure might have been achieved.

Arne Hoff gives pressures of 30 - 40 atmospheres for the famed Girandoni (Austrian Army) airgun of 1780, and tells us 1,500 pump strokes were required by the official description to fill a 45-cubic-inch reservoir for 20 shots. He measured a pump with a 19-inch length of tube but does not give the bore. More recently Geoffrey Baker and Colin Currie have beautifully photographed and privately printed some complete dissections of several antique pneumatics, and they measured a Girandoni pump bore at 13.5 millimetres, with a stroke of 19.8 inches. In theory such a pump would develop 146 atmospheres with that many strokes, but we all know that pumps rapidly lose their heads for arithmetic as the pressure goes up. Hoff reports Danish trials of 1820 with Danish-made Girandoni copies which resulted in pressures of 50 atmospheres.

Wesley describes in detail the pump of his Lowenz airgun – a civilian copy of the plainer military Girandoni – of 1792; it too has a bore of 13.5 millimetres, but a working stroke of 17.25 inches. Applying my body weight of 150 pounds to such a pump, I would arrive at a maximum pressure of 677 psi, and Wesley says he was able to produce a pressure of 600 psi 'without Herculean effort'. In mild conflict, however, and describing a walking-stick pneumatic rifle, Wesley says the highest pressure to which he personally hand-pumped an antique air rifle – an air cane – was 580 psi using a pump of ½-inch bore and a 15-inch stroke.

The importance of the valve in my contraption was vividly demonstrated when one of the inner-tubes got itself slightly twisted, resulting in a small soft intrusion of rubber between the air reservoir and the copper barrel. The velocity dropped from an expected 381 fps to an erratic 162, 227 and 276 fps.

By extension, we can see that for efficiency's sake the smallest part of the exhaust valve's cross-section needs to be larger than the back of the bullet, and this introduces the second basic principle. The force contained by the air reservoir is measured in pounds (that is, pounds force) per square inch. The valve relying on a cloth bag surrounding a rubber bicycle inner-tube limits the pressure to that which will not burst. Bicycle tyres have been made to withstand pressures of 160 psi and at some point above this things get a bit hazardous. However since the inlet valve is that for a bicycle-pump, we are more severely limited by the pressure we can obtain with our pump. In my experiments I used a bicycle track-pump, which is used vertically, and has a long narrow bore, a foot-stand and a tee-shaped spade handle; an altogether easier thing to use than a common bicycle-pump. Nevertheless pumping became nearly impossible above 175 psi.

We are talking of very low pressures for an airgun. If you have few pounds per square inch, you need to have a lot of square inches on which these few pounds can act. At one time there were a series of lead pipes laid out under the pavements in the business sector of London and other capital cities through which small containers were sent with messages inside them, the system being known at the time as 'Pneumatic Dispatch', under which title it features in encyclopædias dating from the first half of the twentieth century. The bore was about two inches, the pressure about 10 psi, and the velocity of the containers was about 50 fps.

As the bore diameter increases, the area on which the air can act increases in proportion to the square of the diameter. Double the bore, and four times as much force acts on the back of the bullet. However the weight of a spherical bullet increases according to the cube of the bore; double the diameter of the bullet, and it will weigh eight times as much. We might therefore expect the performance to diminish as we increase the size of the bore, but it is a general principle that as the weight of a projectile increases, so the efficiency of a pneumatic gun increases. This relates to the law of the preservation of momentum. A moving object, whether air or a lead bullet, has momentum which is the weight of the moving object times its velocity. If there is a collision, the total momentum before the collision is the same as after the collision. This is quite different from the energy, which is proportional to the square of the velocity. But as the weight of the bullet increases, a greater proportion of the energy available in the compressed air is transferred to it.

Momentum is needed to get the ball flying, and momentum is provided by a large mass of air under compression. Since we are using low pressures, we have to use large volumes to achieve enough energy, and since the conservation of momentum applies to everything after the collision, the air that escapes in the wake of the bullet will still have velocity, but this velocity cannot be recovered, hence the inefficiency. Here we have an explanation for the otherwise curious fact that shot from a pneumatic airgun a lighter bullet has more speed, but less energy, than a heavy bullet. The lighter the bullet, the more it approximates to just another air molecule, and the closer it comes to the velocity of the air on exit, and by implication the more of the momentum is still left with the air rather than the bullet. The heavier the bullet, the more momentum it absorbs leaving less total velocity to be shared out between escaping air and bullet.

(Sadly you may find that this is not the explanation at all, because I am painfully aware that my grasp of physics falters and weakens as it wrestles with momentum and energy. It is a fact that if you shoot a bullet at a stationary block then the momentum may be the same afterwards but quite often half the energy will have vanished – some day some kindly soul will explain to me where the other half went. The explanations from my friends who are mathematicians, chemical engineers and physicists are wholeheartedly unconvincing. They mumble into their coffee about heat, and entropy, and Newton's second law of thermodynamics. The one aspect that is lacking is clarity, and more than once I have found that the most confident of the physicists have made fundamental mistakes in their basic maths, and they don't much like it when you point it out to them. It all makes me terribly nervous about being too dogmatic myself.)

That, then, is the home-made airgun in its elemental form. But the discerning reader will already have gathered that I am of experimental disposition, unable to leave anything alone until it has been thoroughly meddled with. We have already discussed some factors which contribute to its efficiency: the pressure of air, the smoothness of flow from air reservoir to barrel, and the bore.

Results and Conclusions

Almost the first thing my generation learnt as schoolboys in a chemistry lab, after discovering the penalties for turning on the gas taps and what happens if you surreptitiously insert your neighbour's tie into a Bunsen burner, is that good experiments should have Results and Conclusions.

There is a straight-line relationship between air pressure in the reservoir, and muzzle energy. The pressure of air is restricted by the valve, which is nothing more than a pinched bicycle inner-tube. A higher pressure can be obtained if the cloth valve-tube is a fine bore, but it must not go below the diameter of the barrel, or the flow from air reservoir to breech will be held up.

Double the pressure, and we get double the muzzle energy (and hence four times the pressure results in double the velocity.) So raising the pressure gives an exactly proportional rise in muzzle energy: using 28 cubic inches of air, a 2-metre barrel, a 340-grain ball in a 16-millimetre bore, at 7 bar pressure I got 344-349 fps, 89-92 foot-pounds and at 11 bar pressure I got 412-420 fps, 128-133 foot-pounds.

Well, it doesn't prove the point, quite. In fact this case is miles out. At 7 bar pressure I should only have been getting 83 foot-pounds, not 89 - 92 foot-pounds. Therefore ignoring for the moment the awkward fact, ever with us and dignified by the title Experimental Error, that results are largely characterised by their lax connection with theory, I avoid fiddling my results but merely hunt out some which are more favourable: using 28 cubic inches of air, a 2-metre barrel, and a 220-grain ball in a 13.6-millimetre bore, increasing the pressure by 1 bar each time produced the results shown. The predicted

Air Volume (cu.ins.)	Barrel Length (cm./ins.)	Bore (mm.)	Ball Weight (grains)	Pressure (bar)	Velocity (fps)	Energy (ft.-lbs)	
						Actual	Predicted
28	43 ins	13.6	220	3	192	18	20.25
28	43 ins	13.6	220	4	234	27	27
28	43 ins	13.6	220	5	264	34	33.75
28	43 ins	13.6	220	6	282	39	40.5
28	43 ins	13.6	220	7	321	50	47.25
28	43 ins	13.6	220	8	332	54	

energy figures were worked out using 54 foot-pounds as the base figure.

There is a straight-line relationship between muzzle energy and the square root of the barrel length. Having a hacksaw, and given that copper pipe comes in lengths of up to three metres, experiments are done very easily on barrel length. Of course this conveys a very wrong impression, which is that there was method to my experiments. There was not. They were entirely random. I shall now bare my soul and admit that as soon as I had established that 15 cubic inches of air would not give me any more velocity in a two-metre barrel than in a 48-inch barrel, I built a trigger mechanism using a modified Chinese crossbow lock for the external valve and through dazzling incompetence managed to make a wooden fore-end five inches too short for the barrel. So I chopped it to 43 inches to fit. Then I made the 28-cubic-inch reservoir, and found to my dismay that a longer barrel suddenly became advantageous. It was a haphazard business, and the only merit in these random trials was my keeping accurate results, because it was afterwards in comparing the figures that the theories began to emerge.

For example, one evening when alone in the house with the children sleeping angelically (a circumstance calculated more to encourage the perusal of figures than further trials in the garage), the startling fact hopped out at me that there was a direct mathematical relationship between performance and barrel length – that of the square root. I suddenly noticed that a 31-inch barrel with a 28-cubic-inch reservoir at 7 bar and a 220-grain ball, gave a muzzle energy of around 40 foot-pounds, and with the same reservoir and pressure a three metre piece of copper pipe had given a muzzle energy of 84 - 94 foot-pounds.

Air Volume (cu.ins.)	Barrel Length	Ball Weight (grains)	Pressure (bar)	Velocity (fps)	Energy (ft-lbs)
28	31 in.	220	7	288	40
28	31 in.	220	7	290	41
28	31 in.	220	7	284	39½
28	3M.	220	7	425	88
28	3M.	220	7	438	94
28	3M.	220	7	414	84

What was this? Why, exactly twice the energy. Well of course it wasn't quite, but I have lived long enough to know that we mustn't expect too much accuracy in our science. So of course I examined what ought to happen if this was the case – if a 31-inch barrel gave 40 foot-pounds, a 62-inch barrel should give 1.414 times as much energy or 56½-foot-pounds. Why 1.414? Because this is the square root of two, and the barrel was twice as long. I didn't have a 62-inch barrel, but I did have a 60-inch barrel, and lo! - looking it up in my results: 28 cubic inches of air at 7 bar pressure, a 220-grain ball, and a 60-inch barrel gave these results.

Air Volume (cu.ins)	Barrel Length (ins)	Ball Weight (grains)	Pressure (bar)	Velocity (fps)	Energy (ft-lbs)
28	60 in.	220	7	345	58
28	60 in.	220	7	348	59
28	60 in.	220	7	344	58

Near as dammit, and enough to convince me that this square root relationship is pretty accurate. Of course it cannot be precise, because the short barrel should really have a smaller reservoir; but it showed me that I hadn't lost much by cutting five inches off my 48-inch barrel.

This – the excessive accuracy of mathematics – is an aspect seldom explored. It took 12.5 strokes of one track-pump to achieve 7 bar pressure in a steel rifle-reservoir which contained 28 cubic inches. The bore of that pump is 1.25 inches and its stroke is 16.75 inches, so it should pump 20.555 cubic inches of air in a single stroke. If there is any correlation between theory and practice, the reservoir would be 36.7 cubic inches. As we saw with the Girandoni pump, there isn't. I filled the reservoir with water and tipped it into a measuring cylinder and it contained 28 cubic inches. Granted the webbing-and-inner-tube valve added a bit, but it was only a cubic inch or so. But since a variation of just one cubic inch could lead to anything from 6 to 9 foot-pounds difference in stored energy, any efficiency figures which I arrived at are barely accurate to within even one per cent. My computer calculated them to a hundredth of a per cent. Computers fondly imagine that figures are accurate; in life we may hope that they approximate to reality just about enough for us to make moderately dependable predictions.

So if we want twice the muzzle energy without altering the air pressure in the reservoir, we need a barrel four times as long. A 31-inch barrel is about a quarter the length of a 3-metre barrel, and gives about half the muzzle energy.

Though complicated by the need for an adequate volume of air in the reservoir, a mathematician might write:

muzzle energy is proportional to reservoir pressure x √barrel length.

It is irritating to note that both high air pressure and longer barrels give higher velocities than those predicted by the theories. The Cardews published graphs of small-bore air rifles at very high pressures showing a tapering off of performance at very high pressures and with very long barrels. It suggests, like Hooke's Law, that our theories are only true in the middle range of our parameters.

Too long a barrel for the volume of air in the reservoir gives inconsistent velocities. The barrel length is important, but a long barrel is only of any use if the volume of compressed air is sufficient to fill it and to keep accelerating the bullet all the way from breech to muzzle. A long barrel may increase efficiency, but there comes a point where there is insufficient air to overcome uneven barrel friction.

The volume of air in the reservoir shows a relationship to increased performance analogous to the size of a spring. A large spring will have the potential for greater power than a small spring. If we squeezed a two-inch spring by an inch, it would be highly compressed, and the initial shove it would impart would be far larger than the final shove it could give. If on the other hand, we squeezed a 12-inch spring by an inch, there would be very little difference between the shove at the start of releasing that one inch's compression, and the shove at the end.

Clearly if the volume is tiny there will be little compressed air ready to accelerate the bullet; there will be an initial very high force on the bullet which will peter out as it occupies the increasing volume of barrel behind the bullet. But once the volume of compressed air reaches a sufficiency to give the bullet a more or less constant shove on its way down the barrel, nothing is gained by increasing this volume.

Taking a 2-metre barrel, 15 cubic inches of air compressed to 7 bar produced erratic results ranging from 229-271 feet per second, or 25½ - 35½ foot-pounds. There wasn't enough air to overcome irregular drag along the barrel – the results are in the first part of the following table.

Cutting the barrel to 48 inches gave both higher and more consistent figures, proven over a ten-shot string, still using 15 cubic inches at 7 bar and a 220-grain ball; the second part of the table gives these results.

We need to note that the barrel acts as an expansion chamber. A two-metre barrel of 13.6-millimetre bore contains almost 18 cubic inches of air. Reservoir plus barrel therefore contain 33 cubic inches of volume. When the ball reaches the muzzle the pressure behind it has dropped from the initial 15 cubic inches at 7 bar, to 33 cubic inches at 3.2 bar.

With the 48-inch barrel, the 'expansion chamber' is of less than 11 cubic inches, so the pressure has dropped to 4 bar by the muzzle. To get the equivalent thrust, a two-metre barrel seems to want a reservoir of 25 cubic inches, which allowing for the expansion of air down the barrel would also end up with a pressure of 4 bar. Again, leafing through my notebook for some relevant results, I found 28 cubic inches pumped to 7 bar, with a 2-metre barrel

Air Volume (cu.ins)	Barrel Length (ins/M)	Ball Weight (grains)	Pressure (bar)	Velocity (fps)	Energy (ft-lbs)
15	2M.	220	7	254	31½
15	2M.	220	7	269	35
15	2M.	220	7	229	25½
15	2M.	220	7	271	35½
15	2M.	220	7	244	29
15	48 in.	220	7	280	38
15	48 in.	220	7	274	37
15	48 in.	220	7	277	37½
15	48 in.	220	7	279	38
15	48 in.	220	7	286	40
15	48 in.	220	7	287	40
15	48 in.	220	7	282	39
15	48 in.	220	7	279	38
15	48 in.	220	7	287	40
15	48 in.	220	7	286	40
28	2M.	220	7	398	77
28	2M.	220	7	402	79
28	2M.	220	7	411	82½
28	2M.	220	7	378	70
28	2M.	220	7	401	78½
50	2M.	220	7	403	79
50	2M.	220	7	386	73
50	2M.	220	7	392	75
50	2M.	220	7	391	75
50	2M.	220	7	400	78

and a 220-grain ball, shown in the third part of the table.

Parity between reservoir volume and barrel volume therefore seems to give inconsistent results. The pattern that emerges is that the reservoir wants to be at least one and a half times the volume of air in the barrel. Increasing the volume of air beyond this does not give a corresponding increase in velocity, but it may well give an increase in consistency, because the thrust along the barrel is more even. Increasing the volume of air to the point where there was almost three times as much air in the reservoir as the barrel – to 50 cubic inches – resulted in no velocity gain at all (the velocities ranged from 386-403 fps), but it took twice as much work to pump the reservoir up. However, the fourth part of the table shows there was less variation in the velocities.

In order to use this greater volume of air, a much longer barrel would be needed; so we conclude that there is an optimum reservoir size for any barrel length. But the larger the reservoir the smoother the push along the barrel, and the greater consistency in velocity may be worthwhile.

The efficiency is proportional to the cube root of the bullet weight. This is a remarkably bold assertion, and one made on the following very dubious grounds. I have two bullet moulds, one for .451, and the other for .527-inch balls. I took a .451 ball and wrapped it in a sabot cut from denim and soaked in molten paraffin candle-wax, with a patch of cotton between the ball and the wax to ensure they separated in flight (again, this sounds intelligent, but it was based on the discovery that a waxed denim patch was too tight for the barrel, while a waxed denim sabot stuck to the ball throughout the flight and gave poor accuracy. The interposition of the cotton patch ensured separation and a slight improvement in accuracy. Given the price of a chronograph, accuracy was always an important consideration).

I fitted a 50-cubic-inch reservoir to a 3-metre barrel, and pumped it to 10 bar pressure, or 140 psi. The .451 ball shot at 599 fps, or 109.5 foot-pounds. It also went straight through a builder's plank of fir, 34.8 millimetres thick, clamped rigidly to the bench-leg, and after crossing a gap of an inch it made a 5.5-millimetre indentation into the fir upright of the workshop bench. The entry hole was small and the exit hole enormous. I kept it as a trophy.

If the cube root rule exists, then a .527 ball should develop, under the same conditions, 128 foot-pounds. (This we get by finding the cube root of the mass of the .527 ball, dividing it by the cube root of the .451 ball, and multiplying the figure, 1.17, by the muzzle energy of 109.5 foot-pounds.) So I loaded up the 3-metre barrel

$$\frac{\sqrt[3]{220}}{\sqrt[3]{137.5}} = \frac{6.04}{5.16} = 1.17$$

$$1.17 \times 109.5 = 128$$

with a .527 ball, pumped the 50-cubic-inch reservoir once more to 10 bar pressure, and shot it at the builder's plank. This, too, went straight through, and again after a gap of an inch, made a dent 2.7 millimetres deep in the bench-leg. The chronograph read 508 fps, or 126 foot-pounds. But if overcome with an eagerness to build yourself a simple air rifle capable of shooting a half-ounce bullet at over 500 fps, reflect first on the inconvenience of a 3-metre barrel. This length of copper pipe meant my clamping it in the Workmate bench with the muzzle in front of the chronograph, and as an experiment it was successful, but it would be hopeless to use it as a gun. The stiffness of a fore-end to support such a length, being proportional to the cube root of the length, would make it intolerably heavy; I found it impossible to move the copper pipe without snagging the ceiling of the garage.

As I say, a bold assertion made, as a scornful statistician would say, where N=1. Sadly he's right. Looking elsewhere for comparable figures, I find one where a 50-cubic-inch reservoir charged to 8 bar shot a .451 ball at 471 fps, 68 foot-pounds. If this rule is applied, a .527 ball should fly at 80 foot-pounds, but it didn't; in the event it flew at 426 fps, 89 foot-pounds. Hence the heavier bullet gives greater efficiency than that predicted.

A more accurate conclusion is:

I don't yet know what mathematical rule applies, though a heavier bullet is definitely a bit more efficient than a light one. Oh well, we have to season our conclusions with a flavour of honesty.

In my earlier catapult studies it had proved necessary – essential, as my wife put it, she having a taste for the biting remark – to cast heavier bullets than half an ounce, and I also possess hand-made moulds in which I can cast shapes approximating to spheres of greater weight than this. I took a 340-grain ball and hammered it round its equator until it became reasonably cylindrical. I introduced it to a 13-millimetre-bore steel tube, and with a plug at either end squeezed it vigorously in a vice. It took a good deal of pounding to get it out again. I expected it to shoot slower, but with more energy, than the lighter 220-grain ball. In fact it was a tight fit in the bore, and shot slower but with less energy than the lighter ball. There are many complications and a simple thing like friction in the barrel can cancel out any other theoretical advantages.

A long barrel eventually leads to inaccuracy. The flexibility of a beam being the cube of its length, a 60-inch barrel is about twice as stiff as a 2-metre barrel. Given that we are playing with flexible copper pipes, the fore-end needs to be very stiff to give accuracy. A 2-metre plywood fore-end distended 2 millimetres in the middle when suspended by its ends, and, sure enough, cut to 60 inches it only distended half a millimetre.

The reservoir shape has a direct effect on the efficiency. I welded a 28-cubic-inch steel reservoir with a gentle cone towards the exhaust valve, and another stumpy 28-cubic-inch steel reservoir with the exhaust port emerging from a flat plate [Fig. 7.4].

The second reservoir gave a less smooth air flow and resulted in a drop of the equivalent of two-thirds of a bar pressure. At 7 bar pressure,

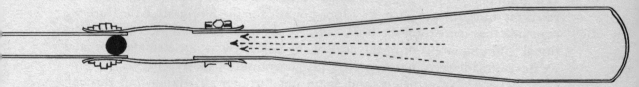

7.4 Angularities in air flow have the effect of a constriction.

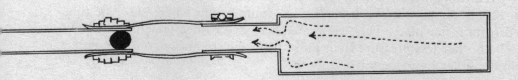

shooting a .527 ball from a 31-inch
barrel, the coned reservoir gave the first
set of results, and swapping the reservoirs
but keeping everything else the same, the
stumpy reservoir gave the second set.

**A bigger bore gives a
higher efficiency than a small bore, even
though the bullet weight is increased.**

Coned shape		Stumpy shape	
Velocity	Energy	Velocity	Energy
(fps)	(ft.-lbs.)	(fps)	(ft.-lbs.)
288	40	273	36½
290	41	272	36
284	39½	274	36½

The idea of a heavier bullet did not go
away, and one morning I fetched down a 2-metre piece of PVC electrical
conduit from where it had hung unnoticed below a rafter in the garage, and I
was pleased, you may depend, to find the bore was 16 millimetres. The 340-
grain ball fitted this, though being from a home-made mould it was slightly
irregular and did not do so smoothly. Nevertheless, with my 28 cubic inches
pumped to 7 bar, it produced 89½ - 92 foot-pounds, compared with the half-
ounce ball's 77 foot-pounds from the same length barrel.

The 16-millimetre bore being bigger than the 13.6-millimetre
bore of the copper pipe, we can calculate how much more square inch there is
for the pounds-per-square-inch of pressure to work upon – the force should be
1.384 times as much. This extra force should therefore have produced an
energy of 106½ foot-pounds, because 1.384 times 77 is 106½. But again there
is the complication that as the bore increases, so the area increases according
to the square of the bore, but the mass of the bullet naturally enough increases
as to the cube of the bore.

Tantalisingly, however, the energy of the 340-grain ball is the
square root of 1.384: 77 foot-pounds x √1.384 = 90.6 foot-pounds. A 2-metre
barrel and the 28-cubic-inch reservoir at 7 bar gives 77 foot-pounds for the
220-grain ball while the 2-metre long, 16-millimetre-bore barrel with the same
reservoir and pressure gave 90.5 foot-pounds for the 340-grain ball. Dare we
conclude that increasing the bore, with a ball to fit, gives an increase proportional to the square root of the area of the bore? It was but a single shot, and
we have already seen that where N = 1, generalisations are rash.

Nevertheless, and again not through any design but through
chance observation, it happens that a glass marble also has a diameter of 16
millimetres. Glass marbles are inconsistent in size, so some were a smooth fit
and some a loose fit and some wouldn't go in at all. With 7 bar pressure and
28 cubic inches, an 84-grain marble achieved 69 – 70 foot-pounds out of a 2-
metre barrel, though it should be pointed out that the reservoir was not my
smooth coned shape, but the less efficient stumpy one where the exit tube
emerged from a flat plate. This, we remember gave a shot which was equivalent to half a bar less pressure than those from the smoothly-coned reservoir
I used in the other figures quoted.

Now a glass marble is sometimes a handy thing in the garden, but a glass marble travelling at 607 fps is not going to educate Tosca so much as to extinguish him, and in doing so alienate my good friend Simeon, who chose this peculiar feline name and who lives next door. 'Tosca, Tosca!' I hear him call every evening, tapping a knife on a plate and summoning him to eat what I will find, suitably reprocessed, the following morning among the tomato plants. I cut the piece of conduit to 31 inches and, true to the theory that the energy relates to the square root of the barrel length, found that the velocity of an 88-grain marble was 467 fps which is 42½ foot-pounds. Perhaps it should have been 44 foot-pounds but this was satisfyingly approximate; however it was still too powerful to risk on a cat. I cut the pressure to 2 bar, and the velocity went down again as predicted to 224 fps, or 10 foot-pounds, though for the theory to be perfect it should have been 12. Carefully aiming to bounce this marble about a foot to the right, for one becomes less sanguine with the years and though Simeon's cat catches the baby birds I harbour it no ill-will, it was gratifying to see Tosca sprint for the fence as the marble boinged past his feet. Oddly enough, I found that the marble had shattered on impact with the paving slab; even at this low velocity, these missiles need to be treated with profound respect.

Repeating the experiment with a piece of large-bore plumber's copper pipe, 37⅛ inches long and of 20.3 millimetre bore – not a planned set of dimensions, but the only bit of pipe to hand – it turned out that this needed a pressure of 155 psi to shoot a Brown Bess musket ball (of 483 grains weight but well wrapped up in tissue to seal the bore), at the magical 300 fps or 100 foot-pounds of energy.

Performance

Blackmore tells us of an experiment of 1905 in which an *'air rifle from the arms collection of Schloss Pfaffroda in Saxony was carefully tested at the government experimental station of Neumannswalde. The 9.5mm lead ball was wrapped in thin paper for each shot. At 35 m. a fir board 3 cm. thick was penetrated and the conclusion was reached that big game could be killed at distances up to 100 paces.'*

Wesley shows photographs of bullets shot at a steel plate and although they are too small to give a reliable measurement, the Girandoni would appear to have turned a ball into a disc 2.5 times its prior diameter. He experimentally charged an air cane using carbon dioxide to 900 psi – this implies a warm day, given what we know about the pressure of carbon dioxide, but it is a reliable estimate of the pressure. This latter produced a flattening of the ball into a disc 3.6 times its original diameter. Using my apparatus, I shot a series of spherical bullets of 13.38 millimetres diameter not at a steel plate but rather at a brick wall. The results, plotted on a graph, show that the relationship of ball-size to flattened-disc-size is proportional to velocity, and it is a surprisingly good straight line.

Velocity (fps)	Diameter (mm)
192	16
234	18.5
264	21
269	20
282	22.5
321	23
332	25
401	32.5
443	36

By projection, it is possible to hazard a guess that the Girandoni shot its bullet at around 375 fps, the Lowenz at 417 fps, and Wesley's experimentally-charged 900 psi air cane at 615 fps. Arne Hoff mentions some experiments in 1820 with Danish copies of the Girandoni giving 330 fps; no doubt they used the ballistic pendulum to measure bullet velocity. There is further contemporary evidence that the Danish army considered this a low velocity, in that when an air machine gun (a cumbersome device) was tested in 1840, the artillery officer considered it would have little military value until given the same muzzle velocity as conventional firearms. In contrast, Baker and Currie give initial figures of 508–523 fps for the first shots from freshly-pumped air canes, the subsequent shots diminishing in velocity as the pressure dropped. We would be bold, perhaps, to agree with the government experimental station of Neumannswalde that big game can be killed at 100 paces.

However there are no laws of physics, though in many countries there are laws of politicians, to prevent us shooting items other than lead bullets. A particularly satisfying missile can be made with a plug of fruit, obtained by impaling an apple with the copper muzzle. A velocity of 349 fps results from a 2½-inch long apple core of 20.3-millimetre bore where the barrel is 37⅛ inches long, the volume 28 cubic inches, and the pressure 120 psi. It explodes on hitting a corrugated iron fence. Such an apple core weighs 340 grains and possesses the surprisingly vivacious kinetic energy of 92 foot-pounds, which is more than enough to cause serious personal injury if one is tempted to shoot it at those passing motorists who so irritate the rest of the community with their whoomphing bass loudspeakers; wherefore, albeit with some reluctance, we have to curb our more exuberant passions.

Conversely, if we are actually in serious need of meat, a glance at the history books reveals the shooting of arrows from the gun. The hunter's broadhead acts as if it were a wing, and as it is at the front of the arrow, desta-bilises the flight. The idea of razor-sharp steel fletchings has occurred to many people, but their use is precluded in a barrelled weapon. Any hunting arrow, therefore, requires very large fletchings at the rear so that the heightened drag at the back of the arrow will stabilise it in flight. Clearly three feathers will compress when an arrow is loaded down the muzzle of a large-bore airgun, but equally clearly they will not seal the bore against the compressed air; for that we must use a wadding of tightly-rolled cloth or tissue paper, or whatever else comes to hand. A piece of kitchen roll, cut to half size so that it measures 4½ inches by 10½, will neatly seal the nock of an arrow in a 20.3-millimetre-bore piece of copper pipe, and a variety of velocities can be obtained by choosing long or short arrows. Using blunt heads which safely bury themselves in the moist soil of the lawn, I found that at 120 psi, and a barrel length of 37⅛ inches, a 618-grain arrow reached 236 fps, 76½ foot-pounds, penetrating 12 inches into the soil. One of 400 grains reached 288 fps, 74 foot-pounds, penetrating 16½ inches, while a little 155-grain crossbow arrow reached 433 fps, 64½ foot-pounds, and snapped in two when it hit the soil. Quite decent accuracy can be attained if one discards any arrow that will not group, or if we limit ourselves to shooting but a single arrow. Naturally the wadding will have to be identical too, and as a small square of cloth commonly falls to earth a few feet in front of the gun, this is sometimes easier than might be thought.

An alternative to the arrow, and indeed to the musket-ball, and ideal for whoever is too lazy to rifle a barrel, is to make short wooden darts and tip them with some kind of weight. The front of the dart needs to fit the bore smoothly – but not tightly – no less than the back of the dart, and this dictates a certain shape. The front portion of the dart needs to be rounded into the classical 'tear-drop' shape, the rear of which tapers and forms a long cone. This cone does not terminate in a point but rather merges into a short and abrupt cone, facing the opposite way, and the rear of this second cone is cut off perfectly flat at right angles to the direction of flight [Fig. 7.5].

Such a cut-off will have extremely high drag, and since the front of the dart has the low-drag shape of a tear-drop, the high-drag rear will stabilise the dart in flight; the more so if the nose of the dart has been weighted. The shape is that of the classical – if that isn't too grand a word – bomb as dropped from aeroplanes, and for the same reason.

Many happy hours can be spent at a woodworking lathe making these darts, and many hours of frustration spent experimenting with them and finding that the wood has either expanded with moisture since it was made so it won't enter the bore, or shrunk with drying so the dart, rattling in the barrel, won't hit what it is aimed at. Ideally one machines a set of identical darts out of acetal or some other plastic, but enquiring as to the price of acetal dampens enthusiasm for

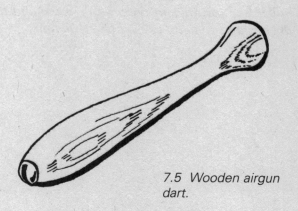

7.5 *Wooden airgun dart.*

this solution. Darts turned between centres fly true if the weight is applied to the front of the centred holes, but as in bench-rest rifle shooting, accuracy depends primarily on the care with which the dart is made. A heavy wood-working screw will focus the weight in the nose of the dart, and to ensure it is aligned and centred in the wood, a hole will have to be bored the length of the dart before it goes in the lathe between centres.

How short a dart will work is a matter of experiment, but the aerodynamicist's recommendation of a length-to-diameter ratio of five:one does tend to mean that one's drills are examined with considerable irritation because they always seem to be too short to run along the required length of wood. Then we are reduced to swearing before stopping thoughtfully to consider that the Penan of the Borneo rainforests manage to drill six-foot holes in pieces of wood to make their blowpipes, with nothing more than a long rod of iron and a tree for a guide. A woodworking lathe is a great convenience, and if not to hand it is very easily built; the simplest can still be operated with the foot, a loop of rope – ideally rawhide – running from a treadle on the ground, round the work, to an overhanging branch above the lathe. The lathe itself need only be two nails hammered into two vertical stakes in the ground, and lest we who cannot use sandpaper unless it has an electric motor and a trigger-switch attached mock, it is always worth remembering that prisoners of war in Colditz Castle in Germany in the 1940s managed to build themselves a glider in the roof of their prison.

Complexity has a cost, and there is much to be said for simplicity. The eventual relegation of the full-bore air rifle from its position as a serious gun was partly because of the difficulties of obtaining a valve airtight at high pressure - metal on metal needle valves were sometimes used, as were cowhorn on metal valves - but also because an enormous amount of effort was required to pump air into the reservoir. As Blackmore, commenting on the ball-reservoir drily observes:

'it was difficult to gauge the right pressures; too little and the bullet had insufficient power, too much and the ball or the barrel burst. Then the airgun suddenly lost all its attractions.'

CHAPTER 8

Low-pressure airguns: the practical

So much for principles – now to the altogether more dangerous business of practicality. I cannot prescribe how to do this, for there must be many ways. Some may even be safe.

As we have seen, the simple airgunsmith imitates the pressurized vessel by sewing two lengths of webbing into a short tube, inside which lies a length of bicycle tyre inner-tube complete with inlet valve which is then pumped up with a bicycle pump [Fig. 8.1].

The inner-tube seals the air; the outer casing of webbing maintains the pressure. If of an imperfect fit the end of the inner-tube within the webbing casing develops what a surgeon would term an aneurysm – a localised swelling – and bursts. It happened several times before I overcame the tendency by leaving the ends of both inner tube and webbing sausage open, and applying a clamp to squeeze them closed together between paired plates of angle-iron. I have speculated that it should be possible to do the same with blocks of wood bound with stout string, the closing pressure being applied with wedges, rather as woodworkers of old managed without the screw vice [Fig. 8.2].

8.1 *Sewn air reservoir of sailing webbing and cycle inner-tube*

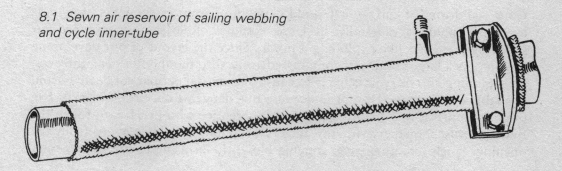

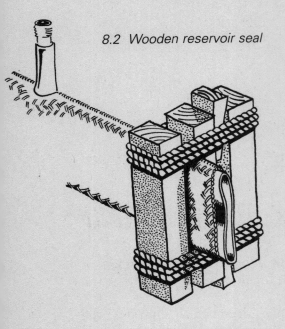

8.2 Wooden reservoir seal

If we want a high mass of air, one obvious and effective option is to increase the pressure of air. Seat-belt webbing is designed to withstand immense longitudinal force, when such car drivers as presume to drive into wayside trees are subject to abrupt deceleration. Unfortunately, as we have seen, a tube is twice as likely to split along its side and with no sideways strength, tubes sewn from seat-belt webbing burst commonly a four-inch split open along their side with an immensely loud bang at pressures of around 116 psi. I don't suppose I need say how I come to know this. I did have some three-inch-wide parachute webbing, very thin stuff, and a sewn tube almost two inches in diameter burst at 40 psi. Doubling the thickness of this parachute stuff resulted in the two layers suffering unequal stresses, and I had no faith in it. Sailing harness made from a nylon webbing seems equally strong about its width and its length, and I have sewn one-inch-diameter tubes of this material capable of containing pressures of 160 psi. For the thread I use waxed dental tape which is both strong and easily sewn. The webbing was sewn with delicate little stitches (by hand using a needle), as close as possible to one another, and it took forever. I hate sewing.

As we aim for the smallest diameters of this webbing tube compatible with getting a smooth flow of air into the barrel, it can be sewn as a helix, which may have any diameter you choose. Experiments are needed to get it exactly right and the sewing must always be very sound, though it is intriguing to see with what few stitches the racing cyclist gets away with high-pressure sew-up tubular tyres.

Another health warning. You can't have too many of them. Guns – all forms of gun – burst, and kill people. Compressed air, as I found, is extremely painful, especially in large volumes. Releasing compressed air suddenly is exactly like exploding a bomb. Since the layout of our developing airgun puts a large volume of compressed air next to the shooter's ear and eyes, an exploding air reservoir is likely to cause instant and permanent deafness and probably eye damage. Do not under-rate this danger. I once took a small bag of air, pumped it to 12 bar and, like the apprentice who just has to touch the flywheel, discharged it with my fingers a couple of inches away from the opening. It felt like a massive, stinging blow; the bruising to my fingers took two days to go away. And fingers, largely composed of connective tissue, are tough organs compared with eyes and ears.

The standard in industry where compressed gases are used is first to fill a vessel with water, and then attach a pump also full of water, and pressurise it. The water theoretically conducts the pressure throughout the reservoir, but there is no air present and should the reservoir burst all that is supposed to happen is a large mess of water. The standard in industry is also, loosely, that a pressurized vessel should have a working pressure of never more than half its bursting pressure. Of course, the standard in industry is to limit the pressure to 30 psi for all blow-guns used for cleaning swarf from machinery. If you are unable so to test the affair, then err on the side of caution and err by a very long way. Once success has been achieved at a given pressure, the temptation will always be to try to get the pressure higher. The pioneer aviator Otto Lilienthal said *'Sacrifices have to be made'* but only on his deathbed. Before his final glide went wrong, you may depend he was more optimistic.

Because I needed a large volume of compressed air, I took to cheating [Fig. 8.3]. It is straightforward if time-consuming to weld steel tube into a variety of volumes of bottle reservoirs, and since fitting the barrel requires only that the valve-tube be lashed to the breech – we do not trouble ourselves to make anything other than a muzzle-loader as the pumping process takes so long that breech-loading would scarcely shorten the loading process – all things can be varied and tested to our delight and satisfaction.

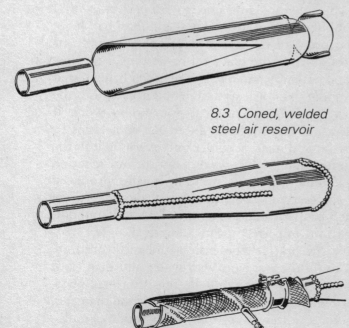

8.3 Coned, welded steel air reservoir

I used 2½-inch mild steel tube of 1.6-millimetre wall thickness; with a small MIG welder I sealed one end, and cutting a long vee-slot into the other hammered and beat this into a bottle-shape, then welded a short length of one-inch steel tubing, sawn from an old bicycle frame, as the exit tube. The bicycle inner-tube, within the sewn webbing outer tube, was pushed onto this exit tube, which because it has a smooth exterior can give an air-tight seal with the outer layers held in place with a hose clamp. The antique airguns made by Girandoni had reservoirs with a wall thickness of 2 millimetres, but of course the required strength depends on the pressure. A higher pressure needs a correspondingly thicker wall. We are certainly not going to exceed 200 psi, because our bicycle pump won't go to pressures as high as this. Very few will go as high as 160 psi.

It sounds simple enough, but two points are important. First, the very best quality of hose clamp was required, not the sort with a worm-thread to tighten it, but rather one with a 6-millimetre minimum diameter lateral nut and bolt. In trying to attain adequate closing pressure, a 5-millimetre bolt either sheared off completely or stripped its threads when tightened. If you don't get enough closing pressure, there is a hissing noise of escaping air and eventually the exciting prospect of the reservoir powering itself off the back like a torpedo. For a good air seal, it sometimes helped to bind a thin spiral of rubber around the outside of the webbing tube before putting the hose clamp in place. The smallest, tightest possible hose clamp had to be used, and getting it on, even loose, was generally a half-hour wrestle accompanied by a good deal of cursing.

Second, when the webbing tube and the inner-tube, complete with intact valve, had been clamped in place and the other end sealed – two bits of angle-iron were adequate at this stage, held resolutely in place with a G-clamp – it was necessary to pressurize the steel bottle and plunge it into a bucket of water. Weld seams which before appeared to be perfect, would suddenly reveal tiny streams of bubbles issuing forth. These pinholes had to be carefully dried of the water, the pressure released because any internal air pressure would blow molten steel all over the place on re-welding, and they needed to be welded up, slowly and patiently and one by one, each being tested by the tedious business of re-pumping the bottle and plunging it back into the bucket of water. If things went well, it only took three or four hours' work. If things went badly it took longer, and impatience reduced me sometimes to putting soldering flux on every seam and melting solder into every joint in the hope that this would seal the damned thing. It always did, but the introduction of the impurity of solder meant I could not later re-weld it. Brazing produced no air leaks, but brazed antique air reservoirs sometimes burst, though I know not at what pressure. Quite what a proper solution might be I never found out, managing all my experiments with the imperfect means described.

How big to make the bottle? The easiest and most accurate way of measuring the volume is to fill the reservoir with water and then tip it into a measuring cylinder. Unfortunately you can only do this after making it.

The standard formula is the internal radius (half the diameter, of course, which when I stupidly forgot threw everything into a muddle) multiplied by itself, multiplied by π which is 3.14159 (this gives the area of the bore of the steel tube) then multiplied by the length to give the volume. Coning one end down to the diameter of the one-inch tube reduces the volume of that end, and a close study of Euclid in a maths book will tell you by

$$\text{Vol} = \pi r^2 \times \text{length}$$

$$\text{Vol} = \pi r^2 \left(\frac{\text{height}}{3}\right)$$

how much: a cone occupies a volume of a third its height multiplied by 3.14159 multiplied by the square of the radius of the cone's base. What you end up with is about four-fifths of a pint or 28 cubic inches, for a 13.6-millimetre-bore copper pipe barrel. I made reservoirs larger than this – one of 50, and one of 62 cubic inches, but they took for ever to pump up and yielded little extra benefit. For a 15-cubic-inch reservoir it was easier to sew the entire reservoir out of the sailing webbing. The gentler the coning, the better. Smooth airflow is surprisingly important.

Chemical engineers, of course, have made detailed studies of this coning and have published often conflicting and always complicated formulæ as to how best to calculate it. Fluid dynamics is one of the hardest subjects in conventional physics, and we have to deal with laminar and turbulent flows. If the flow of air along a pipe is laminar, then the velocity at the middle of the pipe is double the average velocity; if the flow is turbulent, the velocity in the middle is about one and a quarter the average velocity. Whether turbulent or laminar is to do with velocity, and surface roughness of the tubing. Airgun tubes are almost certainly turbulent because laminar flow requires low Reynolds numbers, and low Reynolds numbers are rarely to be had at high velocities. From somewhere, I cannot now remember where, I garnered the figure that a coning of 8° from air reservoir to barrel would convince the air that there was no coning at all, and the result would be as if there was no pressure drop. Illustrations of Venturi tubes show inlet cones of around 11° and outlet cones of around 6° taper. There are any number of books on these abstruse matters in any university library, though it does have to be said that if you find yourself relying on me for this information, you will struggle to make headway in reading them. Physicists commonly labour over their studies, not over their communication of same to us mortals.

When all was done with my steel reservoir, I took a candle and poked it into the reservoir and applied a flame to the outside until the steel was so hot that smoke came out of the end - the rubber tube and webbing, of course, being removed for this operation. Swilling the molten candlewax round and round until I was happy that every bit of the inside of the reservoir was waxy, I then emptied the remaining wax out. It is an unfortunate fact that the explosion of compressed air results in everything becoming instantaneously icy cold, and there is so massive an amount of condensation when one of these airguns is shot that if you take the barrel off immediately afterwards, the rubber inner-tube has beads of water inside it. These will rust the reservoir if it is left uncoated. Antique airguns were lined with grease, and the pumping generates heat which may make the grease produce volatile vapours. The nervous engineer worries if any of their many recorded accidental explosions were a result of the diesel effect, where the pressure caused the grease itself to explode. Candlewax seems safer. But Cardew, fount of wisdom in matters pneumatic, states that a gradual increase in pressure and temperature such as we attain with a hand-pumped air reservoir cannot create an explosion even when the pump and the reservoir are oiled. (However, we are warned against charging a reservoir with compressed oxygen, for any volatiles in such a mixture will certainly explode and kill us.)

On this, of course, it is worth reiterating that we are dealing with low pressures. At some point, the steel tube will rupture. The webbing, if kind, will rupture first. That at least is only very dangerous – perhaps only an ear-drum will be ruptured, leaving you deaf. An exploding steel reservoir is much more something to avoid. Many of the antique reservoirs were spherical, and of course the larger the diameter of the sphere, the greater the stress on the walls and the more likely they were to explode, but some burst out of their valves. Blackmore records an instance of a valve, presumably soldered, bursting out of a copper ball reservoir and killing the unfortunate who was pumping it. Copper solders easily, but it is not very strong.

The home-made airgun requires a home-made barrel whose two vital dimensions are diameter and length. Both qualities are to be found in plumbers' copper pipe, which is to be found throughout the civilized world with an external diameter of 15 millimetres and an internal diameter of either 13.6 millimetres or, bizarrely, half an inch. Copper is a soft metal, and we are therefore limited to low pressures of air. The .303 rifle develops a pressure of forty tons to the square inch, which is more than thin copper pipe can stand. We limit ourselves by bicycle-tyre technology to the pressures sustained by bicycle tyres. The finest quality hydraulic copper tubing of 15-millimetre outside diameter and 13.6-millimetre bore has a burst pressure of 350 psi, and therefore its working pressure is only half of that. Plumbers' copper pipe is of more uneven quality, and the burst pressure is probably lower. Bicycle pumps will struggle to reach 175 psi but even so the danger of an exploding barrel makes us tread very carefully indeed. For higher pressures a completely different technology is required, and completely different materials.

Copper pipe is made by an extrusion process and a glance down a pipe will reveal ripples round the bore, which will give uneven friction on a bullet. I found when loading the ball that different lengths of the same barrel will allow a smooth, even loose sliding fit, but the ball will then encounter a tight patch. This I thought could be overcome by making a small tight plug of hardwood – I used a rosewood plug an inch long turned on a lathe to exactly 13.6 millimetres diameter – covered in fine grinding paste sold by car accessory shops for grinding valve seats, and hammering it down the bore half a dozen times. Such a wooden plug can only be used the once: over a period of time moisture will distort its cylindrical shape and what was a cylinder on a warm dry Monday can very easily have an oval cross-section on a rainy Tuesday. Unfortunately, there is the rather irritating fact that actually it had no effect at all on the barrel.

What is wanted is something a bit better – a proper barrel-making process. *The Model Engineer* magazine of 1912 and 1913 goes into this in some detail, including rifling, though this was for model guns which conveniently have short barrels. But there is a hidden bonus to an unevenness of bore. Modern airgun barrels have the last 3/4-inch of the muzzle choked by about a thousandth of an inch. This ensures that the pellet leaves the muzzle at a tight spot, and gives a more accurate rifle than one where any slack at the muzzle allows the pellet to drift away from the rifling rather than snap out of it cleanly. Provided the intended barrel is half the length of the original piece of copper pipe, it is possible to cut the pipe at the tightest spot to become the muzzle, ensuring a choke. We find the spot by feel, with a ball wrapped in waxed cloth, and by marking a ramrod where the ball is at its tightest. Obviously with extruded copper pipe the choke may be more than a thou' deep, but copper pipe is a fiftieth the price of a barrel. Moreover, it does not rust.

Availability may restrict us to a bore of 13.6 millimetres and we find, fortunately, that this is a perfect size for a half-ounce bullet of .527 calibre which, wrapped in a thin paper patch, will give a reasonable sliding fit. Experimentation may show that a better fit is obtained if the paper is cut away to a sort of flower shape, a central circle of 14-millimetre diameter, and six radiating petals of 9-millimetre length and 7-millimetre width. It allows all the surface circle of the ball to be padded – because it is only the circle of the equator of a spherical bullet that makes contact with the barrel's bore – without the complication of creasing of the patch to over-compress a number of points round the circumference of the ball. A tight-fitting ball gives a poor velocity compared with one which slides smoothly, but equally a sloppy fit of bullet to barrel gives poor accuracy.

It is possible, of course, that a .527-inch bullet mould is not available. A smaller bullet can be used provided the patch is made sufficiently thick to occupy all the space around it yet still have a good sliding fit. A patch, cut to the above shape, but made from two layers of cloth and dipped in molten candle wax, will wrap round a .451 calibre ball and give a very good fit indeed. The ball is hard to get started in the muzzle of the barrel, but once it is moving, the wax lubricates the bore and an excellent air-tight fit is achieved, with perfect sliding on discharge. Better yet, the patch grips the rifling, and some accuracy (depending of course on the barrel) can be achieved. But lest we become smug, the waxed patch is adhesive and will often grip the bullet tenaciously during the flight and ruin the accuracy, so a good deal of experimentation is required to find the right thickness of cloth. I resorted at one point to making a circular patch of thin dry cotton, wrapping the ball in this before putting it into the pre-soaked flower shaped cloth, and this at least seemed to allow the patches to separate from the ball within the first five yards of flight. Since we have encountered complication, let us start calling our flower-shaped patch a sabot to distinguish it from a circular patch. Why don't we simply do as muzzle-loading black-powder riflemen do, and use a thicker patch for a tighter grip? Mostly because our pressures are so low that a tight grip has a serious impact on muzzle velocities.

We see that I have introduced the concept of rifling. The very first muzzle-loading rifles appear to have been made with straight, not twisting, grooves, and it has been surmised that the grooves were cut to allow the powder residues somewhere to go after each shot. It is very difficult to cut perfectly-straight grooves along a very long tube, because any cutter that is pushed along the tube has to have the cutting edge very precisely aligned with the bore. It seems almost certain that the twisting of the rifled grooves first came about because the cutter was not longitudinally true to the bore, and would have slowly spiralled up the barrel as it was pushed through. It did not take all that long before riflemen observed that a twist gave a dramatic improvement to the gun's accuracy.

To cut rifling, then, a long plug is made with a misaligned cutter, such that the cutter is at a slight angle. Pushing the plug along the inside of the barrel, the cutter will rotate according to the angle it possesses, and as it emerges from the muzzle, behold, it leaves a rifled groove in its wake. Repeating this as often as the gunmaker wishes, one ends up with a rifled barrel.

I, being adventurous and not a little foolish, made a rifling tool by taking six inches of half-inch diameter wooden dowel and cutting a lengthwise slot [Fig. 8.4], very slightly angled in the same way that the feathers

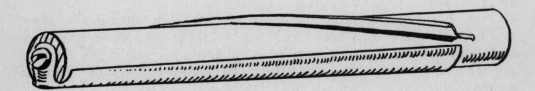

8.4 *Wooden rifling cutter, with hacksaw blade mounted at a slight angle.*

132

of an arrow are very slightly angled. Into the slot was glued a single short length of broken hacksaw blade, using epoxy resin glue. The degree of angling determined the degree of rifling.

The hacksaw blade was ground using a bench grinder until it just gripped the inner surface of the copper pipe, and as it was hammered in, it cut a spiral groove along the length of the barrel. It did not cross my mind that this would very dramatically lower the burst pressure of the copper pipe. How much lower must depend on how deep the grooves are, and you won't find that out until it does burst and you are horribly injured. That it hasn't yet happened to me may be because I have only used low air pressures. I secured a shoe of thin steel cut from a coffee tin to the side opposite the hacksaw blade; the end was folded over the front of the tool and screwed in place with a tiny woodscrew, and the front part of the shoe was glued with more epoxy resin.

Liberally greased, this tool was gently hammered into the back of the copper pipe. When the back end of it was flush with the pipe, another short length of half-inch dowel was hammered in behind it, the pipe itself being securely clamped in a Workmate bench. Secure clamping was generally not secure enough because of the force used in hammering the rifling tool through, so the breech end of the embryo barrel was tightly lashed with a rubber strip to jam it. Then things went more smoothly. Successive short lengths of dowel were hammered in until ten minutes later the rifling tool, along with a fine wiry swarf of copper, emerged from the other end of the barrel. The tool was rotated a little, reintroduced to the breech, and hammered through again, cutting a second groove. It was hard work, but cutting half a dozen rifling grooves in a two-metre barrel took about two hours and it presented a handsome sight to the educated eye when finished. But if the bore is less uneven than plumbers' copper pipe, adequate rifling can be introduced by smearing valve grinding paste on a plug and twisting this through the barrel (see Chapter 10).

How steep the rifling? My rifling cutter describes a complete circle in 18 inches. You measure the pitch of the rifling by marking an arrow on the end of a half-inch dowel which will subsequently become the ramrod, and wrapping a patch of cloth on the end that is pushed into the rifled barrel; as the ramrod is pushed home, you watch the arrow rotate and mark off on the ramrod how far it has penetrated by the time the arrow has described a full circle. The ramrod need only be a half-inch dowel, but a handle is wise because then the ramrod can be cut to the barrel length minus one bullet's length. Too long a ramrod pops the bullet into the reservoir, which is unhelpful. The round ball does not need much rotational speed to lend it accuracy and modern muzzle-loaders commonly use one turn in 48 inches. This is much sharper than a black-powder muzzle-loading rifle but our bullets are much slower than a powder gun, and accelerate more gently. Kentucky rifles had a rate of rifling of around 1 turn in a metre, a muzzle velocity of around 1,500 fps, and a bore of around .36 of an inch. At 100 yards, four-inch groups were common and two-inch groups quite possible. Firearms books give formulæ involving the sectional density of the bullet and the velocity, these needing to relate one to another for good accuracy, but for a decent velocity from low-pressure air the bullet needs to be relatively slack in the barrel and therefore the chances are slight that the rifling will much alter the grouping. Unfortunately, bullets need to be tight-fitting to be accurate.

Although I have shot a four-bullet group of 17 millimetres (centre to centre) at 13 yards, groups do tend to be bigger than this. About two inches at 20 yards; the same accuracy as delivered by the British Army's Baker rifle at the beginning of the nineteenth century. To kill a wild goat grazing the lettuces you'd have to be close enough to put the bullet where you want it. My lettuces have never been harassed by goats, so this is pure speculation.

Regardless of any rifling, the muzzle needs to be crowned. The direction of the bullet depends on the very last thing it touches before free flight. At the exact moment of quitting the barrel, the bullet should be touching the entire circle of the bore, so any burrs left will have to be very carefully and evenly removed, and in the absence of a hollow-spindle lathe it is an agonising task. A good engineering workshop will do the job in a couple of minutes, and probably chuckle heartily at the project if you are so misguided as to allow them to peer down the bore at the rifling.

Into the end of our short webbing-and-inner-tube sausage of the compressed air reservoir is inserted the breech of the copper barrel, and this is bound into the air-sausage with a strip of rubber cut from another inner-tube. All that is then required is the means of separating the compressed air from the breech of the barrel until it is wanted.

Any gate clamped around the outside of the unsealed section of air-sausage will seal it, and to act as an efficient valve between reservoir and breech it must be possible to slip this loose at the flick of a trigger. A mechanism which works well is the toggle, or over-centre release [Fig. 8.5], though frankly it is so dangerous it shouldn't be used. It has three advantages. First, the mechanism itself acts as a lever allowing the valve to be closed firmly. Second, there are no delicate sears to be made. Third, it is very simple. I found that any bearing pin needs to be at least a quarter of an inch in diameter or it will bend. The forces of air at 100 psi, our safe upper limit, over time are quite capable of bending steel. Naturally the trigger, once nudged, will move of its own accord and will need to describe a very large movement to effect the full and instantaneous opening of the valve. As it will be opened with the whole force of the escaping air it must be arranged so that it cannot scissor any fingers whatever. 28 cubic inches of air compressed to 100 psi represents 450 foot-

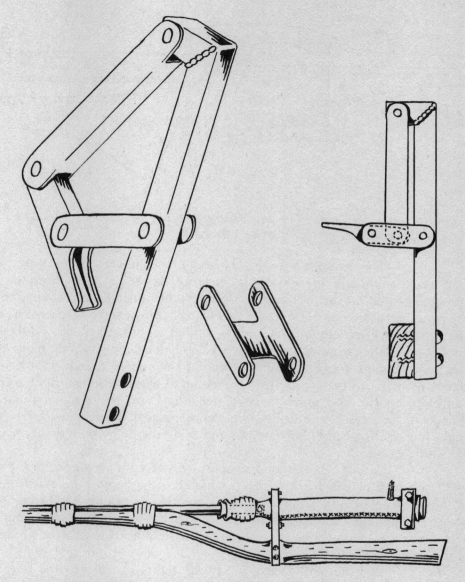

8.5 *Simple airgun but with a very dangerous over-centre release mechanism.*

pounds of energy, which is ample for an amputation. However there is another caveat – if the trigger pull is to be delicate, then the pinions will have to be so closely aligned with one another that the mechanism will have a tendency to go off inopportunely of its own accord. A fatality need only occur once to negate all its advantages. Therefore this mechanism ought to have a safety catch. I abandoned it before adding one.

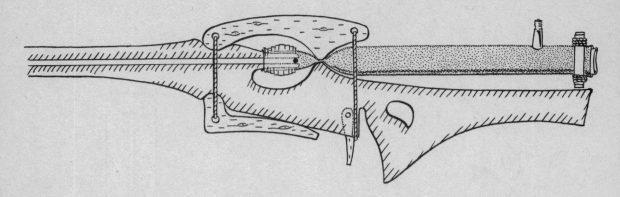

8.6 Idea for a wooden airgun. I've never made this, but the top lever flies up on release, and the shooter's head must be kept back.

The weight of the closing mechanism appears to be unimportant, although some of the pressure of air in the reservoir is undoubtedly used to throw the gate open. Being outside the webbing-and-inner-tube there is no objection to the gate being made of some very strong and dense wood such as lignum vitae and a skilled woodworker can doubtless think of some other wood that might work. A challenge might be to make the entire gun of wood, rubber and cloth [Fig. 8.6]. We have already seen that a Penan tribesman can make a six-foot barrel out of a hardwood without access to an electric drill, and unlike a twist drill the D-bit (beloved of amateur engineers in the days before drills were commonplace) will follow a perfectly straight line. Rifling can be obviated by replacing the bullet with a very short dart of stiff wood.

A post foresight and an aperture rear-sight are sufficient for the limited accuracy of which the barrel is capable. Anyone with access to mild steel box-section of different sizes and a few metal-working hand-tools – a hacksaw, a drill and a thread-cutting tap – can derive much satisfaction out of devising a means of adjusting the position of one sight horizontally for windage and the other vertically for range.

One normally seeks to lay the sights as close to the bore as possible, but again there is an advantage in arranging for the sights to be much higher where the velocity of the ball is low. If, for example, the ball flies at around 300 fps and the barrel is capable of reasonable accuracy between 25 and 35-yards range, putting the foresight ten inches above the line of the bore should ensure that the line of sight lies along a tangent touching the long, gentle curve of the trajectory from a range of 15 yards all the way out to 35 yards. The ball will be about an inch high at 25 yards, and spot-on at both 15 and 35 yards. To a great extent this will minimise the problems of aiming any low-velocity weapon, which is to say range estimation. Since we are building the low-pressure airgun from first principles, there is nothing to stop us from deliberately designing it upside-down, and if we play with the wooden airgun design exercise we can see that it can readily be laid out in any number of different ways [Fig. 8.7].

Those familiar with the design of crossbow locks are likely to be able to think of some means of making the valve-closing mechanism, for the same principles apply. The crossbow has a string held against extreme force, and it will be found that extreme force is required to hold the webbing sausage closed when it is charged with compressed air. In order to render the valve air-tight, it needs to be held very tightly closed, and a good deal of effort is required to close it. Nevertheless, this force must be released with the minimum of disturbance to the line of aim. Crossbow locks on release commonly drop down into the stock out of the way of the crossbow string; if a steel bar is arranged over the top of the airgun's webbing tube, another can be raised from below to effect the closing pinch. This second bar can be dropped using an identical mechanism to that of the crossbow lock. The only complication is that some kind of lever will be needed to apply enough force to close the valve, and as this lever will need to be removed before the gun can be shot, it may be developed as a safety catch.

That indefatigable enthusiast Douglas Elmy, now President of the Society of Archer-Antiquaries, once gave me an example of the Chinese crossbow lock, of which he had made several. Exchanging the twin claws holding the string for a bar pressing upwards and thus closing the valve, worked perfectly for the airgun [Figs. 8.8, 8.9].

Now a copper pipe is a bendy thing, and bendy rifles are not noted for their accuracy. Not only does a butt for the rifle need to be made – a large and robust piece of wood between the rifleman's head and the air reservoir

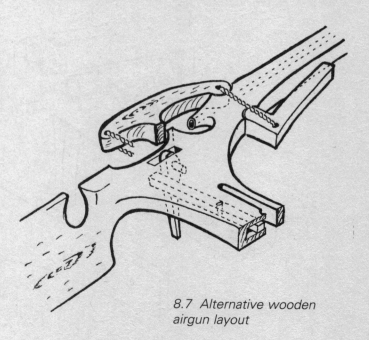

8.7 Alternative wooden airgun layout

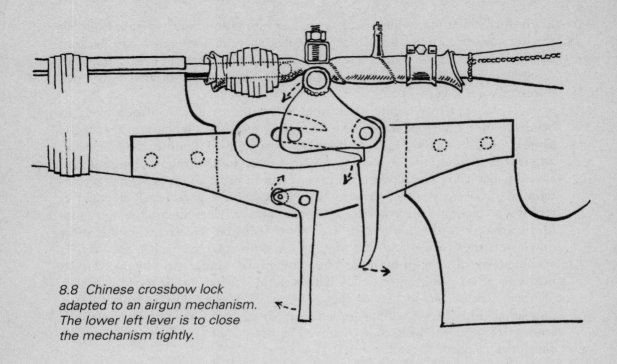

8.8 Chinese crossbow lock
adapted to an airgun mechanism.
The lower left lever is to close
the mechanism tightly.

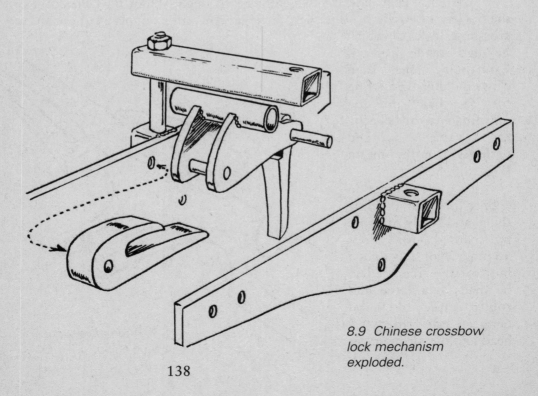

8.9 Chinese crossbow
lock mechanism
exploded.

– but also a full-length fore-end needs to be made and it must be stout enough and stiff enough not to flex when the gun goes off. The copper barrel has no intrinsic stiffness whatever, and it cannot be allowed freedom at the muzzle because of course it is the lack of movement of the muzzle that determines the predictability of the shot. These barrels need to be long – the longer the better: absurdly long in fact – and therefore the fore-end has to be long. This will made it heavy. It will also make it flexible, for a beam bends according to the cube of its length. Make the fore-end twice as long, and it will be eight times as flexible. My very first experiment had a barrel two metres long encased in a split bamboo tube for stiffness; actually it had no stiffness at all, to which a veteran car domiciled in my garage, where my early experiments were conducted, once owed an impromptu indentation.

Seasoned hardwood cut from a quarter-sawn plank has the least likelihood of warping. $1^1/8$-inch wide is stiff enough, an inch deep at the muzzle, and four inches deep at the breech. With infinite care, and using 1-inch box-section steel as a straight-edge, clamped to the fore-end at only two points so that the wood of the fore-end is not unnaturally straightened during the grooving, I run a router down the wood to cut out a perfectly straight V-sectioned channel in which the barrel is to lie. It would be nice to have cut a semi-circle of exactly the outside diameter of the copper pipe but it would not remain a semi-circle because wood changes shape according to the humidity of the air.

Routing, to those who have never tried it, sounds a pleasant and easy task, but it is a noisy business and throws large amounts of wood shavings into the eyes even behind safety glasses, and generally the router doesn't run smoothly along minding its own business but suddenly lunges sideways into the wood, gouging out an extra little bit here and there just to assert its independence. Such has been my experience, anyway. Fortunately these extra little bits don't much matter, so long as there is a central clear straight channel. The extra gouges do matter of course if they are taken out of the tip of your thumb, and I can assure you that they hurt a great deal too. One woodworker in two ends his life with fewer than ten digits in these days of cheap power tools. A wooden top-section to the fore-end, similarly grooved, will protect the soft copper from inevitable blows and may add a line of defence if, in an act of folly, higher pressures are attempted and the barrel bursts.

By far the best method of holding the copper barrel in place, though it would shock any real gunsmith, is to lash the top wooden section to the bottom wooden section with strips of rubber. The lashing is both tight and secure, and it is easily undone to change the barrel for the next experiment.

Strips of rubber are obtained with scissors. Inner-tubes of bicycles are common, and car tyre inner-tubes of vulcanised rubber or butyl can be found, as can tractor tyre inner-tubes and those of any other vehicle.

Bow-builders cut these into strips half-an-inch wide or so, making them almost infinitely long by the expedient of cutting a huge spiral from a car inner-tube as one peels an orange. Bow-builders lash laminates of freshly-glued wood and glass-fibre together with them, and once lashed, the force they exert is immense. The width of the strip does not much matter – it is best to be as wide as possible while still allowing you to be able to stretch it until it feels solid. Cutting the strips is tedious, and since infinite length is a handicap, it is as well to cut them so they no more than touch the ground when dangled from waist or shoulder. The first lashing runs over itself so there is no need for a knot. The final lashing can be hooked under the penultimate and if done in a loop, the whole can be pulled apart almost in an instant, though that does not necessarily render any advantage. It is critical that the muzzle of the copper barrel is least moveable, and wise therefore to lash the muzzle for four inches or so back. Then lashings only need be spaced every foot down the fore-end. The barrel needs to be somewhere about four feet long – shorter is stiffer and more handy, while longer is more powerful.

All the woodwork makes the apparatus heavy, which turns out to be an advantage. The kick of a full-bore nine-pound airgun is enough to disturb the accuracy; increasing the weight of the assembled gun to 12 or 14 pounds makes it very much more resistant to the recoil of the blast of a large volume of compressed air. Lashed between two pieces of grooved wood, the whole clamped in a Workmate bench, I found I often did not need to alter the aim between shots.

Is there a point of equilibrium, where the barrel is as long as will give velocity without losing practicality, the air volume is as small as possible without losing velocity, and the pressure is as high as possible without bursting the reservoir? The flintlock shooter of old was advised that a six-foot barrel was not too long, but I am inclined to think that subsequent history, in reducing this to a more manageable length, has proven the advice doubtful. When first I developed this thing, it became known among my friends as The Jezail (a jezail being a long Afghan matchlock gun) and much evil I had to resist, they egging me on to shoot it at all sort of doubtful targets including one adjacent to the office window of our estimable secretary. Manoeuvring two metres of barrel, plus stock, in and out of the doorway, the jezail inevitably incurred bumps and the shots bore no relation to the point of impact as tested previously. On every occasion I demonstrated the long gun, Poomph! and dammit, I missed completely.

Cutting the barrel to 43 inches I found the slight loss in velocity was compensated by increased regularity, so instead of getting wildly fluctuating velocities, all came out within 10 fps of each other. I had a 31-inch length of tube left over, and using this found the velocity went down to 225–237 fps.

Obviously two metres is too long, despite the theoretical advantages of a long barrel; 43 inches is okay, and 31 inches is too short. An unforeseen advantage of the 48-inch barrel was that it was stiff; it didn't bend under its own weight as did the 2-metre barrel.

There were a mere 35 deaths (including suicides) worldwide from air weapons in the thirty years since 1956. But with a four-foot barrel and 140 psi of pressure, a 28-cubic-inch reservoir sent a half-ounce lead bullet 10 inches deep into the endgrain of a rotten log. We need to be aware that the principles I have laid out create something far more ferocious than the conventional airgun, and it must therefore be treated with appropriate care.

CHAPTER 9

High-pressure airguns: the theory

Before we entirely abandon the idea of the low-pressure airgun, perhaps it is worth digging out our history books. The airgun is far older than most of us imagine: from as early as 1608 there have been written records of them. The twin requirements of the pump-up airgun (surprisingly, vacuum airguns have been built, though since a vacuum cannot exceed a pressure of minus one bar, they must necessarily have been of limited power) were a pump and at least one valve. The earliest forms had two valves, one from the pump into the reservoir, the second from the reservoir into the barrel.

Those of us who have the bad habit of frequenting the local pistol or rifle club range can, if we are unobtrusive about it, pick up abandoned brass cartridges of all manner of useful sizes, and with only a limited amount of ingenuity and some plumbers' copper pipe, can bring a very simple airgun into being by examining how our ancestors managed it. Flimsy soft solder joints seal everything together except the moving valves themselves. Given cleanliness and lashings of flux they are easily made airtight, and good for 100 psi but not very much more. But 100 psi is ample to blow a pea down a rattly microbore copper pipe, or if we don't bother with the pea, a little blast of compressed air is a diverting way of dispatching flies in the kitchen. (A damp rag is a vital accoutrement, lest the owner of the kitchen asks awkward questions afterwards as to the red splodges on her walls and ceiling.)

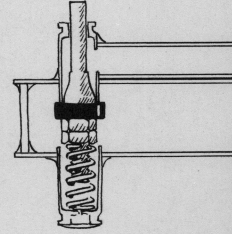

To harness a bicycle pump for the power source, the inlet valve needs to be a Schrader valve because the working parts of the Schrader valve can be unscrewed from the front and that allows us to solder it without damaging the seals. Schrader valves can be had for free from old inner tubes, though the rubber must be removed carefully before solder can be applied. In the history books the valve into the barrel is a disc of leather soaked in oil. Rubber is better, but even a disc of rubber rarely affords a perfect seal. It will, however, usually hold the pressure for a couple of hours. The benefit of using an old brass cartridge as a valve seat is that the front opening is perfectly circular and perfectly square to the bore, so it isn't too difficult to get the rubber valve disc to sit neatly in place. The Kolbe airgun enclosed the barrel within the reservoir, but it is easier to pop the barrel outside [Fig. 9.1]. Fitting the valve spring inside an opposed brass cartridge is only possible with soft solder − brazing requires so high a temperature that the spring would lose its temper.

A number of people have been making high-pressure full-bore airguns openly in America and, unless human nature has radically changed since my youth, in − er − seclusion elsewhere. Full-bore is anything from 9 mm to half an inch, and though this conjures up museum specimens, most antique airguns were of ¼-inch calibre: only with the advent of the familiar modern spring airgun, developed by Pettengell in America, did the .25 lose favour, as these airguns had a low velocity. The advantage of the conventional smallbore airgun is that it is now powerful, accurate, reliable and increasingly cheap, and ammunition is gloriously inexpensive. There is therefore no excuse for building any conventional airgun, other than the desire to do so. To make an airgun will occupy many more hours of labour than is financially worthwhile, and if we simply want the gun, the only sensible advice is to buy one and have done with it.

It was the Cardews who, in finding that upwards of half its energy derived from the dieseling of oil vapour, showed that the conventional spring airgun does not always come within the compass of human-powered bullets. The true airgun is the pneumatic, in which the pellet is expelled by air previously compressed and held in a compression chamber called the air reservoir. Although, as we shall see, accuracy depends mostly on the matching of a rifle's velocity with the best choice of pellet for that rifle,

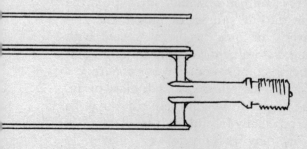

NOT for high pressure. Simplified from the *Kolbe* airgun, this is soft-soldered from copper *tube*. The valve is a rubber disc and the valve-*seat* a .38 pistol cartridge. A Schrader valve *allows* the use of a car foot-pump.

the pneumatic has the advantage that it has slight and often indiscernible recoil. The recoil of any gun depends on an exact division of momentum between everything moving forwards – always the bullet but in spring airguns also the piston – and the mass of the gun moving backwards. Among firearms the recoil can be calculated by knowing the weight and velocity of the shot, and the weight of the gun. Using as a yardstick the fierce kick of a 12-bore shotgun, which we have all experienced, we only need know that it weighs about 6½ pounds and shoots 1⅛ ounces of shot at 1,200 fps, to assess other guns accordingly. The former military NATO rifle, whether the .303 or the 7.62 (.308 Winchester), delivered a kick of about 60–65% of that of a 12-bore. The new NATO 5.56 (.223 Remington) has more than halved that to match the mild kick of a .410 shotgun. My pneumatic weighs 7 pounds and shoots a 21-grain pellet at 740 fps, so its kick is 2½% of that of a 12-bore. A 10½-pound target rifle shooting a 7-grain pellet at 600 fps reduces this to under ½%.

The single-shot pneumatic incorporates a pump, and with the exception of single-stroke pneumatics, a number of strokes of this pump are required to bring the pressure up to what will yield a useful velocity. Smallbore pneumatics have a lower efficiency than powder rifles – commonly between 5% and 10% – and this is one of the pump-up's two great drawbacks. The marksman who has just exerted over 200 foot-pounds of muscular work pumping the gun up, is seldom in that relaxed condition necessary to capitalise on its lack of recoil. The second drawback is that pumped air contains such debris as may be floating in the wind, and it is this debris which is responsible for almost all air-seal failures.

The modern pre-charged pneumatic overcomes both difficulties by the use of filtered and dried compressed air, which is commercially available in the form of pressurized tanks used for scuba diving. 'Scuba' stands for 'self-contained underwater breathing apparatus', and although it introduces the new drawback of being dependent on an outside source for power, the pre-charged pneumatic powered from a diver's air-tank has been greeted with acclaim, and the type is rapidly assuming a dominant position among adult airgun users. As the air is dried before being compressed, the barrels are less prone to rust from the condensation effect of the release of each blast of air. Another advantage has been found in the degree to which these rifles may be silenced by using a sound moderator; especially useful in the vicinity of livestock, and perhaps other neighbours one may wish not to – er – alarm.

The pre-charged pneumatic is of course anything but new; it is a reversion to the very early airguns. The Austrian army had equipped a regiment with pre-charged pneumatics of .44 calibre in 1782. What was new was the development of the O-ring – a circle of rubber that is itself of circular cross-section – which made it extremely simple to create a perfect air seal.

Patented by Niels Christensen in 1937 for hydraulic sealing of automotive brakes, it came into widespread use only with the needs of the aircraft industry in the Second World War. An O-ring will sit in nothing more complicated than a machined rectangular-sectioned groove, and provided the clearance between the plug and the bore is small, it will seal pressures easily up to 1,500 psi and, if a harder rubber compound is used, up to 15,000 psi.

Any number and variety of pre-charged pneumatics are now available, the principle being that a gun is supplied with a large chamber of highly-compressed air, a small amount of which is released at each shot. The gun's large air chamber is replenished from time to time, and if there is no diver's air bottle available (itself periodically filled to a pressure of 3,000 psi), shooters can use a hand-powered pump. Depending on the gun and the power required, from a couple of shots to several hundred can be taken on a single charge of air.

The advantage of the pump-up, as opposed to the pre-charged pneumatic is cost. One buys the gun; that is all. With a pre-charged pneumatic, the gun is only one bit of the package. The diver's bottle may be two-thirds of the price of the rifle, while the high quality of hand-pump required to develop these pressures, if one cares to risk damaging the air seals, is a similar price. A telescopic sight and its mounts, plus a silencer, can also amount to a healthy sum.

That a rifle is pneumatic does not guarantee its accuracy, and for all the common reasons that compromise the accuracy of any rifle. The shortcomings of a poor barrel, or a poorly-mounted barrel, or poorly-mounted sights will be further compounded by the fact that any compressed gas, suddenly released, results in a dramatic cooling which will cause condensation of the water vapour ever-present in the air, rusting the rearmost five inches of steel barrels. Even in pre-charged pneumatics using dried air it has become standard practice to oil pellets to help control this problem. I add a teaspoonful of ordinary motorcar engine oil to a tin of pellets, roll the tin from side to side for two minutes, and mop any residual oil out of the cavity of each pellet before shooting it. It is often commented that pneumatics are made with very thin barrels, and match riflemen who are used to heavy barrels in their bench-rest or target rifles are astonished at the thin-barrelled pneumatic's accuracy. But pneumatic pressures are so low that a thick barrel is not called for, and whereas a firearm generates heat with each shot, and the barrel can utilise a lot of mass to absorb that heat without materially altering its point of aim, the pneumatic suddenly cools with each shot, and a thin barrel has the advantage of rapidly returning to the ambient air temperature.

Spring airguns have the advantage of simplicity and ease of shooting; nothing need be done other than to cock the weapon, load it with a pellet, and shoot it. I cheerfully admit that I shoot a spring-powered rifle more than all my other weapons combined. I like spring-powered air rifles. They are durable and avoid the greatest drawback of the pneumatic, which we only discover when, 500 miles from home, an air seal develops a leak. They do not forgive the slightest error on the part of the rifleman because the pellet leaves the barrel after the kick. Since shooting technique is critical when using them they are fine training for any other form of rifle shooting.

Like all other target riflemen, I find that the rifle wanders about according to my pulse for the first four seconds of the aim. There follows a lull of about three seconds in my pulse, and if I can squeeze off the shot in that period, the rifle shoots accurately. If I delay, accuracy vanishes and it is a matter of chance where the shot lands. In the course of a morning's experiments, I have just shot my old, battered recoiling spring gun – a Weihrauch HW 85 – with the pellets it likes, and lying prone I got a 22.5-millimetre group at the 13-yards range my shed affords. While seated and gently resting my left arm on a cushioned stool I reduced this to a 15-millimetre group. But a gentle relaxed hold and perfect technique will sometimes give me half-inch groups at 13-yards range, and its ease of shooting allows for plenty of practice. It doesn't shoot much better than this, and therefore if using it to mete death upon rabbits, I should have to limit my range accordingly. The simplicity of loading and the discipline of practice explains why, despite the better accuracy of the pneumatic, the spring gun retains my affection.

Spring airguns can be tuned, though 'tis a chancy business, and most endeavours are made merely to increase velocity – a misguided aim unless it corresponds with an increase in accuracy. It frequently doesn't. The amateur gun-tuner has a special talent for wrecking the spring airgun, usually starting from the premise that it did not cross the mind of the designer to use a powerful enough spring. He therefore fits one the wire of which has a square cross-section. Unfortunately, too powerful a spring allows too little time for the aerosol mist of oil to form, and he is vexed to find that the velocity goes down. Moreover any coil-spring expands in diameter on compression, and the squared corners of these springs have a habit of making momentary contact with the bore of the air cylinder, which – spring-steel being very hard – may thereby be chewed up. One must take a view on whether this is a good or a bad thing, and the arguments are by no means on one side of the question. A roughened bore will better hold combustible oil. If one is not deterred by the thought that with no experience whatever one might not be more expert than the makers of the guns, then the spring airgun is at least not a very uncommon article to chance wrecking. One would be wise to acquire a copy of the Cardews' book, which has the most detailed experimental evidence as to where one might first devote one's attentions. Investigating spring airguns they discovered that unless elaborate precautions were taken to ensure that oil did

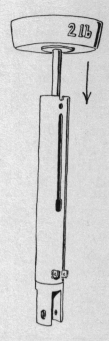

not reach the compression chamber, up to 40% of the power was derived from the combustion of a minute amount of oil, the gun acting on the same principle as the engine we know as the Diesel. They found that with modern synthetic piston seals, maximum consistent power can be obtained when a 2-pound weight placed on a vertically-mounted piston sinks the piston into place [Fig. 9.2]. Roughening the internal bore of the air cylinder has a similar effect.

Just to demonstrate to myself the effect that the oil has on the velocity – and to prolong the pleasure of the morning's trials – I extracted some diesel oil from the tank and, without cleaning out the old lubricant, dripped half-a-dozen drops onto the spring of my Weihrauch. First shooting fifty pellets so as thoroughly to stir up the lubricants and mix in the lighter grade of oil, I then put ten Hobby pellets through the chronograph. On a diet of a single drop of SAE 20/50 motor oil every week its muzzle velocity had been 675 fps. With the small addition of this lighter oil, the average velocity went up to 688 fps. In neither case did the velocity vary by more than 10 fps. Then, on the suggestion of a friend, I took some dry pellets and stood half of them on the oiled tin lid so each had the smallest circle of diesel oil on its base. Again, there was a jump in velocity amounting to another half a foot-pound for each oiled pellet as compared with the dry pellets.

9.2 The Cardews' finding: if a 2-pound weight pushes the piston down, power is greatest. If a lighter weight pushes the piston down, power becomes unstable.

I had hoped to get away with this bald statement but a gimlet-eyed editor, to whom the reader ought to be grateful and the author certainly is because she has saved him from a string of errors, wanted to know why the sudden change to foot-pounds that are not readily directly compared by the reader? There was a sneaky reason. And the sneaky reason was this: the earlier experiment was done with RWS Hobby pellets which weigh 12 grains. On discovering that oiled pellets group more closely, with impetuous delight I had oiled all my Hobby pellets, and in consequence when this experiment was suggested I had to cast around for some which had no oil on them. The second experiment was therefore done with as close a match as I could find, a dry unopened tin of Bisley Practice; but these weigh 13.6 grains. Half were stood on oil and half were left dry, with me meticulously alternating them to ensure the figures were directly the result of the oil. I couldn't repeat the first experiment using the heavier pellet as the rifle was now lubricated with the lighter oil. One does one's uttermost to avoid these embarrassing disclosures about one's experimental incompetence, but at least, by switching to foot-pounds, we save the unfortunate reader having to endure a set of twenty figures, and their analysis, to arrive at this conclusion.

This particular rifle had also proven instructive as to a significant difference between spring-piston air rifles and pneumatic air rifles. One day when innocently measuring the drag of different pellets, I felt moved to use the powerful pneumatic to measure drag at high velocities, and to compare them with the less powerful spring-piston rifle, shooting the same pellets at lower velocities. I took three pellets weighing 12 grains, 14.35 grains, and 21 grains; the pneumatic shot them at higher velocities, the spring rifle shot them at lower velocities.

Pneumatic Rifle		
Pellet Weight (grains)	Velocity (fps)	Energy (ft-lbs)
12	893.5	21.28
14.35	847	22.87
21	739	25.47

Spring Rifle		
Pellet Weight (grains)	Velocity (fps)	Energy (ft-lbs)
12	682	12.4
14.35	613.7	12.0
21	488.5	11.13

Analysing the muzzle energies, the astute student of airguns will inevitably notice that the pattern of efficiency in the spring rifle is the exact reverse of what happens with a pneumatic airgun. In a pneumatic, increase the pellet weight, and the efficiency goes up. In the spring rifle, increasing the pellet weight results in a drop in efficiency. It fairly weeps for an explanation.

In a pneumatic, a certain law of physics tells us that before and after a collision, the momentum will be the same. Releasing compressed air behind a light-weight pellet gives a collision 'twixt a great many air molecules and a plump slug of lead. All rush up the barrel at the same velocity. Releasing the same air molecules behind an even plumper slug of lead means that the overall mass after the collision is greater, so the overall velocity is less; but because the heavier slug absorbs a great deal more of the available momentum, it has a much bigger share of the energy that is there to be had.

With the spring gun, the position is rather different. Pulling the trigger results in the piston hurtling forward, gathering up a mist of oil droplets as it goes. When the compression reaches a certain point, the lot goes bang. At this point two things happen. Another law of physics tells us that any action is equal and opposite. The force of the oil going bang therefore acts both to shove the pellet down the barrel at a brisk rate of feet per second, and to shove the piston backwards against the spring. The spring being powerful and the piston heavy, the latter doesn't get shoved backwards very much at all, but the shove is there nonetheless.

If the pellet is heavier, its inertia is greater, and therefore more of the force is transferred to the equal-and-opposite piston. Hence less is available for augmenting the pellet's velocity.

The fact that forces are equal and opposite suggested to several makers the use of pistons moving in opposite directions on firing, and precisely this principle has been used successfully for target air rifles. Such a system gives both the advantage of simplicity – no delicate air seals to leak, no divers' bottle requiring refilling – and that of an absence of recoil. One hunting rifle used the system, but it is an expensive mechanism and it did not survive commercial pressures.

The fact that forces are equal and opposite suggests an even more simple system. Two pistons moving towards one another are inevitably complex; some means of linking the pistons to one another must be devised, and if one of the pistons is producing no power, as in some target air rifles, it is surplus baggage. If we imagine the centre of the spring to be the neutral point, then an equal and opposite reaction can be arranged by having the piston fly forwards and the cylinder-and-barrel fly backwards. Several designs, including a target rifle have used this, which we might call the sledge principle, with great success. Other than the mechanism allowing the metalwork to slide backwards slightly on being shot, which makes the recoil indiscernible, there remains to be overcome only the small problem of allowing for vertical shots to be taken.

Pneumatics are better understood and more easily tuned. In Britain, where firearms restrictions have spurred a flurry of airgun development, the authorities eventually noticed that most pneumatics were very easy to tune to powers above the British legal limit of 12 foot-pounds muzzle energy. Consequently British manufacturers, worrying that Parliament could make everything very difficult for everyone were this to continue, tacitly agreed to make it a good deal more difficult for hardy young souls to tune their airguns in the future. Nobody with any feel for human psychology will be surprised to learn that as soon as a government sets a legal power limit, the enthusiast regards it solely as a challenge. The pity is that only a small proportion recognise that tuning the velocity is one of the most critical aspects to realising the potential accuracy of an air rifle. Spring rifles may have earned a reputation for poorer accuracy because of the limited scope for altering the velocity to that which yields greatest accuracy. As there is always an optimum velocity at which accuracy is at its best, choice of pellet is even more critical, as it may be the sole means of reducing a spring rifle's grouping.

It needs to be stressed that for any barrel + pellet combination, there is a velocity at which the accuracy will be greatest. Sometimes the accuracy increases with velocity; sometimes it increases and then diminishes. This aspect of accuracy afflicts all rifles, firearms included. The effect of velocity on accuracy is not widely appreciated, even among those who make a living by use of the air rifle. One writer, who describes his profession as a pest controller, advocates varying the power of the rifle to match the quarry. It is clearly bad practice.

All sorts of airgun ammunition can be bought, from dome-headed to hollow-nosed, from pointed to flat-nosed, and from heavy-weight conventionally-shaped pellets to solid bullets. For any airgun (and this to some degree includes two of identical make and model), the best accuracy can only be obtained by testing a variety of pellets and selecting that which delivers the tightest groups. All writers mention the long business of pellet testing which is required before one brand of pellet is found which groups most closely for any particular rifle. Being primarily interested in the physics of these things, I built a big single-shot .22 pneumatic rifle the power of which could be varied by the sophisticated expedient of counting the number of pumps. It was a purely experimental rifle, and had a bipod on a rubber mount which gave pretty well an identical hold for each shot, thus making accuracy comparisons very straightforward. I tried several brands, as one must, before settling on 12-grain RWS Hobby pellets, lightly oiled. Lightly coating each pellet in a film of oil had a significant effect on accuracy, reducing the big rifle's group size by 25%.

At 7 pumps, the velocity was 586 fps, the power 9 foot-pounds, and at 13 yards a five-shot group was 12.5 millimetres from centre to centre of the widest shots. At 12 pumps, the velocity was 710 fps, and the group shrank to 9 millimetres. At 16 pumps, the velocity was up to 782 fps, but the group had widened out again to 15.5 millimetres.

No. of pumps	Velocity (fps)	Group (mm)
7	586	12.5
12	710	9
16	782	15.5

Hence for any rifle and pellet, there is an optimum velocity. But – a caveat. Velocity alone is not the key. Testing this just now, I took some heavy Bisley Magnum pellets and shot five at 20 pumps, which is a velocity of 710 fps, a power output of 23.5 foot-pounds. The group was 17 millimetres at 13 yards. Note that the velocity was the same as that which gave the 9-millimetre group with the light Hobby pellets. Therefore merely containing the velocity by using a heavy bullet does not mean that accuracy can be depended upon.

In America, a haven for those with a technical bent, there developed from 1944 onwards a discipline of building powder rifles of extreme accuracy for shooting purely from bench-rests. From the writings of an early participant, Col. Townsend Whelen, it became clear that riflemen had arrived at the conclusion that both bullet length and rotational mass had an effect on accuracy, and each needed to be carefully selected to match the particular twist of a rifling.

We can demonstrate this with a spinning top; a short one does not need to spin so quickly as a tall one to remain balanced. Broadly speaking, so it is with bullets; a long bullet needs to spin faster than does a short bullet. The speed of spin is determined by the rifling and the muzzle velocity; a rapid rate of twist is required for a low velocity. Equally, a light bullet requires less spin than a heavy one, so muzzle-loading black powder authorities admonish us to use a slow rate of twist for a ball (the lightest form of missile), and a fast rate of twist for a heavier conical bullet. The renowned accuracy of certain smallbores, notably the .222 centre-fire, is thought to be related to the fact that it is more difficult to make a bullet very much heavier or lighter than that for which the barrel's rate of twist was designed. A bigger bore allows much more variation in weight for comparatively small variations in bullet length. The .303 rifle was designed about a 220-grain bullet; it is possible to buy bullets to fit of only 150 grains, but accuracy must suffer.

Whelen had access to a then virtually unobtainable book of 1909, *The Bullet's Flight from Powder to Target*, by Dr. F. W. Mann of Milford, Massachusetts, now published in 1980 by Wolfe Publishing of Prescott, Arizona. Without wishing to reduce a lifetime's meticulous work to a few sentences, Mann showed that a major accuracy problem arises from a bullet so seated in the breech that its centre of gravity is even the slightest amount offset from the centre of rotation. The barrel, of course, keeps it rotating round its outer diameter, but when it leaves the muzzle there is nothing to stop the rotational centre reverting to the bullet's centre of gravity. If the spin is already eccentric to this, it follows a pattern which we can happily conjure

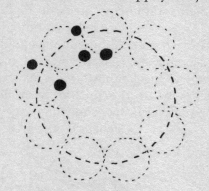

on the kitchen floor with a toy spinning-top: the base of the top describes a small circle, and if spun on a sheet of glass dusted with flour, where it goes on spinning as if there is no friction, the small circles describe in turn a much larger slower circle. The bullet will hit the target at whatever point these two circles choose to land it [Fig. 9.3], and the seemingly random dispersion of a five-shot group can often be explained by the fact that each bullet's seating might be a whisker different from that which went before. The smaller circle varies in size and its position around the larger circle also varies. This pattern of movement is common in any free rotating body;

9.3 Dr Mann's finding: a grouping is the result of a double circle dispersion, and random chance will sometimes throw up a very tight, but misleading, focus to the group.

astronomers like to exchange remarks about precession of the equinox. From time to time the two circles of dispersion will land all the shots in a very tight group, which the rifleman will display to an eager and admiring throng, erroneously congratulating himself on his rifle, and equally erroneously regretting that his skill is not up to a regular reproduction of such accuracy.

If we add to this the fact that accuracy can be affected by a bullet being a mild or a tight fit in the rifling, and that air rifle pellets are an intoxicating aerodynamic nightmare, it becomes apparent that predicting a good pellet for any airgun is virtually impossible. To an extent we can relate speed with pellet weight – add weight, and the velocity comes down. But weight alone is not a sufficient predictor, because pellets all have different shapes and as every aerodynamicist knows, the smallest imaginable differences in shape can have enormous effects on drag. Airgun pellets are broadly of the waisted variety so there are two points at which the pellet is of greatest diameter, and the interaction between these two (in which the air is swept out by the first and sucked in behind in an eddy and then blown out and sucked in again by the second) makes everything very difficult to predict or even to study. It is irritating that because of this vigorous nest of complexity, the best we can say is that any newly-acquired air rifle has to be tested methodically with a variety of pellets until the most satisfactory brand is found. It is even more irritating that some of the most accurate pellets turn out to be those with the highest aerodynamic drag. In itself this tells us that not the least of the air rifle's accuracy is to be found in the fact that the diabolo shape, with its flared trailing skirt, acts a bit like an arrow; rather than the high drag of the feathers which serve to stabilise an arrow in flight, it has a high drag rear surface [Fig. 9.4].

Air rifles commonly come in four calibres: .177, .20, .22 and .25 of an inch, although engagingly in the USA where perhaps there is a tacit acceptance of a sufficiency of firearms, there are custom builders, notably Dennis Quackenbush, who make fullbore air rifles of remarkable power and accuracy. At the time of writing there are also one or two South Asian commercial firms producing large-bore air rifles.

Pellets of the first of the above calibres are the cheapest and

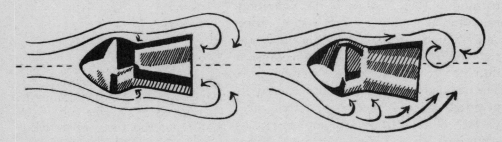

9.4 The high drag skirt of an airgun pellet tends to straighten it in flight.

allow, as light pellets do, quite high velocities – around 850 fps is not all that uncommon. Some .177 rifles have been marketed with a muzzle velocity of 1,250 fps to tempt the newcomer who is invariably unacquainted with the fact that airgun pellets do have an appalling drag coefficient. The .177 is the worst culprit for this, having little weight and a large surface area. Even worse than this, at the high muzzle velocities offered by a light-weight pellet, the drag is generally three times that of lower velocities. In all pellets, the cut-off to very high drag is in the 800 fps zone. In one example, losses of 38% of energy over a flight of just 10 metres were measured in a 7-grain pellet, and launched at a little over 1,000 fps it was found to be travelling at 800 fps just 10 metres down-range. Below 800 fps, this same pellet lost 18% of its energy over the next 10 metres, where it was travelling at 730 fps.

Nevertheless all target air rifles are of .177 calibre, although their muzzle velocity is usually lower, at around 600 fps. As they are very much more accurate, albeit at a limited range, than any other shooting weapon, the rewards can be dramatic. A famous advertisement of thirty or forty years ago showed a very expensive, recoilless spring target air rifle of .177 calibre with a comparatively low velocity, which was used one summer evening to shoot more than 300 rabbits from a single warren, the precision of accuracy allowing for humane brain shots to be taken. The value of such a tool to the farmer does not need stating. It has been said that ten rabbits will eat the grazing for a single sheep, and as sheep are of commercial value and rabbits generally are not, the rifle must have paid for itself in that one evening's shooting.

The .20 calibre is frequently found in American single-shot pump-up pneumatics, but is uncommon elsewhere.

The .22 is the most widely-used hunting calibre, and for this reason it and the .177 have the greatest available variety of pellets. Lightweight .22 pellets weighing 12 grains can be had, all the way up to solid bullets weighing as much as 30 grains. It is popular for pest control, the larger pellet head area reducing the tendency to penetrate straight through a target. For those whose need is to control rabbits, and it has to be said that one of mankind's most stupid acts was to turn the rabbit loose on continents where its reproductive attributes subsequently made it an environmental disaster, there is much to be said for a pellet that hits but does not penetrate, as it means that the energy of impact is retained by the animal, and thereby tends to a humane kill. High velocity and penetration may leave an animal injured with a puncture wound rather than dead. I recall shooting a pellet from a very low-powered .22 air rifle, deliberately trying to drive off rather than kill a starling that kept the children awake every night, and being appalled to see it drop stone dead as the slow, heavy pellet imparted all its shock to the unfortunate creature. When I went to bury it I found the pellet hadn't even broken the skin, and was jammed in the feathers.

The .25 calibre was common among the makers of eighteenth and nineteenth century airguns where the power was supplied by compressing air into a chamber and subsequently releasing it behind each bullet, but for a long time it was virtually unavailable. However as higher power pneumatic airguns have developed it has regained a following, and offers the combination of a heavy pellet and a large frontal area; a combination conducive to a very clean kill. It does have to be said that the large frontal area can be duplicated by either a flat-nosed or a hollow-nosed pellet, both of which to some extent mushroom on impact. The heavy weight of the .25, anything from 18 to 25 grains, can also be duplicated by the wide range of pellets available in .22, so where the .25 does pay off is in the pneumatic, where the larger bore area allows for a 29% greater force to develop behind it on its way up the barrel.

Both the .25 and to a lesser extent the .20 calibres suffer from the fact that few types of pellet are made for them, limiting the variety from which to select an accurate barrel + pellet combination. Again and again, we come back to the importance of accuracy. The small momentum imparted by any airgun pellet limits it to use on small quarry, and a well-directed shot commonly has ample energy to kill. It has often been pointed out that killing ducks and rabbits with shotguns only requires three or four foot-pounds of striking energy.

Accuracy at the longer ranges can be decided by the wind, of which very little is required to blow a bullet cumulatively off course. If the wind is constant a skilled shot can shoot accurately, but small gusts and eddies can wreck an otherwise perfect shot.

Testing the accuracy of the Sharp Innova, a renowned single-shot pump-up, with every pellet brand I could lay my hands on, I concluded it shot best at ten or eleven pumps using lightly-oiled RWS Superdome pellets. When cold, it needed eleven pumps, but after two shots the pump had warmed up and it only needed ten. At this pressure the velocity was around 700 fps, or 15.6 foot-pounds. Any slower, and the groups were not quite as tight; any faster, and the pellets rapidly started to spray all over the target. Shooting strings of five consecutive shots, and measuring the centres of each hole from one another, it shot a 6-millimetre group at 13 yards.

Fremantle reported that Sergeant Instructor Wallingford, the finest shot in the British Army, shot a 330-millimetre group at 300 metres in the International Match at the Hague in June 1899, which would represent a 13-millimetre group at 13 yards. It follows that this little air rifle was dependably capable of double the accuracy of the .303 – and so it proved out to a range of 40 yards. On a still day I shot a 12-millimetre group at 20 yards, and a 26-millimetre group at 40 yards. But at 50 yards the group opened out to 37.5 millimetres, and worse, to 97 millimetres at 60 yards. Of this last group, four pellets fell within 37.5 millimetres of one another; coincidentally the same as at 50 yards, but the outlier is the one that tells us the degree of predictability of the rifle.

As every book on target shooting tells us, 'tis the worst group that governs everything, not the best. A trying quality of pointed pellets was the tendency towards fliers. I found with the Sharp that I could shoot truly astonishingly good groups with pointed pellets – four would achieve a group of as little as 2 millimetres at 13 yards. But the fifth would turn out to be a 'flier', and land an inch outside this tight group, wrecking the dependability. Most published reports will give the best groups of any gun/bullet combination, and quite commonly state that they ignore the fliers. Alas, the one thing that could be depended on is that I could not consistently replicate these very tight 2-millimetre groups because it was never certain until after the shot that a pellet was not about to be a flier. I had reluctantly to conclude that it was better to be certain that a shot would land within a quarter an inch of the point of aim, than to know that though it would probably land right on the point of aim, every fifth shot would miss completely. A centre of gravity a thousandth of an inch out can upset the dispersion by over two minutes of angle, and the point is very vulnerable to damage.

The group sizes again demonstrate that the factor that limits range is accuracy, not power. The Sharp starts with 15.6 foot-pounds at the muzzle, has about 12 foot-pounds at 25 yards and about 9 foot-pounds at 50 yards. 9 foot-pounds is double what is required to kill a rabbit. Many spring-powered air rifles are capable – in still air – of one-inch groups at 25 yards; and some of today's pneumatics have the potential to reduce this to $\frac{1}{2}$-inch groups at the same range. But even a gentle breeze will open an air rifle's group out, and at longer ranges, dramatically so. Using the Innova, I shot a 102-millimetre group at 50 yards on a windy day, a group that compares very unfavourably with the 37.5-millimetre group in what was comparatively still air. The shots were all within 18 inches of the ground, but the wind velocity was still sufficient, and sufficiently variable, to fling the grouping. We must assume that long range for an air rifle is anything above 30 yards unless the air is very still indeed.

As a necessary digression, it is always worth reminding ourselves that the gun is only the delivery system, and it is the projectile that does the work to the target. To shoot holes in paper targets the smallest pellet offers the highest velocity, and high velocities tend to minimise the greatest mistake of the rifleman, which is estimating the range. If a rifleman guesses a target to be 30 yards away and in fact it is only 25 yards away, an otherwise well-aimed pellet may easily fly an inch above the anticipated point of impact. But as Benjamin Robins discovered in the eighteenth century, and as everyone has subsequently found, high drag is the penalty for high velocity.

The gently-curving graph showing the loss of energy to air drag is a familiar one in reputable rifle books from Fremantle on, and is broadly similar regardless of the bullet. Of course some bullets do have much lower drag than others, depending on their shape, weight, and frontal area, but the pattern is very clear. Above 800 fps, and increasing as the velocity reaches up past the speed of sound (1,080 fps), the air drag is very much higher than at the velocities airguns commonly achieve. The reason why can be seen wherever bullets have been photographed in flight – a technique over 100 years old and performed by arranging for the bullet to connect two wires and set off an electrical spark of immense brightness and remarkable brevity. Above the speed of sound the bow wave of the air, radiating out from the nose of the bullet, can be seen; it is not there when the bullet is slower.

The air rifles with which I grew up developed about 6 or 7 foot-pounds of energy. The most powerful .22 spring air rifle of Wesley's era, a Webley Mark III or a BSA Airsporter, developed only 9.7 foot-pounds at the muzzle. When chronographs became available I and many others of an enquiring disposition began finding that higher velocities generally extend the range (measured by the kinetic energy of the projectile) by only around ten yards because of this enhanced loss of energy to air drag. If higher velocity results in the pellets being blown all over the target, the extra speed reduces the range: it does not extend it. Those with very powerful spring air rifles find themselves having to tame the velocity with heavier and heavier pellets until the best accuracy is found.

To the drawing-board. Spring airguns require special steels, most obviously in the spring. The amateur gunsmith, starting afresh with raw materials, therefore concerns himself with a single-shot pump-up pneumatic airgun whose workings and necessary accessory – the integral pump – are at least comparatively straightforward to understand, and if he possesses a lathe and has faith in O-rings are relatively easy both to design and to make.

Above all else the pneumatic airgun requires valves. It should be mentioned that there are pneumatic airguns where the piston-head of the pump acts as one valve, so that only a single stroke of the pump is possible. These operate usually at low pressure, the pressure at the pump rendering even a lever hard to bring home if a high pressure is to be attained. The most famous using this principle was the Walther LGR, a very fine target rifle. The excellent but commercially unsuccessful Dragon used a sliding pivot in the lever to obtain a mechanical advantage towards the end of the compression stroke. An engineering friend who had a powerful single-stroke Titan Mohawk observed that they didn't catch on due to this effort required to charge them, which he likened to using a set of bolt croppers on something too thick; "eyes bulging and the "snap" as the action goes over centre". Otherwise, in pump-up pneumatics, air must be compressed into a reservoir, and it can only be introduced via a valve.

Air must then be released behind the bullet, and this too is only accomplished with a valve. The early airguns resorted to a single valve serving as both inlet and exhaust, which necessitated a detachable air reservoir. Old pump-up airguns relied on a cowhorn cone sitting in a hole. The most famous of these, the only one with a military history, was variously spelt Giradoni, Girardoni or Girandoni. (As linguists inform us, 'correct' spelling is but a recent idea – even Shakespeare used several spellings of his own name.) The cone was momentarily dislodged back into the air reservoir and air escaped through the circular gap round the cone. After leaving the reservoir, the air had to bypass the spring and hammer, which lurked between reservoir and barrel. Bartholomew Girandoni used a brass casting incorporating a curved hole to convey the air from the reservoir to the breech of his barrel, but unfortunately for the efficiency of the device, this hole was only a 1/4-inch in diameter, and posed a constriction in the airflow before the pressure hit the back of a ball which was of around 1/2-inch in diameter [Fig. 9.5).

Cowhorn, if a good fit, is airtight and the good fit was obtained by making the horn into a cone, with a conical seat of metal. Some writers speak of bone, but bone is porous and will not totally seal air. I tried it. The valve seat screwed into the mouth of the reservoir, and this screw-thread was rendered airtight with the aid of plumbers' artifices, doubtless a paste of white lead and thin string and much testing and much cursing and many attempts. Today this can be obviated with the use of rubber O-rings which are of proven reliability. The cowhorn plugs frequently became leaky; pumped air is full of motes of dust. Rotating the cowhorn in the valve seat 'until it squeals' was recommended by the nineteenth century maker Reilly to correct the fault, but these were always high-maintenance guns. Again, rubber O-rings overcome this fault, and although leaks still occur and for exactly the same reason, the O-ring accommodates a good deal more filth before it becomes leaky. A number of today's makers have used plastics, of which acetal (machineable nylon) and PTFE have been praised.

A difficulty is that any soft material has to be robust enough not to be blasted out of the hole simply by the air pressure, and although there is sense in reinforcing the sealant

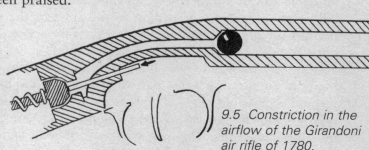

9.5 Constriction in the airflow of the Girandoni air rifle of 1780.

with metal, a hole drilled through the middle of a piece of plastic to accommodate a threaded metal rod may not itself be airtight. Some of the leakages of antique airguns attributed to the horn material are by the air seeping through the hole occupied by the steel valve rod, rather than past the valve seat.

Chemical engineers spend a great deal of time studying the effects of gas flow at high pressure along tubing, and though the basics are relatively easy to grasp, a detailed analysis requires the deepest study and an intimate knowledge of mathematics. It is, however, clear that anything that impedes direct flow of air uses some of the energy of the air, and this reduces the efficiency. The word 'bottleneck' has a very real meaning in the inhibition of smooth air flow.

I once had a Crosman .22 Medalist, a cheap gun when new and very cheap indeed when I came by it, as it then had a leaking valve. For a time it became a test-bed, to see what operations could be performed to alter its power. Although replacing the plastic pump piston rod with an incompressible steel rod had an effect in allowing the pump to develop higher pressures, and although boring out the inside of the air reservoir to increase its volume also had an effect, it was not until I opened up the exhaust port that the improvement became dramatic. The initial power of this gun was around $5^1/2$ foot-pounds, and the first two operations took this up to $8^1/2$ ft-lbs. But when I opened the interior exhaust port and the one going from the air reservoir to the back of the pellet, to an equivalent diameter of 5 millimetres, just half a millimetre less than the pellet itself, the power leapt to $14^2/3$ foot-pounds.

The only disadvantage of a large exhaust port is the need for a large exhaust plug, and as we are dealing in pounds per square inch, raising the number of square inches on which ultimately the trigger has to operate, raises the prospect of a heavy trigger pull. The designer has to be careful of this, especially if choosing the simple blow-off valve plug.

But before going on, the inevitable word of caution. We can't have too many of them. Compressed air is an extremely dangerous medium. There is no difference whatever between a blast bomb used to kill people, and an explosion of an air reservoir. The pressure and volume of air available to kill or maim reduces according to the cube of the distance from the bomb. Because an airgun positions the air reservoir very close to the shooter's head, a burst reservoir can be very dangerous indeed.

When I was busy amusing myself by inventing a low pressure big-bore airgun, this was a particular worry. I had experimented and found it just about possible to go as high as 190 psi, but I had also burst a good many reservoirs in the process. A large volume of air compressed even to 100 psi is horribly dangerous. There was a case not long ago of a truck driver whose

head was blown off his shoulders when he was inspecting a tyre – and truck
tyres are run at pressures of around 150 psi.

Large-bore airguns have a number of advantages. First, they
shoot large bullets, conveying large amounts of momentum to the target.
Second, the larger bore allows a correspondingly larger force on the bullet; the
corollary is that for a given energy output, the larger bore will allow the use of
a lower air pressure. Third, it is straightforward to obtain large-bore hydraulic
tubing from which to rifle a barrel. It is, of course, incumbent on us to check
that the materials will withstand the pressures to be applied: as the price of
copper goes up so the plumbers' suppliers become more parsimonious and the
current 0.6 millimetre wall thickness standard 15-millimetre copper tubing has
a burst pressure of only about 350 psi, and therefore its working pressure is
half of that. Nineteenth-century air canes may have had brass barrels but the
pressures reached by the pumps of the time did not exceed 600 psi.

We can only use a barrel with a low burst pressure by
containing it within the reservoir itself: antique 'barrel reservoir' airguns ran
the barrel through the middle of a larger tube which contained the compressed
air, and of course a tube compressed from its outside acts like a circular arch.

In its simplest form [Fig. 9.6], with an O-ring to seal the breech
of the barrel, there cannot be rifle grooves at the rear because they will leak air.
But do not despair. A smoothbore barrel is sometimes an advantage. The local
plumbers' supplier has an elegant solution to metrification: he simply had all
his copper pipe stamped with the new measurements. His '20 mm' copper pipe

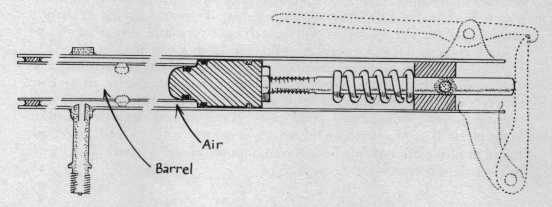

Air

Barrel

*9.6 About as simple as it gets, if you have a lathe and can solder. Barrel reservoir,
single-shot, muzzle-loading airgun. Be very cautious about copper pipe as a
pressurized air reservoir. Even the best quality, 20-millimetre tube of 1-millimetre
wall thickness, will burst and kill you at around 400 psi. Ordinary copper pipe
commonly has flaws, and any thin part will concentrate a stress and, like a
malformed party balloon, burst at lower pressures.*

is in fact ¾-inch bore, and his '15 mm' is actually ½-inch bore. (We really do have to do our own checks and calculations and measurements, and do them on the actual materials to hand.) Therefore to make my .451 ball an airtight fit in a ½-inch barrel I have to wrap it in a patch. Any sabot has to be of perfectly even thickness around a bullet, or the centre of rotation of the ball will be different from its centre of gravity, and as soon as it exits the muzzle, as Dr. Mann taught us, all manner of interesting spiral motions are going to ensue and accuracy can very easily be worse than if it emerged into the sunshine without a spin. Naturally, a smoothbore precludes long-range shooting – perhaps 20 yards? – but other than in our fantasies, long-range shooting with any of these human-powered bullets is likely to be out of the question.

Although the importance of volume of the air reservoir is not as significant in smallbores at high pressures as it is with large-bore low-pressure airguns, it does have some effect. Most commercially available pump-up pneumatics have a reservoir of about a fifth of a cubic inch. A 20-inch barrel of .177 bore contains half a cubic inch of air, while a .22 barrel contains three quarters of a cubic inch of air. This volume of air in the barrel is around 2½ to 4 times that of the reservoir. If we are tempted by big-bore high-pressure airguns we can scale up from this, so that, for example, a 10-millimetre bore barrel 20 inches long would require a reservoir of one cubic inch to be equivalent to a .22. However a .22 with a 20-inch barrel will benefit from a reservoir of up to one cubic inch, and the enhanced volume will allow a similar power output from air pumped to a lower pressure. It is always easier to pump a lot of air to a low pressure than a little air to a high pressure, regardless of what the theoreticians may tell us, but it is also more time-consuming. If we are seeking to shoot a heavy bullet at pistol speeds, we will have to use a very large volume of air and a very high pressure, and this will be tiring indeed to pump up.

The problems are not new, and account for the fact that most eighteenth-century airguns were of small bore, and though we all tend to believe that an antique airgun must be a large-bore weapon, this is only because the large-bore airguns excite museum curators enough to win a place in the glass cases. Museums, on the whole, have nine-tenths of their collections stored in cardboard boxes in back rooms, untouched and unseen except by the privileged, or persistent, few.

CHAPTER 10

High-pressure airguns: the practical

To work, then.

To make a high-pressure airgun, a lathe, so far as my experience goes, is essential. No engineer requires an explanation for that statement, but there is such a great variety of lathes and my experience is so slight that no discussion of the subject will serve a useful purpose. The most astonishing thing to me in an age of abundant machinery is that my father's generation did not balk at this; if they wanted one they built a lathe, of wood if nothing else was to hand, or of hand-filed cast iron if they could get it. He who truly wishes to build an airgun will not be greatly deterred by the lack of a lathe. But perhaps it is worth saying that a hollow spindle is an advantage if barrels are to be made, for the muzzle really ought to be square to the bore.

First we need appropriate tubing. Seamless steel tubes may be obtained with a hacksaw from a bicycle but are not much good to us. High-quality frames are useless because the frame tubes are butted, which is to say they are thickened internally at the ends, and the middle of the tubing has walls very much too thin to accept high pressures. Low-quality frames are useless because the tube is made by rolling it from flat sheets and joining the edges together by a process (electronic resistance welding) which leaves an irregular welded ridge on the inside. This ridge prevents airtightness. Aluminium tubing is worryingly prone to catastrophic failure, so application must needs be made to the local steel tubing supplier. Hydraulic steel tubing is both seamless and – vitally – supplied with data on its safe working pressure. For airgun building it is ideal, and I would be terrified of using anything else. We cope with rust, or try to contain it, with liberal embrocations of oil.

Seamless tubing will both seal and withstand high pressure. Pneumatic engineers regard anything in excess of 150 psi as high pressure, and as modern pneumatic airguns work in the region of ten to twenty times that, we are operating at very high pressures indeed. An advantage lies in a capacity to hold a high volume of air; and here we need to tax our memory about pressure vessels. I have used phosphated hydraulic cold-drawn seamless tubing of 1¹/₈-inch outside diameter, and 1.2-millimetre wall thickness. With a bore of 26.175 millimetres, it holds a working pressure of 1,500 psi. Since an ordinary nitrile O-ring will seal pressures up to 1,500 psi, it was a good match. The steel will bulge somewhere above that pressure, and burst at around double, killing or blinding or blowing the fingers off the amateur gunsmith. Such accidents do happen.

Were the walls of the tubing twice as thick – 2.4 millimetres – it would have a working pressure of twice this. Were the tubing twice the diameter, it would have a working pressure of half this. These are basic engineering formulæ to be found in any appropriate textbook. Some activity with a pocket calculator suggests that a working pressure of 2,000 psi can be had with a tube of 22-millimetre outside diameter and ³/₄-inch bore – heaven knows why such mixed measurements occur in the world of engineering, but they do. These measurements are relevant because they are used by at least one commercially-available pump-up airgun.

Unless you are wholly credulous, you will never believe on first inspecting one that an O-ring can work in the way that it is said to work, but nevertheless it does. That fact, and the availability of cold-drawn seamless steel tubing, makes building a high-pressure airgun possible wherever there is access to a workshop.

The textbooks on the subject of pneumatic seals (and there are dozens to be found in any university library) tell us that O-rings require precise fitting if they are to work successfully. *'O-rings are not very tolerant of incorrect tolerances'* is one of my favourite quotations from one such, and one hopes the author was better able to construct his seals than his sentences, but my own experience has been that he, and the other textbooks, err. O-rings tolerate almost intolerable tolerances. My only serious failure, which needlessly caused me endless, and thereby valuable, experiments on an inlet valve, turned out not to be the O-ring but rather the soldered joint, and having discovered that fact I abandoned the structure and replaced the soldered joint with a plug screwed in place and sealed with O-rings – and it worked perfectly. Perhaps, however, my machining is more accurate than I credit it, so it is as well to give the tolerances, and perhaps we should also ignore my relaxed attitude to these seals. After all, I have been lucky, and everyone knows we learn from our failures, not from our successes. Professional pneumatic engineers are – well – professional, and have a great deal of experience, whereas I am the rankest amateur and, frankly, not to be trusted.

How does an O-ring work? It is a circle of rubber, commonly

nitrile (black 'rubber' – acrylonitrile-butadiene rubber, or NBR, if you must know), and of circular cross-section. If it is sandwiched in a groove between two pieces of metal – a tube on the outside and a solid cylinder on the inside – and air pressure is applied to one end, the O-ring is sucked into the gap between the two, and seals it [Fig. 10.1].

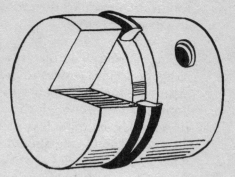

Suppose you take a plug of brass and machine it on your lathe until it fits into the seamless tubing. To slide within, it will need a clearance of about two thousandths of an inch, not least because even seamless steel tubing is of

10.1 An O-ring sits in a groove and seals by distorting into the gap.

variable bore along its length. Air can easily pass through such a gap, so the gap is plugged with the O-ring. All that is necessary is a circular groove cut into the brass plug. The groove depth will need to be about 75% of the thickness of the O-ring. The outside of the O-ring needs to be compressed by the tube in which it sits, and provided the groove is sufficiently small to nip the O-ring on three of its four available sides, it ought also to slide up and down a tube, as is required by a pump or a valve plug, without suffering the common spiral failure of O-rings. Spiral failure occurs if the O-ring is loose enough to act rather like a roller when subject to reciprocating movement, or to the sudden arrow-like movement of a valve-rod down its centre; then the O-ring will tear and make you wish you had paid more attention to what the professional engineers say about tolerances and had treated what I have to say with appropriate disdain. However, taking the size I have used, the O-ring will be of 2-millimetre thickness and have a bore of 22 millimetres. The groove will therefore be of 1.5-millimetre depth, which will nicely stretch the O-ring across its diameter by a millimetre. Some textbooks tell us that stretching should not exceed 6%, but a practical engineer who has worked with drilling apparatus of 15,000 psi tells me that anything up to 10% is admissible.

The groove has to be 30% wider than the thickness of the rubber to accommodate distortion as the rubber fills the gap 'twixt brass plug and seamless steel, and since O-rings work by being wedged by the force of compressed air into the gap, this too need not be desperately critical. The compressed air is, after all, only trying to go one way. But we do keep the groove dimensions a whisker tight wherever we are afraid of spiral failure; which is wherever the O-ring is acting as a dynamic, rather than a static, air seal. Every junction in the groove needs gently rounding smooth. The internal angles are a jolly sight harder to round off, and luckily a jolly sight less critical, than the outer. I apply an appropriately rounded-cornered, sharp, parting-off tool to the inside of the groove, rounding the outer sharp edge with very fine crocus paper.

As the brass needs to be smooth, so too does the seamless tubing. O-rings will tolerate a surface roughness of 0.4-0.8 microns, which can easily be seen as ripples round the inside of the tube. The chances of your ever again needing to be able to measure tenths of a micron of roughness are limited, so it is enough to say that if you cannot feel any roughness with a fingernail, even though you may be able to see roughness, then you should be all right. The O-ring should seal. This gem is also from my engineer friend, who spends his days working with them rather than writing academic textbooks. A rougher surface may damage the rubber of the O-ring as the sealed plug is slid into place.

Two further things are needed.

First: oil. The O-ring needs lubrication to help it slide gently into position when it is being mounted. Gunmakers commonly use hydraulic car transmission fluid, and financially astute gunshops will sell tiny amounts in tiny bottles with some curious label of their own devising for sums of money which vary only according to their avarice. I use a drop of car engine-oil, knowing that this will have the additional advantage of rust prevention inside the air reservoir, and when you have seen the beads of water that condense after an airgun is discharged, you grasp the need for rust prevention.

Second: smooth, gentle, polished slopes to slide over. My lathe is large and heavy and 100 years old, and previous owners of it filched all the change wheels so I can't easily cut screw-threads. This is not a problem, for if the seamless steel tubing is threaded, the jagged edges of the threading will shred the O-ring and it won't seal for long. So holes are drilled into the tubing from the side, and into the brass plug; then the brass plug-holes (if that is not too confusing a phrase) are tapped so that the plug is retained in its allotted position in the seamless tube by screws entering from the side. The holes in the steel need to be very carefully smoothed and chamfered and polished from the inside. This, though difficult, is by no means impossible and just wants a great deal of patience, a lot of crocus

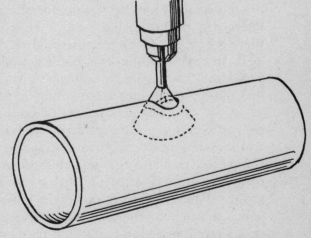

10.2 *Holes in the wall of a tube must be polished smooth to stop sharp edges damaging any O-ring that has to be slid past them.*

paper cut into tiny semicircles and glued onto tiny roughly-carved wooden cones which are mounted, wide side distally, on 3-millimetre steel rods so that they can be poked and jiggled down the steel tubing. When the rod protrudes through a hole, it is popped into an electric drill and spun round and round gaily but carefully until boredom sets in or the wooden cone slips off inside the tubing, whereupon cursing and repetition takes place. The aim, ultimately, is a hole so polished that the O-ring, compressed slightly by the tubing in which it is sliding, can pass the hole without being scratched and thereby damaged [Fig. 10.2].

It is as well to stagger any holes in the seamless steel tubing. As the brass plug is introduced – into a tube end chamfered and polished – it must needs be pushed past a lateral hole, and rubber being squidgy, the local bit of O-ring will try to extrude through the hole and must be chastised with a smooth, rounded off (on a fine oilstone) screwdriver and poked right back again. It is as well not to have more than one of these holes to deal with at a time.

If higher pressures than 1,500 psi are anticipated a harder O-ring (maybe 90 on the Shore A scale) might be required, and a smaller gap (maybe a thousandth of an inch), between brass plug and steel tube. The Shore system is a rating of hardness which pneumatic engineering textbooks enjoy describing in paragraphs of tortured English, and any attempt to go to the high pressures offered by diving bottles requires us to consult them and actually grasp what they have to say. A fatal explosion can be the consequence of getting it wrong. I have always stuck to the lower pressure, relying for performance on efficient valving and moderately large volumes of air, rather than on my arithmetic and calculations of shear strength of the nuts and bolts I trust to hold the various brass plugs in place.

Regardless of how obvious it seems, it needs to be stated: pounds per square inch is exactly that, so if a brass plug has double the area exposed to an air pressure it is twice as likely to come bursting out of a tube, and I am acutely aware that my body will not be an obstacle to its flight. Similarly, doubling the pressure doubles the chances of it bursting out. This does have to be emphasised. Modern airguns are reliable and tempt us to complacency, and complacency has an unfortunate habit of breeding mishaps. Of course pump-up airguns tempt us to one more pump-stroke to see if it will enhance performance, and this ambition too can lead to disaster.

We discover from the fact that I have not touched upon it, that the design of a high-pressure airgun needs no introduction. Probably I am right for no-one who troubles himself with the long and tedious process of reading this is likely to have failed, at some point, to acquire a pump-up airgun – they are very cheap – and to have pulled it apart to see how it works.

This fantastic assumption belies the possibility of there being more than one design, and since there are many, let us see what it is we are about to make.

Antique pump-up airguns, if at all powerful, had an air reservoir that was detachable from the gun, for pumping. The pump was applied; the charged reservoir was attached to the gun; a hammer rotated a cam onto the exhaust valve which popped open; following a blast of air, the pressure within closed the valve again, retaining most of the compressed air. Thus many shots could be taken with one pumping. The antique gun, capable of shooting twenty shots without attention, was an effective weapon indeed. Modern pre-charged pneumatics are usually smaller bore and commonly shoot more than this at one charging. They have, like their predecessors, an independent air supply; either a diver's air bottle or an independent pump.

But this requires complexity, and complexity always has a cost. Anyone who tackles the business of a simple airgun and survives, will gain experience enough to tackle that of the complex airgun. I confine myself to simplicity. Simplicity is the single-shot weapon, and the simplest is that with an integral pump, invented by Paul Giffard in the 1860s. Giffard applied the over-centre lever mechanism such as was used on crossbows for hundreds of years before airguns were developed, to make a viable, integral high-pressure pump.

The simplest high-pressure pneumatic is therefore a rifled gun-barrel lying on top of, and parallel to, a larger diameter tube [Fig. 10.3]. At the back of the barrel is some kind of bolt action so that a pellet can be introduced into the breech, the bolt having a small rubber O-ring towards its front end, with a long pin protruding in front of the O-ring. As the bolt is closed, the pellet is pushed forwards by this long pin, so it passes above and comes to rest in front of, a transverse hole in the rifled barrel, bored from below. This transverse hole communicates with another probing deep into the large diameter tube, and marks the route through which high pressure air is released from the air reservoir.

The air reservoir is found at the back of the large diameter tube, and in bores of up to .22 it is of small volume, well under a cubic inch. In front of the air reservoir is a pump occupying the rearmost half of the

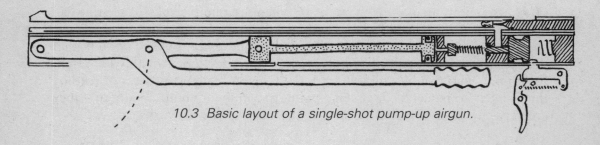

10.3 *Basic layout of a single-shot pump-up airgun.*

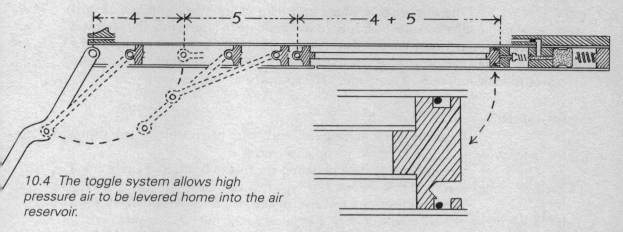

10.4 *The toggle system allows high pressure air to be levered home into the air reservoir.*

available length of the large diameter tube: the front half is marked by a long slot allowing two levers, hinged about their middle a little like the letter V, to drop out of the bottom of the assembled gun. The primary lever, hinged at the muzzle, extends to the breech and is commonly used, when the pump is closed, as the fore-end of the gun. A secondary lever hinges to the piston and the action of closing the fore-end forces the two levers into a long straight line which in turn forces the piston up hard against the air reservoir, and the air reservoir admits the air thus compressed through an inlet valve [Fig. 10.4].

To keep things airtight the piston must be sealed, and usually some kind of rubber piston-head is used. The piston head for the pump needs to be airtight for a very short period so oiled leather, accurately cut, may suffice. Sometimes, astonishing to the modern engineer, the pump piston of the antique pneumatic was nothing more than a block of lead cast in place and sealed only by a film of oil. Again, today O-rings can be used in place of oiled leather or cast lead, and because there must only be a seal on the forward stroke, the groove for such an O-ring can be made quite deep, so that the O-ring is loose. A long hole is drilled from the front of the piston head backwards, communicating with the inner part of this deep groove, and this prevents the O-ring sealing the piston on the rearward stroke, where it would otherwise create an annoying vacuum [Fig. 10.5]. The textbooks tell us that a long stroke, plus a slow movement and a loose O-ring, ought to lead to the O-ring being spiralled against the bore and failing, but thus far I have not found it so. Oil on the bore will reduce the friction of that part in contact with the pump cylinder.

10.5 *Pump piston head must be made to seal perfectly, but only on the push-stroke.*

There is what we have learnt to call a small amount of 'lost volume' in the inlet valve, which is hard to eliminate in converting the plans on the drawing-board into engineering reality. When the pressure of air in the reservoir equals the pressure of air in front of the closed piston head, the pump ceases to have any effect and the air reservoir is to all intents full.

Several things need to be noted:

First, the lost volume exists even with perfect machined fitting, for there must be a hole between pump and reservoir.

Second, at very high pressures the piston head, if of rubber, will itself be compressed and this will increase the lost volume.

Third, of necessity the area of the air reservoir's inlet valve is a bit larger inside the air reservoir than it exposes to the outside, for otherwise it would be blown out of the hole and into the pump. For the sealing surface to be at all reliable, this increase is around the circumference, and of course a tiny increase in circumference will involve a massive increase in area. If, as is often the case, the valve comprises a cone sitting in a coned hole, and if the coned fit is perfect then there is more valve area affected by the pressure inside the reservoir than valve area affected by the pump. I have one inlet valve which sits in a hole 1/4-inch in diameter, and on the inside of the air reservoir it sits in a hole 3/8-inch in diameter. The area exposed to the compressed air inside the air reservoir is therefore nine times as big as the area exposed to the piston head. Accordingly, the pump must achieve a pressure nine times as great as that in the reservoir, before it will introduce any more air. This is a particularly bad example, but probably not as bad as the figure suggests, because it is most unlikely that the cone is sealing perfectly throughout its height. It is more likely that there is simply a circle somewhere along its length where it is wholly air-tight, and if this is the case the pump pressure need only just exceed the reservoir pressure to admit air transfer.

These points are vital to our understanding because they explain why a pump-up airgun always has an upper mechanical limit on the pressure possible. You cannot simply go on pumping and make the device ever more powerful. There always comes a point where the pressure inside the reservoir equals the pressure of the lost volume at the head of the pump piston.

As with the low-pressure airgun we can, to an extent, compensate for low pressures (though even 500 psi is hardly low) by large volumes. For a big-bore airgun a large volume is essential, but even if we choose to make a smaller bore airgun a large volume of air in the reservoir gives a consistent push to the pellet, whilst a small volume will give a sharper initial smack followed by a reduced push as the pellet travels down the barrel.

A larger volume is not a direct compensation, and some gentle arithmetic affords an explanation. We can calculate the area of the back of a .22 pellet; it is almost 24 square millimetres. This is about a twenty-seventh of a square inch. If the pressure is 1,000 pounds per square inch, the force on the back of the pellet is a twenty-seventh of 1,000, which is just under 37 pounds.

If we make the barrel 27 inches long, it will contain one cubic inch of air. If we then use an air reservoir of one cubic inch, the force on the back of the pellet at the muzzle is half of 37 pounds, and the total energy applied will have been 62 foot-pounds.

It is more common to use a reservoir of about a fifth of a cubic inch, and a pressure at the muzzle will therefore be not half, but one-sixth of its original pressure, there being five times the volume of air in the barrel. If we now start with an initial pressure of 1,500 psi the force on the back of the pellet would initially be half as much again, 55 pounds, but because there is so little air in the reservoir, at the muzzle the force is only 11 pounds. However the total energy applied will have been 72 foot-pounds.

Naturally in neither case can we expect that much energy in the flying pellet. All energy transfer involves a loss somewhere, often a very large loss. Steam engines are about 5% efficient; internal combustion engines about 30% efficient.

By experiment, always more dependable than mathematics, it can be shown that 1¼ cubic inches at 1,500 psi works very satisfactorily in a 20-inch .22 barrel, even with the inefficient indirect valve that the below-barrel reservoir layout requires. An experimental rifle yielded 20 foot-pounds with a 12-grain pellet, 22⅓ foot-pounds with a 21-grain pellet, and 24⅓ foot-pounds with a 28-grain bullet – a roughly linear increase in efficiency as the projectile weight goes up.

Grains	ft.-lbs.
12	20
21	22⅓
28	24⅓

A larger bore needs a correspondingly large volume of air and as, for example, a 10-millimetre bore barrel contains more than three times the volume that a .22 barrel does, we are guided by this direct relationship. Big-bore airguns need a large amount of air to do the work we require of them. Of course a reservoir of 4 cubic inches takes more than three times as much pumping to get it up to pressure, so there is a good argument for making the pump as long as possible. If the pump is longer, then there is no reason not to make the barrel longer, for a longer barrel enhances the performance. But a longer barrel benefits from a slightly bigger reservoir, so we are left with choices again. The pump could be made of a larger diameter tubing, which clears more air through it at a single stroke. As this means harder work on the poor soul doing the pumping, it may be better to use a smaller diameter pump barrel, and settle for a good many more pump strokes, each of which is easier to accomplish.

Because the exhaust valve needs to remain strictly airtight, and yet be capable of instantaneous opening, its design has gone down the limited routes these requirements dictate, each of which some enterprising designer has doubtless patented.

The Three Commercial Systems

Almost the earliest system is to tap the valve from the outside with a hammer. The antique gun used a rotary cam movement to displace the valve a set distance. Today's systems largely deal a blow from a free-flying hammer, the closing of the valve being effected mostly by pressure of the air in the reservoir [Fig. 10.6].

Either system allows for many shots being taken from a single charging of the reservoir, always provided the reservoir is sufficiently large. As the air pressure goes down at successive shots, so more air is released at each blow on the valve, and for a limited number of shots the velocity remains reasonably constant. The air reservoir needs to be large, or the pressure difference between shots will be great. But suppose one were to start with a reservoir containing 20 cubic inches, and allow half a cubic inch out per shot, starting from a pressure of 1,500 psi, the first five shots would lose around 35 psi per shot (as shown in the table), and there is a fair chance accuracy would not suffer too much. In the field, a capacity for five shots is usually ample. The valve needs to be faced and of a hard plastic material: rubber may compress too much and give a sluggish valve opening if the design is unwholesome.

psi
1,500
1,462
1,426
1,390
1,355

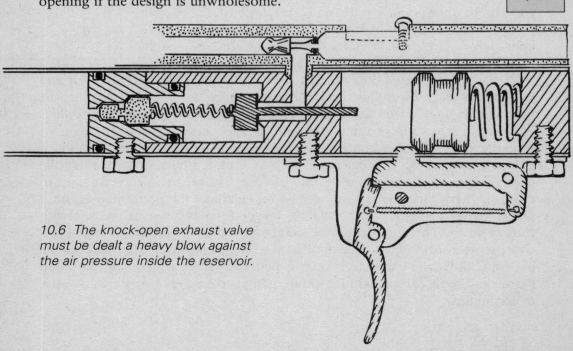

10.6 The knock-open exhaust valve must be dealt a heavy blow against the air pressure inside the reservoir.

The chief disadvantage of hammering the exhaust valve open is that some of the space through which the compressed air flows to the back of the bullet is occupied by the means – usually a rod – of transmitting the blow from the hammer of the gun to the valve. Compressed air does not like to flow along cluttered passageways, and there is always some loss of efficiency.

If the reservoir is very small the entire reservoir contents are released at each shot. This we have learnt to call the 'dump system'. For subsequent shots it requires a pump integral with the gun, but it is a simple mechanism and is the cheapest common airgun in circulation. America is awash with them. Provided the same number of pump strokes is applied per shot, and a decent interval is allowed between shots, they are capable of very fine accuracy. The decent interval is both to allow the shooter to recover from the exertion of pumping, and to allow the pump and the reservoir to cool. Hot air develops higher pressures.

Avoiding a hammer, the O-ring allows the use of a very simple exhaust valve; nothing more than a rod sitting inside a stationary O-ring surrounding the exit hole. The rod plugs the hole; pulling the trigger allows the rod to shoot out of the hole and the air to blast its way back, and up, and down the barrel [Fig. 10.7]. Because it is so simple to make, and needs only an O-ring for a seal, this is the layout I prefer. It is always associated with the single-shot dump system, unless an elaborate secondary pressure chamber is somehow incorporated with its concomitant costs and increased opportunity for malfunction.

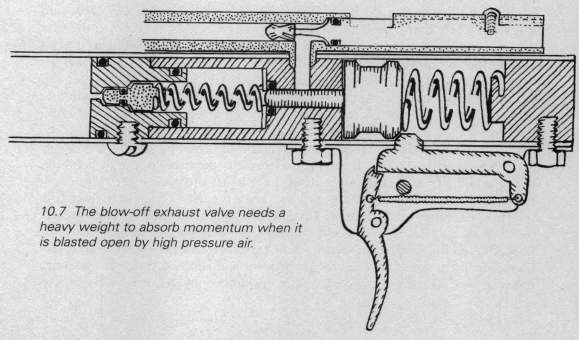

10.7 *The blow-off exhaust valve needs a heavy weight to absorb momentum when it is blasted open by high pressure air.*

It is as well to place a large steel weight behind the rod, and indeed to use this steel weight as the sear; a substantial spring will absorb the shock of the weight, and the momentum of the weight reduces the speed of exit of the rod, so that this rod too does not hurtle out of the back of the gun and impale the shooter, which would be unkind. It is not just a hypothetical danger. The Paterson Colt was a good deal more popular than other revolvers not because Colt had patented the concept of mechanical rotation of the cylinder, but because other revolvers did not always mount the cylinder pivot in line with the barrel. The Cochran patent of 1837 mounted the axle of the revolver vertically rather than horizontally and it was commonly known as a monitor, or turret gun. In a very unfortunate incident, Patrick W. Porter was actually demonstrating to Samuel Colt his revolving rifle in which the cylinder rotated in the same plane as a bicycle wheel, when the flash ignited all the chambers, including that pointing through the breech towards Porter, who was killed. The drawback was immediately evident to Colt and prevented the concept becoming popular.

Removing the rod from the passageway into a cul-de-sac means that the air must turn at least one corner before it can push the bullet down the barrel, and this gives a loss of efficiency. In the commercial pneumatic airgun the holes are simply drilled: there is no effort to round off the internal corners, and the turbulent eddies have a fierce effect on airflow. Any chemical engineer will tell us that this will reduce the effect of the compressed air. In actual guns, comparing like volumes these losses are very large; as much as 40% compared with the potential of a straight-line valve. It follows that if the compressed air is released directly onto the back of the pellet it will be far more efficient, and it is quite likely that a pressure of about 1,000 psi applied directly to the rear of the pellet, will act as if it were a pressure of about 1,500 psi applied backwards and upwards and forwards, from an initial point below the barrel. Even the reversal of air flow required by the barrel reservoir airgun (see fig. 9.6) leads to an astonishing drop in efficiency compared with the straight-line valve. I have measured this in a .535-inch bore barrel, and it yielded only 83 per cent of the muzzle energy of a straight-line valve.

Precisely this efficient straight-line valve approach is used in air cartridge systems, where a tiny brass reservoir is pumped to a high pressure, with the pellet fitted directly in front of the exhaust valve, each cartridge being loaded separately into the airgun as if it were a firearm. The air cartridge rifle was first patented by Giffard in 1872, but it was reintroduced with greater commercial success by Saxby and Palmer 100 years later. It is now made by Brocock, and illustrations of sectioned air cartridges can be seen in their advertisements in the press. The valve comprises a rod running through the entire reservoir, and as the hole at each end is the same diameter, it is being sucked out of the reservoir at both ends to exactly the same degree, so it goes nowhere. The gun trips the rod forwards, and the air escapes around the dislodged front plug. The trigger could pull the rod backwards just far enough for the hole at the breech to open. But once this happens, the rod will fly backwards with immense force, and again it needs to be caught securely and cushioned. The penalty for failing to make this sufficiently strong is of course that suffered by the unfortunate Mr. Porter – you shoot yourself.

Some Theoretical Designs

A good engineer can create a straight-line valve by putting the air reservoir behind the barrel, and not underneath it. A communicating port (a hole) between pump and reservoir is needed, and provided there is an external clamp holding the pump and the barrel together, this can be made air-tight with solder.

With the air reservoir a tube, and the plug running through the middle and emerging at both ends through O-rings, if the rear hole is slightly larger in diameter than the exhaust the larger end will have the greater thrust and will want to be blown outwards, sucking the smaller end of the sealing rod into the air reservoir. Provision must be made not to suck the bullet into the reservoir too, or much cursing will ensue. The force on the larger end will depend on how much larger it is than the smaller end. Of course, if the bullet makes an air-tight seal, this force has to have an additional 14 pounds for every square inch of valve-rod, because the pressure has to overcome a vacuum, and a vacuum is worth about 14 psi of suction.

If the pressure is 1,500 psi, and the smaller end goes into the back of a .22 barrel, the force on that smaller end is 57 pounds, which we calculate by working out the area of a .22 circle in square inches and multiplying it by the pressure. Pressure is conveniently measured in pounds – that is pounds force – per square inch. If the pellet makes a perfect seal, we have to regard the pressure as 1,500 minus 14 psi, so the force on that end is reduced to 56.5 pounds. If the larger end is 6 millimetres in diameter, the force trying to blow it out of the reservoir is 66 pounds, so the total force trying to open the valve is 8½ pounds, and a sear at the bigger end can be designed accordingly [Fig. 10.8]. Unfortunately, as soon as the valve is released the air forgets it is trying to push the smaller end down the barrel, and the big end momentarily develops the full thrust of 66 pounds and has to be caught in an appropriately robust mechanism. If the pressure is 3,000 psi, all these forces are doubled. If we make a mistake in our calculations and the valve bursts out of the back of the gun we get killed, so the arithmetic and the engineering is really rather important. Emphasising the word 'reliable', a *reliable* means of stopping it flying out of the back of the gun is required.

The reservoir will remain sealed if a sear is introduced behind

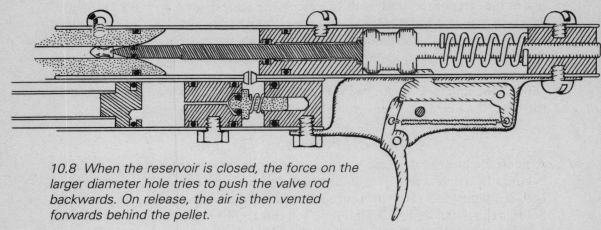

10.8 When the reservoir is closed, the force on the larger diameter hole tries to push the valve rod backwards. On release, the air is then vented forwards behind the pellet.

the central rod valve. Using separate front and rear brass plugs there will be great difficulty in lining up both central holes with one another, because the method of fixing them in the tube of which the reservoir is made means that the air pressure tries to turn the retaining screw into a pivot, so the face of the plug will not be square to the bore [Fig. 10.9]. Although the O-rings may seal for a time as very slight ovals, the central valve-rod won't appreciate being bent, so there must be clearance for the valve-rod to prevent metal rubbing against metal and rapid wear. Lengthening the brass plug, or using three retaining screws distributed round its circumference, or very careful execution of workmanship to give a very close fit should all reduce this alignment difficulty.

The most urgent problem however is still to ensure that any springs behind the valve rod are adequate to catch it without it flying out of the back of the gun, yet are not so powerful as to pop the rod back into the barrel before all the air is discharged. From what I already know it seems that only extensive experiment will determine the right impact-absorbing springs, and their choice will depend on the bore of the barrel, because a large bore will clearly need a big valve to capitalise on its potential power, and in turn this will require a large rearward hole, which of course will deliver a more substantial rearward blow on release. Spring failure I find difficult to predict, but too weak a spring will usually reveal itself, after a few shots, by the coils of the spring collapsing on one another. I have never suffered too strong a spring and can only guess that it will show itself by a reduced velocity, indicating that the valve is being closed prematurely.

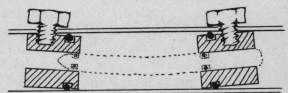

10.9 The disadvantage of doing without screw-cutting equipment. However good a fit, a side-pinned plug will pivot against the retaining bolt in the bore, distorting the central hole.

It is possible to echo the forward-moving plug of the air cartridge, but it will have to move into a large chasm so that the air can flow round it without being unduly pinched before it hits the back of the bullet.

The air cartridge depends on machining both ends of the plug absolutely equal in diameter, and this includes machining the grooves at each end of absolutely equal diameter, and it includes machining the holes at each end of the reservoir of absolutely equal diameter too. There is no room for the slightest inequality of these two ends. The penalty for one end being machined even the smallest bit bigger than the other is that under the high pressure used the valve rod will tend inexorably to move towards whichever end is the larger, and it will suddenly burst free. Whether loaded or not it is a recipe for a fatal catastrophe. But, trying to think how to retain the advantages of this efficient valve, it occurs to me that by having the forward end of the valve rod a little bigger than the rear, the valve will want to move forward into the chasm, and the sear need only hold the rod back. A light trigger pull on the sear could be effected by having the rear-most opening only slightly smaller than the front opening. The greatest problem is likely to be catching – and cushioning – the forward movement of the valve rod without it either popping back and closing off the reservoir, or going too far and jamming in the breech. Needless to say, I've never risked the labour to build such a mechanism, with all its inherent possibilities for causing me to rage about the workshop berating my stupidity in attempting something so hairy. Besides, the valve rod would need to be of some high-tensile material lest it break and go hurtling down the barrel in hot pursuit of the bullet. Machining high-tensile rods is not something you really want to do.

It is difficult to make accurate predictions about efficiency because so much will depend on all that happens at the valve. A gentle coning of the air into the breech is what chemical engineering textbooks recommend. A similar improvement should obtain if the valve rod itself is tapered, smoothing the transition from reservoir to barrel. Both of these cones are needed anyway to locate a long valve rod in the forward exhaust hole of the reservoir. At an angle of somewhere between 8° and 11°, the air doesn't know it is being funnelled into a tight constriction, and there is the least loss of efficiency.

This straight-line valve may require a novel approach to loading the pellet, for air rifles develop their best accuracy if the muzzle is fractionally choked, which precludes the simplest of all forms, the muzzle-loader. A little lateral thinking suggests making the barrel move to allow loading at the breech. Of course the conventional break-barrel spring air rifle does precisely this, but there is no reason why the bolt action should not be applied to the barrel rather than to the bolt [Fig. 10.10]. Provided it does not involve any undue force that might distort the barrel, there need be no reason

why such a system should stop the
sights being aligned with the barrel,
nor is there any reason why the
sights should not be directly
attached to the barrel.

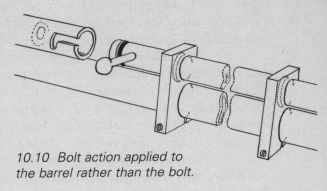

The uninhibited
engineer who chances to find a
double-barrelled shotgun in a dry
barn somewhere, can do worse than
drill a communicating hole between
the two barrels at the breech, and
by means of plugs with valves

*10.10 Bolt action applied to
the barrel rather than the bolt.*

contained within them, convert one barrel into a pump and the rear of the
other into an air chamber, releasing air directly behind a bullet. The firearms
enthusiast weeps at such a suggestion, but we are not interested in his emotions
and the world has an ample number of old double-barrels kicking uselessly
around.

As we have averred, releasing any compressed air always
results in a temperature drop, and this in turn always produces condensation.
The effect of this in a deep mine can be so great, even with the smallest abrupt
drop in pressure, that the mine is instantaneously filled with fog, and for a
moment the miner can see nothing. This I once learnt from a mines site
engineer. In an airgun the condensation will lead to immediate rusting of any
exposed steel. This means that pumps must always be adequately oiled so that
the insides of reservoirs are protected, for steel valve rods and springs are
especially prone to rusting. By way of further reiteration, it has also been found
by bitter experience that the rearmost five inches of a barrel suffer a tendency
to rust because of this condensation of water. Therefore pellets must also be
oiled, or the insides of barrels will rust too. Cardew informs us that the
pressure change is too gradual to give the danger of 'diesel' explosions. I did
once, however, experience a mysterious series of very high velocity shots from
a newly-reassembled pneumatic pistol, which I could put down to nothing else
but dieseling, so a reasonably heavy grade of oil is wise. Among antique
airguns the insides of the reservoirs, commonly made of sheet steel rolled and
brazed, were usually greased, and this has the bonus of being, and may
primarily have been intended to act as, a dust trap.

Turning, at last, to the barrel itself, the easiest plan is to remove
a barrel from some existing arm. The .22 rimfire rifle is the commonest calibre
in the world, notwithstanding the 80-million AK47s that litter the globe's
troubled regions. The longer the barrel the better for a pneumatic arm; it has
the same effect as increasing the draw length of an archer, which is to say,

increasing efficiency and hence muzzle velocity. A barrel four times as long will give twice the muzzle energy. The Afghan jezail had a prodigious barrel, and I have an 1897 photograph of an Arab mounted on a camel outside the Great Pyramid with a jezail whose barrel was four feet long. What nineteenth century Arabs may have shot at among the sand dunes I do not know, but in denser foliage a long barrel may prove a nuisance. It is possible to buy a .22 barrel of 20 inches; my old Winchester Model 67 has a 27-inch .22 barrel.

The alternative is to make a barrel, and it is as well to spend time selecting tubing of an appropriate bore so that one of the four commercially-available calibres of pellet can be used. If a fullbore is contemplated and tube isn't to hand, the only alternative is to go through the extremely long-winded process of drilling the bore with a D-bit.

A D-bit has the advantage over a twist-drill of following a perfectly straight line through a material. The bit itself is made of silver-steel of the correct diameter for the bore and long enough for the whole barrel, though provided twisting can be avoided (something difficult to avoid in a long drill), one might conceivably attach a short D-bit to a longer rod by means of brazing. The D-bit is made by shaving the end section away so that exactly half of it is missing and the end-section resembles a letter D – hence the name [Fig. 10.11]. This is relieved at an angle of 5° in both planes, and provided the cutting edge is always sharp, and shavings are regularly removed, it will methodically bore a hole for as long as you have the patience to turn it.

Professionally one might ream such a hole afterwards, but certainly lapping a barrel is sensible prior to rifling it, and lapping a barrel is not something to undertake lightly. It involves a long, slowly-rotating rod with a longitudinal split at one end, which is the lapping tool. Lapping compound – an abrasive paste – is regularly smeared on the tool and it is slowly rotated for hours up and down the barrel. Then a small wedge, introduced to the split, is tapped in a little way to expand the lap, and the process is repeated until the barrel is perfectly smooth and perfectly uniform along its length.

Hydraulic tubing can be found of all sorts of useful bores, and I have lengths of it in so close an approximation to .22-inch that pellets will fit snugly. Lead deforms permanently, without any residual spring, so that once a pellet is seated in the barrel, no more force is required to push it along the barrel. Hydraulic tubing is never of perfectly even bore throughout its length, and the imaginative barrel-maker pokes a pellet through with a long brazing rod,

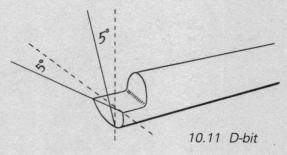

10.11 D-bit

carefully marking where it encounters a tight spot. This spot can then be used as the muzzle, giving a crude form of choke, though one has to cross one's fingers that the tightness is due to a constriction, and not a flattening of the bore into an oval. Hydraulic tubing is ideal for making barrels of a larger bore, though you may have to apply the lathe to making an appropriate bullet mould. Accuracy generally increases with a tight fit, so the relationship of bore to mould is important.

All that is then required is to cut some rifling. Dr. F. W. Mann described a form of micro-groove rifling and the bench-rest riflemen of America in the 1950s tried it in their quest for ultimate rifle accuracy. It works, although you can't see the rifling grooves in the barrel. Dr. Mann wrote that a barrel need only be rifled with the scratching of emery powder rubbed onto a close-fitting lead plug for a bullet to follow the micro-grooves left behind it. A very thoughtful workman, therefore, will devise some means whereby a revolving rod tows behind it a rigidly-attached plug of lead, with some valve-grinding paste smeared all over the plug. How accurate this might be – and how long it lasts – will always remain to be seen, but if a source of tubing is found, it is neither expensive nor time-consuming to repeat the process until a good barrel emerges.

Revolving the rod can be accomplished by referring back to one's juvenile efforts in the school forge. Almost the first thing one makes in metalwork lessons is a poker for the fire, and metalwork teachers being fond of needless complication, the poker is always made of twisted square rod. Schoolboys do not spontaneously make fire pokers but if we, blessed with malicious lateral thinking, humour the metalwork teacher and obtain a square rod at least the length of our putative rifle barrel, we can heat it red hot and, clamping one end in a robust vice, twist the other to match the number of revolutions we want in the rifled barrel. A cap is then clamped to the outside of the barrel, with a square hole in its centre. As the square rod is drawn through this hole on its way out of the barrel, it will rotate, and any cutter or abrasive-covered plug behind it will rotate the same amount [Fig. 10.12].

Of course this is better suited to larger bores, where the square

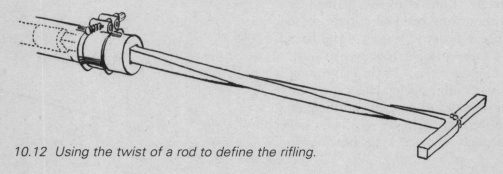

10.12 *Using the twist of a rod to define the rifling.*

rod can be quite thick and therefore stiff. An interesting effect may be obtained if a small-bore barrel is rifled in this way, because the torque on the squared rod varies according to its length. If the guiding square hole is mounted at the muzzle of the barrel, the rifling at the breech is cut when the squared rod is longest. Because of the length of the rod at this point, the twisting of the rifling cutter is resisted by the barrel wall, and the rod slightly untwists. As the cutter moves up the barrel, so this tendency to untwist is reduced, and the rifling twist is more and more strongly guided by the twist of the squared rod. If the balance of depth of rifling cutter is correct, one can end up with an accelerating twist to the rifling, something advocated by Metford in the nineteenth century and actually used on the Carcano military rifle. Unfortunately, despite the theoretical advantage, no benefit has ever been shown by use of an accelerating rate of rifling twist.

It will be seen by the observant reader that I have not touched on certain essential engineering discussions surrounding the strength of pivots, nor the case-hardening of steel, nor the merits of silver-solder and the means of achieving perfect cleansing of metals prior to making any joint. It is assumed that nobody is likely to embark on a project of this dangerous nature unless some confidence already exists in his capacity to undertake reasonable engineering benchwork, and few among us who have invested the sum required for a metal-working lathe will have done so without some judgment as to how basic machining can be done.

*

It remains only to reiterate the warning that compressed air is quite astonishingly dangerous, and that nothing but seamless tube should be used, and further that careful calculations must be done to ensure that the materials are capable of withstanding the pressures. Every engineer will issue the caveat that everything should be hydraulically tested before it is pressurised, and I cannot gainsay this advice, nor would I wish to. Calculations are useful things, but reality has the sometimes disconcerting habit of revealing when they have gone astray, and if an error is on the wrong side of safety, the personal costs can be and will be quite horrible. If you can't do the maths, then don't make the gun. I really mean it. It's just too dangerous.

Chapter 11

Compounding & complexity

The nature of craftsmen is conservative and any new idea is invariably regarded with hostility until the resulting advantage is overwhelming, when it commonly spawns a landslide of imitative experiments. Necessity is no longer the mother of invention; quite the reverse. It is only when we do not have an active daily need for a bow and arrow that we feel free to entertain radical ideas.

A compound bow is one which accentuates the string speed by some subordinate mechanism, and though it includes the bow with wheels at the tips which has now come to dominate modern archery, it does not exclude other forms of compounding string-speed; nor are wheel-tipped bows the first compounds ever produced. It must be stated, as we are always keen to suspend our disbelief when perusing the advertisements, that the laws of physics continue to apply regardless of what some marketing executive might care to publish, and a missile cannot be persuaded to have more kinetic energy than the archer puts into the bow however intricately the strings may be arranged. Compounding the string movement is always a good plan because a large string movement allows greater time for transfer of energy from the bow to the missile, but the total energy for work will still be the incremental draw weight, multiplied by the draw length.

In 1966 W. H. Allen patented what most archers call 'the' compound bow, an arrow-shooting bow having eccentric wheels or cams at the limb-tips and an additional cable connecting the string via each of these eccentric wheels to the other limb-tip. The arrangement gave two advantages – a higher arrow velocity, and a reducing draw weight. Of these, the second has the greater significance, since the feeling of pulling a stiff bow which suddenly yields as the eccentric wheels roll over to the point at which their leverage acts in favour of, rather than against, the arm muscles, is utterly seductive, and allows those of us who are not gifted archers to shoot rather better than we otherwise might. The early years of the compound bow were the usual struggle of a new idea to gain acceptance; its appearance offended many, and the fact that one needed less skill to achieve comparable scores led the authorities who govern target shooting, as authorities in sport are prone to do, to ban it. The fact that the sensation of shooting it was so pleasant, and the fact that it was developed in America where a substantial part of the population use the bow for hunting rather than competitive target shooting, led eventually to its total dominance of the market. Once makers realised that a complexity of design could give tangible rewards, compound bows became bewilderingly complex, with multiple cables and cams positioned in every conceivable place. Eventually a single design – the original one of W. H. Allen, with a single eccentric wheel or cam at the tip of each limb, which indicates his brilliance – came to dominate the field. It gave the greatest simplicity with the most significant advantage of the concept, and there is no longer any doubt that this will come to have as firm a place in the history of archery as the English longbow or the Turkish recurve bow.

There should be no especial difficulty about inveigling the compound to shoot bullets, although it would be important to provide two separate bowstrings [Fig. 11.1]. An obvious way is to put two eccentric pulley-wheels at the limb-tip, one on each side, so that in effect the bow is strung twice over; the double string allows the use of the pouch to house a bullet, and it also prevents limb twist, which is a problem that has always plagued the makers of compound bows. Such an arrangement means, unfortunately, that the wheels and probably the limbs and the handle, will all have to be constructed afresh; an existing bow cannot easily be adapted to do the job. A particularly large sight window would be required in these days of litigation; no manufacturer would

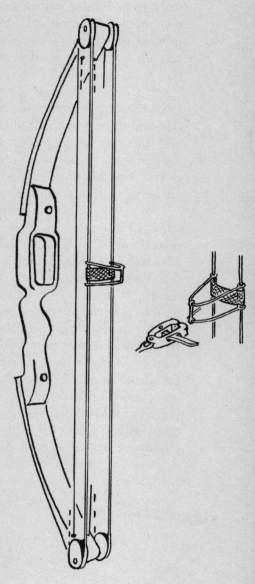

11.1 *Centre-shot compound bow with wheels, strings and cables doubled to allow free flight to a bullet. Note the need for a mechanical release aid.*

want to be hauled before a court by a plaintiff who had bounced a ball off the riser back at himself. A mechanical release is also likely to be essential to prevent the string rolling, as it does, off the fingers. The finger release always sets up a gyratory motion which cannot produce a straight departure of the ball from the pouch.

Naturally, a number of arrow-shooting compound crossbows have been made and sold. But one of the chief reasons for the success of the compound bow is the lightening of the draw weight as full draw is achieved, and there is no need for this in a crossbow, which already possessing a mechanical release device suffers no penalty through a heavy weight at full draw. Yet the idea suggests a number of ways in which unconventional stringing methods might be employed to enhance bullet velocity.

The most ancient is the arrangement of several bows in the stock of a single crossbow, an arrangement already described in the written records prior to Genghis Khan and researched by the great bowyer Edward McEwen. McEwen made a model reproduction with two 40-pound bows, four feet long, opposed to one another, and a third 20-pound bow of the same length, at the front of the weapon [Fig. 11.2]. Thus the two front bows faced forwards in the normal way, and the rearmost bow faced backwards. A single string ran from the tip of the front, light-weight bow, to a pulley-wheel at the tip of the rearmost bow, and thence to a pulley at the tip of the middle bow. It then crossed the stock at right angles and went through a pulley on the other tip of the middle bow, back through a pulley at the tip of the rearmost bow, and finally back to the tip of the front bow. The arrangement allowed a draw length of 42 inches, and a draw weight of 100 pounds. One difficulty encountered was in giving all three bows a brace height. The original drawings were clearly by an artist who didn't have much idea of what the weapon really

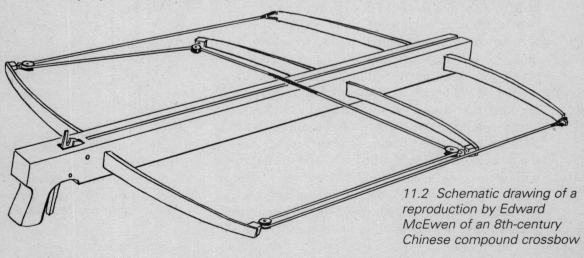

11.2 *Schematic drawing of a reproduction by Edward McEwen of an 8th-century Chinese compound crossbow*

looked like, so he had inserted 'clouds' to mask the bits he didn't know how to draw properly. With no guidance on how the bowstring was mounted, McEwen first tried metal rings, but they gave a jerky movement, so instead he used pulleys. The device then worked perfectly and the performance was impressive.

A simpler arrangement might be to mount a single bow with pulleys at the limb-tips, with the string a single loop, one half of which is stretched and held, the other being stretched and released. This allows a theoretical doubling of the string velocity given identical limb-tip velocities. Since the energy gained cannot exceed the energy put into the system, a doubling of muzzle velocity cannot be expected. But crossbows are rarely more than 50% efficient, where longer handbows are often as much as 70% efficient, so some improvement is certainly possible. Again, it will be found that using this to increase the draw length is the way to improve velocity, because again we come back to the fact that the more time is allowed for accelerating the missile, the higher will its launch velocity be. The efficiency, of course, refers to the amount of energy coming out in the form of bullet-speed, compared with the amount of energy put into the system.

Another point of departure might be the quadrupling of limb-tip velocity which can theoretically be achieved by halving the limb length. Short limbs need not shorten the draw length of any bow; all that is required is a long stiff section between them – hence the whip-ended bow of Ascham, and hence too most modern recurve bows with their cast metal handle sections. Among compounded crossbows this can be done by mounting a half-sized bow on either side of the crossbow tiller, with the inner ends tied to the stock, the

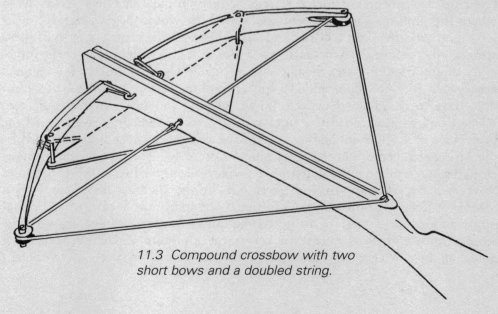

11.3 Compound crossbow with two short bows and a doubled string.

outer end of one bow being attached by the bow-string to the outer end of the other bow. Despite sketching the idea out long ago [Fig. 11.3] I never got round to building such a crossbow, thus saving myself what would no doubt have been considerable lawyer's fees, as a similar arrangement was used in the TSS Quadraflex compound bow patented not long afterwards by Joe Coldwell in California. It should be noted that the pulley wheels I gaily thought I would use are

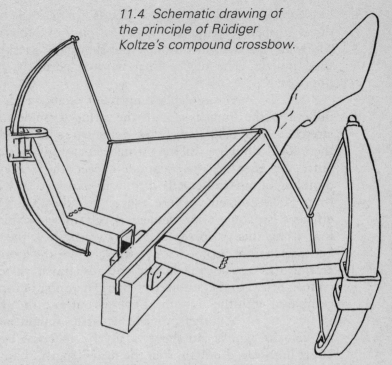

11.4 Schematic drawing of the principle of Rüdiger Koltze's compound crossbow.

not eccentrically mounted; a drop in draw weight is not really needed in a crossbow, and since eccentric wheels require the cable to lock to the pulley, using standard pulleys simplifies the stringing.

The idea of separate bows occurred independently to the German experimenter Rüdiger Koltze, who by attaching bows vertically to where the limb-tips of a conventional crossbow would be, strung each bow separately, and then ran a horizontal string between the centre of each of these strings. His patent is a particularly good idea as it altogether removes the possibility of any friction losses through use of pulley-wheels. Hitherto unimagined arrow velocities are reported: 650 fps, and in one instance 800 fps, though it does have to be added that each individual bow was made by stringing two Barnett bows together side-by side, and he gives a total draw weight for the four bows of 1,000 pounds [Fig. 11.4]. The drawback is the bulk required by the string geometry. Photographs show Koltze wincing at the moment of cranking the string back. I empathise: I wince whenever I span my 196-pound yew crossbow, though wincing never did me the slightest bit of good as a means of securing my safety. Additional complication leads to additional opportunities for something to go wrong, and when we are dealing with the storage and controlled release of very large amounts of energy, something going slightly wrong can be, and in the history of weapon development frequently has been, fatal.

In Dayton, Ohio, the use of pulleys was explored to reduce the crossbow to a much more compact form during the late 1970s by Robert van House. Dispensing with the conventional bow, his patented designs use either a coil-spring or a compressed-gas strut lying inside the butt. A crank feeds the power to pivoted but otherwise stiff bow 'limb' levers, to the ends of which he fits a double pulley. Together with a pulley fitted to the sides of the crossbow tiller, these allow a single string to thread its way hither and yon, and translate a spring movement of 2¼ inches into an arrow movement of 21 inches [Fig. 11.5]. The principle is a very cleverly-applied version of the multiple block-and-tackle.

At the American Crossbow Hunters' Association speed contest of 1978 van House recorded a velocity of 370 fps with a spring-powered version, and later shooting the same crossbow he achieved 427 fps with a 210-grain arrow. Since the weapon is only 14⅜ inches wide braced and 4½ inches wide cocked, and isn't very much longer than the draw length itself, it has to be one of the most practical and intelligent applications of the compounding principle. Again, it is worth noting that high velocities resulted from a long draw.

Holding the string of a heavy crossbow naturally requires a stout mechanism, every bit as strong as the pull itself, and until Leonardo applied the principle of multiple levers to it, the trigger pull tended to be heavy. However the string is retained, a long trigger lever, or compounded levers, can be used to reduce this pull so that the aim is unaffected. The most elegant trigger mechanism I have seen is one designed by Dr. Flewett. Interesting himself in a number of crossbow mechanisms, one of which he patented, he

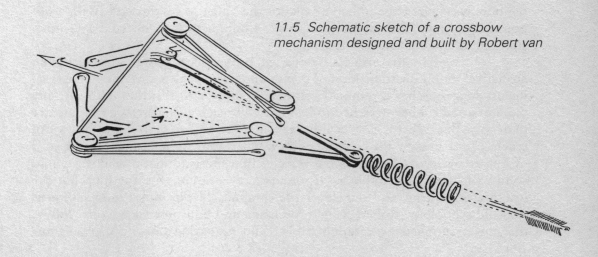

11.5 Schematic sketch of a crossbow mechanism designed and built by Robert van

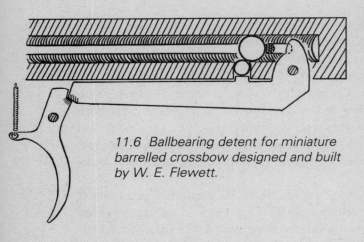

11.6 Ballbearing detent for miniature barrelled crossbow designed and built by W. E. Flewett.

came to consider the slot-sided barrelled crossbow which has always had the attraction of straightforwardness. Complexity always has a cost, and the barrelled bullet-crossbow suffers the inconvenience that the bullet rolls out of the barrel if it is pointed downwards. It occurred to him that the simplest, and therefore best, release mechanism to overcome this difficulty uses the bullet itself to hold the string in the drawn position [Fig. 11.6].

The crossbow is a muzzle-loader, and uses a ram-rod to push the bullet, and with it the string, home to the breech. In doing so, it automatically cocks the release mechanism. Immediately in front of the bullet, and obtruding into the barrel from below, is a ballbearing retained by a long sear lever. The trigger allows the sear and the ballbearing to drop, and the bullet then flies over it. As the bullet in this case is itself a ball-bearing, no distortion results from it being held in this way. Ballbearings are made of tool steel. I have both cocked and loaded, and shot this crossbow, which the designer had built in miniature pistol format, and every part of it worked to perfection. It was fitted with a tiny alloy bow 1/8-inch thick, 220 millimetres between the nocks tapering from 27 millimetres wide at the base of the limb to 3 millimetres wide at the tips, with small protrusions to form the nocks themselves. The middle of the bow was enlarged and had a hole for the bullet to fly through. With a 60-pound weight and a draw length of just 54 millimetres, it delivered a 5/16-inch steel ball at an amazing 196 fps.

To the armchair designer, rubber as a power unit seems an attractive option for some kind of compounding of velocity. My limited experiments suggest it has a terminal velocity of about 270 fps; that is to say, any piece of good rubber stretched to its limit will reach a final velocity no greater than this. But 270 fps is a healthy velocity, far higher than many bows can reach. Unfortunately the creep of rubber, where leaving it strained for periods of but a few seconds reduces the velocity in a most dramatic manner, would seem to make it unsuitable as a primary power source for anything but the instantaneous draw-and-release of the catapult. In the mid 1980s a fifteen-year-old schoolboy, Robert Knight, designed and built just such a 'crossbow', the power supplied by catapult rubber and the string moving a prodigious distance by means of pulley wheels [Fig. 11.7]. Unfortunately, he relates, it was relatively low-powered, though in hindsight this was no bad thing in the hands of a fifteen-year-old, and he remarked to me "As I remember, a serious drawback (no pun intended) was rubber breakage, leaving unsightly welts on the cheeks of the operator...". Clearly, for both reasons rubber was not the best material, but the development of the Allen compound bow has shown us the unwisdom of predicting 'never', and perhaps someone will dream up a delightfully simple mechanism that obviates these limitations.

There will always be a point of equilibrium between the development of higher velocities and the increasing complexity this requires. With complexity come costs both in manufacture, and more significantly in maintenance of the weapon. Henry V inclined to simplicity, and with uncomplicated longbows held an enormous army of French (including crossbowmen) at bay. Military experience suggests that a large number of simple weapons, clearly understood by an experienced and well-rehearsed army, will hold the day against a small number of highly complicated weapons, the trade-off being that complication involves expense, and expense precludes both practice and the amassing of large numbers of the complicated weapon.

There is one final point that needs to be made. The concept of a crossbow is an attractive one for target shooting. It combines the simplicity of the bow, and some of its silence (in fact a powerful crossbow is surprisingly loud), with pleasing mechanical details in the release mechanism. The power source is free, and the ammunition re-useable. It affords accuracy with far less practice than hand-bow or catapult, but achieving its potential requires a great deal of meticulous care and practice. Yet for shooting in the field it is very swiftly discarded. Shot perhaps half a dozen times, the owner discovers that a

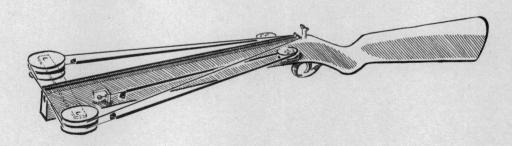

11.7 *Rubber-powered, compound, arrow-shooting stocked catapult, designed and built by a 15-year-old schoolboy, Robert Knight, in 1984.*

rifle – even an air rifle – shoots more quickly, is easier to manipulate, is less unwieldy and does not leave one groping in the grass for a lost missile. Governments throughout history have sought to legislate against crossbows. Laws against crossbows never work and are always unnecessary, since practical experience legislates against them a great deal more effectively.

It has been noted that the Timorese, forbidden the use of guns after a long war, became especially adroit in the use of the shanghai, or catapult. Lacking latex tubing they obtained rubber bands and plaited them into useful lengths. Lacking lead bullets they made do with stones, carefully selected. I will admit that the one regret I have is not having taken the catapult more seriously when in my youth and eagerness I was ever keen to be stalking some wild creature; with practice it is a formidable weapon, having the accuracy and the power of a bow, and with none of the attendant bulk and inconvenience. Besides, it is terribly easy to make, and those who deem themselves worthy to jump through the hoops imposed by self-appointed political parties and (by the default of better people finding better things to do) become our political rulers, will ever be thwarted in a desire to impose a ban on it.

CHAPTER 12

Velocity measurements & the relation of drag to cast

It was said by a great astronomer that an intelligent man could derive a lifetime's interest from a six-inch reflecting telescope. Whether I can be described as intelligent is open to question, but I have certainly found that some amusing physics can be done with an electronic chronograph, comparing velocities measured accurately using different launching methods; different rubber with the catapult, different strings with the bullet-bow, and different volumes of air, pressures, and lengths of barrel for an airgun. The chronograph is to shooting what the telescope is to astronomy. It tells truths – quite often rather tactlessly.

The first scientific method of measuring the velocity of a bullet was that invented by Benjamin Robins and described in detail on pages 25 to 33 of his book *New Principles of Gunnery,* published in 1742 when he was 35 years old. Like all things of genius, it is brilliantly simple, relying on the principle that the momentum of a formerly stationary body after a musket-ball has collided with it – providing that the musket-ball is absorbed into the body and doesn't make an exit – is the same as the momentum of the musket-ball before the collision took place.

Robins erected a robust tripod [Fig. 12.1] and suspended from it a pendulum whose weight was 56 pounds 3 ounces, and whose length (determined by timing 200 swings in 253 seconds), was 62²/₃ inches. The measuring of the length of a pendulum by timing a swing is a pretty bit of applied maths, described in every decent elementary physics book, but since we threw all our text-books away on arriving at the maturity trumpeted by graduation, and since today's text-books shun anything useful on the doubtful basis of not wishing to handicap a child's development by implying it to be other than gifted, it will save looking fruitlessly in a box on top of a wardrobe to state the formula:

$$L = g \ (T \div 2\pi)^2$$

Since I always confuse myself by what is meant by a full swing, and since I can never find the right passage in the right textbook, I always have to check by tying a heavy spanner to a long bit of string and swinging this from a nail hammered into a rafter of the garage roof while peering in the gloom at my wristwatch. It swings backwards and

L is the length of the pendulum in feet
g is the gravitational constant 32.16 (which refers to an acceleration, fps per second)
T is the time in seconds taken for a complete swing.

forwards three times in about nine seconds which, the garage roof being eight feet high, tells me that what we mean by a full swing – three seconds – is from top right to top left and all the way back to top right again. Robins, it will be deduced by those who can be bothered to find a calculator, measured half-swings, that is from top right to top left only. Robins arranged for musket bullets to be shot into a 7-inch thick block of beech wood screwed to a

swinging steel plate so that they would sink into the wood. The immediate thought of anyone whose physics has rusted quietly since school, is that surely some energy from the collision will be used by the bullet making a hole in the wooden plank, and this is so. But momentum is different from energy in that the former is only the mass multiplied by the velocity, and this means that there is plenty of spare energy – which involves the square of the velocity – to punch holes in beech wood. Robins stated that *'in a Bullet moving with a*

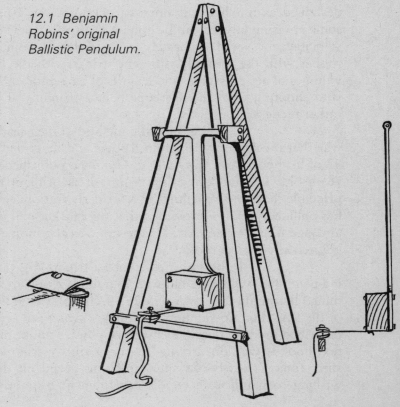

12.1 Benjamin Robins' original Ballistic Pendulum.

190

Velocity of 1700 Feet in 1", the Error in the Eftimation of it need never amount to its five hundredth Part.' As electronic chronographs have become cheap and plentiful we have become rather inclined to be circumspect about claiming an error so small. The Error in the Eftimation of my two electronic chronographs sometimes amounts to its forty-two-and-a-quarter Part when I actually compare one with the other, as we shall see.

Can we therefore rely on Robins' velocity measurements? In 1852 the American 18-bore musket, tested with a balistic (sic) pendulum, was reported to shoot at 1,250 fps, which went up to 1,550 fps when a 17-bore ball was used to reduce the windage. We can never be entirely certain without the means to check one instrument against another. But I have found the ballistic pendulum to give a very good estimation of velocity if a number of shots are taken from which to calculate an average.

The very obvious difficulty of measuring something moving extremely quickly through the air is how to time it over a given distance. Robins' inspiration was to harness the principle of conservation of momentum after a collision, with the knowledge that a heavy object will rise against the acceleration of gravity according to its velocity. So the square of the velocity is equal to twice the gravity, multiplied by the height gained; all of it depending on whatever mass is moving after the collision.

We need to be careful about the measurements, and since we deal in feet per second and foot-pounds, it is as well to measure everything in seconds, or in feet, or in pounds. And, as millimetres are easier to read than feet, we have to convert any millimetre reading by dividing it by 304.8 for the very good reason that there happen to be that many millimetres in one foot. We also have to be very careful indeed about weight, because the exact speed is determined by multiplying a number by the exact weight of the pendulum bob in pounds, and dividing it by the exact weight of the bullet in pounds. A small and accurate balance can be made very easily, and delicate grain weights can be made out of any handy bit of copper wire, an ounce being carefully weighed before being snipped into measured lengths, based on the knowledge that 437.5 grains are an ounce.

Although we measure bullets in grains and there are 7,000 grains in a pound, the calculators we use to supplement our waning mental arithmetic do not measure things in seven-thousandths nor even in those sixteenths which would enable us to use ounces conveniently, so every single weight has to be converted into decimal fractions of a pound. The clever modern physicist circumvents this by operating solely in kilograms and metres, but they rob everything of its charm, and further I never met a rifleman who had the faintest inkling of what a Newton or a joule might be, whereas every single one has heard of a foot-pound and many of us understand the concept too.

One benefit of using a pendulum is that as it moves upwards, so it swings backwards, which swing can easily be measured, and since we want it to swing gently, it has to be heavy. As a rule of thumb, a decent reading for catapult-speeds will be obtained if the pendulum bob weighs around 200 times as much as the bullet. My first was heavier than this, 12 pounds, but it did not swing very far, and the further the swing, the clearer are differences from which we calculate the velocities. A heavy pendulum will not travel upwards very far even when hit smartly by a catapult bullet, so the longer we can make the string, the further it will swing backwards for a given height gain. Mine is limited by the height of the garage roof, and it is 7$\frac{1}{3}$ feet long, which I know by measuring it with a stopwatch, for if mildly disturbed, a pendulum will always swing at a constant rate which is why it is used in clocks. My pendulum completes exactly 20 swings in one minute, and though this does tell me it's 7$\frac{1}{3}$ feet long, in fact I don't need this measurement at all. I can use the number of seconds per swing instead.

The easiest means of measuring how far the pendulum swings backwards is to lay down a piece of ordinary window glass immediately before and just below it. Since a catapult cannot exceed the speed of recoil of rubber, which is around 270 fps depending on the batch, if we use a 7-pound pendulum 7$\frac{1}{3}$ feet long the piece of glass need only be 18 inches long; such a pendulum will only swing back a few inches for a reasonably heavy ball at that velocity. On the window glass some sawdust (of which my garage yields an abundance) is sprinkled. To the front of the pendulum is attached the lightest possible needle, pivoted so that it can move effortlessly up and down. The reason it has to be light is that it will incur some momentum but will not be lifted upwards, so it is a point of experimental error. This needle rests on the glass amid the sawdust, and it will scrape a quite discernable line up and down, which we can measure by ruling a line next to the needle tip when the pendulum is stationary. Robins used a thin ribbon, a datum line being marked by pushing a pin through it, and he arranged for the pendulum bob to pull this ribbon through two lightly-nipping knife-edges of steel, so that the ribbon would slide only one way and it would be held at the furthest extent of the pendulum's half-swing upwards.

Our pendulum bob is suspended by four strings acting as parallelograms, each looped round a nail projecting from the side of the pendulum and its other end being looped over a hook screwed into the rafters. Fremantle, copying William Metford, who was his close friend, used eight strings – wires, in his case – to ensure the pendulum swung straight back, but he was using a .303 rifle, which is very lively compared with a catapult. Naturally the higher the rafters the better, because a catapult can be shot with more velocity if the shooter stands erect than if he has to crouch down on the floor among the bicycles and lathe stools and stacks of wood and old ice skates and half-empty paint pots and all the other clutter of a garage.

The four strings must be parallel so the four nails are hammered into the rafters at precisely the same height. The strings must also be the same length, which is most easily accomplished if four turnbuckles – one to each string – are included at their four ends; this also makes it easy to produce a nice, precise swing of once every three seconds. These four strings weigh nothing and save the wretched business of having to calculate what proportion of weight, and at what height, the thing would swing to were the bullet to hit a pendulum mass focussed at a point, though Robins, a mathematician, derived much comfort and satisfaction from precisely this calculation. Of course his musket balls went a lot faster than our catapult balls, and required a more robust pendulum. Robins had to weigh his steel pendulum,

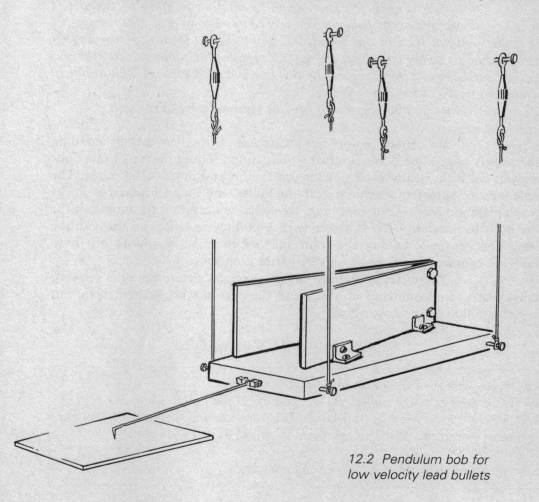

12.2 Pendulum bob for low velocity lead bullets

and by finding its centre of gravity and comparing the centre of impact with the centre of oscillation, calculate the theoretical pendulum length and thereby the weight that would equate to the mass moved by the impact of the bullet. We can enjoy a simpler calculation if we maximise the mass of the pendulum bob and minimise the mass of the link to the pivot, which is why we make this out of thin string. Then we can ignore all these fine details and pretend they don't matter, and if the pendulum bob is squat and heavy and the strings are long and light, we're about right.

It is important that the bullet hits the pendulum and is secured in the bob, and this is not just for the calculation, but also to protect the well-being of the inmates of the garage, among whom the shooter will figure prominently if it happens to be Benjamin Robins. Quoting his inimitable style (page 32):

'When in thefe experiments fo small a quantity of Powder is ufed, as will not give to the Bullet a Velocity of more than 4 or 500 Feet in 1", the Bullet will not ftick in the Wood, but will rebound from it entire, and (if the Wood be of a very hard Texture) with a very confiderable Velocity indeed. .... To avoid then thefe Dangers, to the braving of which in Philofophical Refearches no Honour is annexed...'

— and he goes on to suggest remote firing of the gun.

We cannot remote-fire a catapult, so the best way of avoiding rebounds is to give the bob a floor of wood, and to mount on top of this floor two vertical walls of plywood touching at the far end in a V [Fig. 12.2]. The angle must be sufficiently acute to trap the bullet, and I have found this works if each plywood piece is one foot long, six inches wide, and if the mouth of the V is itself five inches wide. If a couple of 6-millimetre bolts run through the pointed end of the V, holding the point together, they can be undone briefly to allow the captured bullet to be removed after each shot.

There are a variety of formulæ to determine the velocity, depending on the command of algebra of the person who drafted them, but they all amount to the same thing.

The one I use is:

$$V= [(W + w) \div w] \times [(N \times 2\pi) \div T]$$

W is the weight of the pendulum bob (7 pounds)
w is the weight of the bullet (.03125 pounds, if the bullet is a ½-ounce)
N is how far backwards and upwards the pendulum swung: i.e. from the point of rest to the furthest back point it swung to (0.35761 feet)
2π = 6.28318
T = 3 seconds, the time of one pendulum swing

In an actual example shot a few minutes ago, I found the pendulum swung back 109 millimetres when hit by a half-ounce ball.

$109 \div 304.8 = 0.35761$ feet – this represents a velocity of:

$7 + 0.03125 = 7.03125$

7.03125×0.35761 feet $\times 6.28318 \div (3 \text{ seconds} \times 0.03125)$ lbs $= 168.5$ fps.

F. L. English who used one with arrows suggested a correction figure for losses due to friction, and it can be seen that if you set a pendulum swinging, it gradually loses height. After a shot mine swings six or seven times before coming to rest, and at the first swing it loses about 15 millimetres, at the second 14 millimetres, at the third 13, at the fourth 10; and so on. Metford and Fremantle hung their wires on knife-edges to reduce friction. The late J. R. Wiggins believed the correction for my pendulum hovered between 0.6 and 0.7 inches, the smaller for a swing of up to 4 inches and the larger for any swing of over 5 inches. It really was this uncertain.

The biggest caveat is therefore on reliability. Nowhere have I records of shooting more than seven shots. Statisticians wince at depending on an average of even seven pendulum readings, especially where the variation is as great as I found it; and one evening spent bolting and unbolting the spent balls from a ballistic pendulum will convince all but the most diehard experimenter of the benefit of purchasing an electronic chronograph [Fig. 12.3].

Even the electronic chronograph is not as accurate as its digital read-out would have us believe. I have two, to allow me to set up one in front of the muzzle and the other down-range to measure the drag as velocity loss on assorted missiles. There was a deal of fun to be had in calibrating them. I set mine up adjacent to one another, and tilted so that their electronic eyes measured precisely the same bit of flight of a projectile [Fig. 12.4]. The figures revealed that one would show a reading a few feet per second faster than t'other, but it was not all that consistent. Using a Webley air pistol, one would read 332 fps and the other 335 fps, but

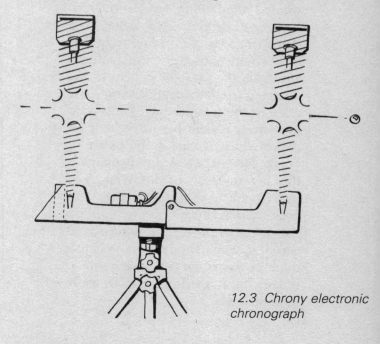

12.3 Chrony electronic chronograph

12.4 Calibrating Chrony and Chronotech chrono-graphs over the same period of bullet flight.

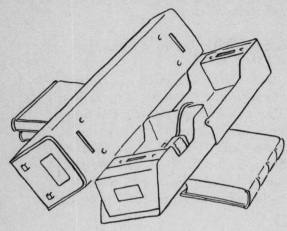

in the same string of shots the slower reading could be 330 and the faster 338. With no other means of calibration, we are probably wise to assume the accuracy of our electronic chronographs is no more than plus-or-minus 2½%.

Before I had an electronic machine, I constructed three physical chronographs, one being the ballistic pendulum, the other two using the known principle that whatever its horizontal speed, a bullet falls at an accelerating rate of 32.16 feet per second per second.

In the first of these a thin paper screen ten feet away fell just as the shot was made; the bullet had to pass through this screen and into one immediately behind it [Fig. 12.5]. The discrepancy between the position of the two holes showed by how much the first screen had fallen, and the elapsed time was calculated from knowing that the distance it dropped was equal to 16.08 feet multiplied by the square of the time measured in seconds. I secured the falling screen via two screw-eyes, and held it there by a taut string. My end of the string was held with finger and thumb alongside the catapult pouch, so the screen started to drop exactly as I released the catapult ball. For a bow, the screen is held by a thin strip of paper which is cut as the bullet or arrow is launched. A disadvantage is the nervousness of knowing you have to hit a falling screen ten feet away, and as often as not I would hit the framework of the screen and smash it. Each shot took about five minutes to set up and the frequent repairs did not make for statistically large samples.

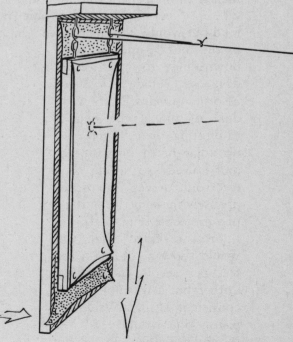

12.5 Falling screen chronograph.

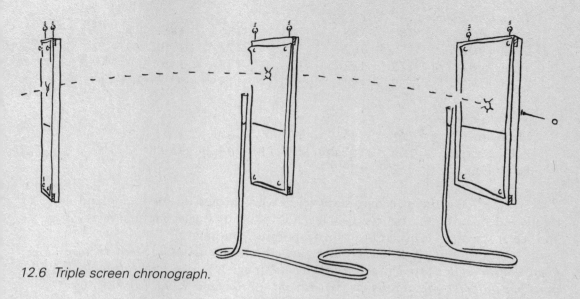

12.6 Triple screen chronograph.

Reflecting that such a method included the period of acceleration of the rubber, I dreamt up a second chronograph, arranging three stationary screens set up at head height, with exactly six feet between each pair [Fig. 12.6]. A datum line which was exactly the same height off the ground on each screen was marked; achieving precision for this was easier than it sounds because all that was needed was a long clear plastic tube filled with water attached to the centre screen – the water level at each end was the same height. The bullet had to be shot through all three screens, and its height accurately measured from the datum lines to show by how much it deviated from the straight. The problems of shooting through the third screen, which obviously couldn't be seen, soon became apparent and usually all that I could say was that a bullet was travelling pretty fast past my head on its way back from the garage wall.

Both of these methods suffered the further disadvantage that a big lead ball doesn't necessarily make a mark that can be measured in fractions of a millimetre, which is necessary for accurate calculations. How dependable these methods are may be judged from the following results, shot with a catapult:

140-grain ball:

Electronic:	194	199	199	198	199		
Falling-screen:	206	187					
Triple-screen:	187	166	204				
Pendulum:	197	200	197	164.5	221.4	183.5	215

220-grain ball:

Electronic:	187	188	185	180	183		
Falling screen:	152.5	162	125.5	172.5	170.5		
Triple screen:	172	152	156	145	159		
Pendulum:	192	184	200	114.7	97.7	204	195.4

376-grain ball:

Electronic:	159	145	141	153	157
Falling screen:	158.3	131.266	136.715	144.25	150.8
Pendulum:	163.2	139.9	135.2		

To the armchair statistician who throws up his hands and – rightly – demands more figures, I shall echo Robins by suggesting that he try it and see at what point his enthusiasm evaporates. Quoting:

'But thofe Experiments which are yet wanting, will require great Leifure and a proper Seafon to execute. [page lv] .... *a Difficulty which none but thofe who fhall attempt Experiments of the fame Kind, can be judges of.'* (page liii).

A simpler method is possible for an accurate air rifle with a good telescopic sight mounted on it. Using a spirit level to make a single horizontal line as an aiming mark a measured ten yards away, I carefully bedded such a gun on its left flank and took five shots with the vertical reticule lying on the line. The rifle was then flipped over, bedded on its right flank, and another five shots carefully taken with the reticule on the line. The average drop from the horizontal aiming line of all ten shots was then worked out, any sideways scatter from the one side being compensated for by that of the other side. The calculated velocity, 479 fps from one side and 432 fps from the other, gave an average velocity of 455.5 fps. How dependable? A subsequent electronic chronograph reading for the same gun was 484 fps. Given the random dispersion of any five-shot group, one can entertain the possibility that more shots would have given a closer correlation.

Among archers, owing to the ease with which the cast of a bow can be measured, only recently has the emphasis switched from how far an arrow is thrown by a bow to how fast that arrow flies. There is no lack of documentation on the distance to which an arrow can be shot, and it consti-tutes the first objective comparison of the performance of bows. How useful these comparisons are is questionable, because early writers gave measure-ments in whatever unit sprang to mind; it was clearer to the ancient than to us what stadia were. The most obvious human measurement is the pace, but it falls short of a desirable degree of objectivity. Nor is it of any value to those of us bred up on muzzle velocities, because the wind resistance varies greatly from arrow to arrow, and plays a more significant part in determining the cast than the launch velocity does. Proof, were it needed, lies in flight shooting records. Wendy Hodkinson, five times British Ladies' National Flight Champion, once told me that her records – shooting over 400 yards – were made with a bow of only 30 pounds or so draw weight. She was, of course, shooting tiny, barely-fletched flight arrows.

The method of J. D. Seagrave of shooting an arrow vertically upwards and multiplying the flight time (measured in seconds) by 17, which gives the approximate initial velocity in feet per second, may be a very considerable approximation. A disadvantage of this method is the slight possibility of the experimenter suffering an unfortunate mishap, although anyone who has tried it will vouch that a greater difficulty lies in finding the arrow afterwards, the slightest breeze leading to drift, and it being difficult to follow the flight of an arrow when staring up into the bright sky. In addition, a shot taken with the body contorted to give a vertical flight may not give the same draw length as a conventional 'horizontal' shot.

We could also measure velocity by penetration. Penetration is proportional to energy. Saxton Pope, a Californian physician of the early part of the twentieth century, became enamoured of archery as a consequence of caring for Ishi, the last Yana Indian, and he describes the simplest method of all for finding the velocity of an arrow. One foot-pound is the energy of a pound weight dropped from a height of one foot. Two foot-pounds is either two pounds from a height of one foot, or one pound from a height of two feet. He made direct comparison of weights attached to an appropriately small arrowhead and dropped into a cake of paraffin. From this we learnt that an arrow from Dr. Pope's 75-pound longbow had 25 foot-pounds of energy at 10 yards, and as he tells us it weighed an ounce, the velocity must have been 160 fps.

Velocity loss

In tests conducted at Chatham in 1846 the approximate maximum range of a musket if given an upward slope of 5° was 650 yards, from which the velocities can be only imprecisely known, given that the windage of a musket ball means that even at the same velocity, some will fly high and others low. The average velocity over the first 200 yards of flight was 1,026 fps, calculated from its drop. The velocity by the time the bullet was flying between the ranges of 600 yards to 650 yards was as low as 362 fps. It suggests that the percussion musket of 1847 had a muzzle velocity of between 1,200 and 1,500 fps.

Robins' work encouraged more trials, particularly among the military. In the 1780s another distinguished mathematician, Professor Hutton, also used a ballistic pendulum but for cannon velocity measurements. Hutton's was necessarily a large affair, the pendulum itself weighing between 600 and 700 pounds, made of elm and requiring very frequent repair due to the effects of being shot at with 3-pound, 6-pound and 13-pound cannonballs at a range of 30 feet and at velocities of 800 to 1,600 fps. Each shot, though adding to the pendulum its own weight, tended by penetration of up to 17 feet (!), to squeeze out water, splinters, and occasionally pieces of the ironwork holding the pendulum bob together. Professor Hutton's tests on 6th and 7th August 1788 with 1-pound cannonballs are instructive. With a 2-ounce charge of powder, he registered the following velocities (*see table*).

We would expect a large cannonball to lose less energy over a given distance than a small musketball, so these figures give us good guidance as to the drag we can expect from our spherical ammunition.

Hutton was not immune to satisfying his curiosity regarding the range to

Range (yards)	Velocity (fps)	
10	877	
20	850	94% of the energy at 10 yard
40	844	98.5% of the energy at 20 ya
60	804	91% of the energy at 40 yard
80	784	95% of the energy at 60 yard
100	765	95% of the energy at 80 yard

which these cannonballs would fly and, imp that he was, sometimes shot cannonballs along a curve of the lower Thames, his safety arrangements being to await a gap in the shipping before each shot. The use of a stretch of water was to enable the splash to be observed from a series of known points, from which the range could be determined through trigonometry. These observations were rendered the more entertaining by Hutton's placing observers – cadet officers from the Royal Naval College – at points along the proposed flight which, as H. A. Baker so delightfully tells us, being far from a predetermined affair occasionally afforded them opportunities for very close monitoring of events. When I lived there I should dearly have liked to see these experiments repeated, not least for the pleasure of shooting naval cannon towards Westminster, where politicians even of the Mother of Parliaments are so frequently apt to forget that they are the people's servants and not their masters. Alas, it seems quite unlikely that such a method of velocity testing would now be allowed.

Sir Ralph Payne-Gallwey too was fascinated by range, and pursued the curious hobby of shooting at the island of Anglesey from the coast of Wales. He frequently hit it, and did so with a bewildering variety of mechanical weapons, some of them constructed on the spot for the purpose. Some of the trials are recorded in his comprehensive book *The Crossbow* (1903). Although a man of means and a fervent experimenter, there is no record of Payne-Gallwey's possessing himself of an electronic chronograph, which had been invented in 1864 – no doubt in a moment's relaxation from his Church duties – by the Reverend Francis Bashforth. So far as we know Payne-Gallwey did not even have a ballistic pendulum. Instead, he contented himself with the measurement of the effective and extreme range of his crossbows, stating for example;

> *'If held at an angle of 45 degrees, a good bullet crossbow will throw a ¹/₂ oz. lead bullet to an extreme range of 300 yards, and if shot at a metal target at 20 yards, more than half of the bullet will be flattened.*

Although this does not tell us the speed of the bullet, it does alluringly give us enough clues to be able to work it out. Were the test to have been conducted in a vacuum, regardless of the projectile we could calculate the launch velocity easily, since the only force is that of gravity which produces a constant downward acceleration. Until Robins, all writers had averred that the resistance of air to the flight of a musket or cannonball had to be so small as to be negligible, and Robins' rebuttal (page xlvi-lii) of their logic is a delight to read.

I shot some balls not at a metal target at 20 yards, but rather through the chronograph at about two yards, at a brick wall. It is impossible to be accurate because of the irregular distortion, but measuring with a micrometer the maximum and minimum diameters, and the maximum thickness, their flattened dimensions are shown in the table.

Velocity (fps)	Diameter (mm)	Thickest part (mm)
332	23-25.5	5.5
321	23-25.5	6
282	22-23.7	7.7
269	19.5-24.2	6.9
264	19.5-20	7.3
234	17.7-18.4	8.3
192	15.9-16	9.2

The two which most closely resemble Payne-Gallwey's description *'more than half of the bullet will be flattened'* were travelling at 192 fps and 234 fps [Fig. 12.7]

However, possessed as I am of two chronographs and an unhealthy curiosity, I found a pressing need to establish the degree of air resistance likely to be offered to a small lead ball. Robins had devised the method of shooting at 25, 75 and 125 feet range – having first determined that the average velocity of a musketball did not vary by more than 20 fps –

12.7 Flattened half-ounce lead bullets shot at different velocities at a brick wall. From a photograph.

'*provided I can direct the Piece fo as to caufe the Bullet to impinge on the Pendulum...*' (page 74). Accuracy was a grave problem, and later Hutton thought up an admirable advance with his cannon, which was to mount a cannon on one ballistic pendulum, and shoot the ball into another. The first would swing to give a reading of the muzzle velocity, and the second would swing to give a reading of the terminal velocity.

Between them they found that the projectile lost velocity much more quickly above the speed of sound than at lower velocities. Robins, concentrating on a ³/₄-inch musketball, is of more interest to us than Hutton's cannonballs, but his short-range tests at 25 feet, only give the result of a drop from 1,670 fps at 25 feet range to 1,550 fps at 75 feet range. We will not see a catapult shoot a bullet so quickly, and because of the enhanced drag at those speeds the result is not necessarily very helpful. Ascher Shapiro showed that there is a certain speed at which the drag on a projectile is less than at higher or lower speeds. It depends not only on the speed, but also on the shape and weight of the projectile. The half-ounce .303 bullet travelling less than 800 fps has 92¹/₂% of its energy left after 100 yards' flight; the half-ounce spherical lead ball has only half its energy left at this distance. Simply, a long narrow pointed bullet spends less energy shoving the air aside than does a round ball. Worse, the ball is a smooth sphere, and its drag changes according to its velocity through a mystery known as the Reynolds number. Here, briefly, I must depart from my own experiences and go into the realms of laboratory tests I have only read about. These, therefore, I might believe but cannot vouch for.

Drag can be read up in books on aerodynamics. We are concerned with turbulent and separated flow, and I know for a fact I shall now get all confused because I am about to start discussing laminar flow which, like everyone else, I think I understand until I try to explain it. Fully to understand drag you need a brain, as somebody put it, the size of a planet, and this precludes your ever managing to communicate it to people like me.

A Brown Bess musket ball pushes aside 0.37 square inches of air in flight, which at low speeds separates behind it and, in a manner of speaking, sucks it backwards like the wake of a ship. If instead of a sphere it was shaped like an air-ship – perfectly streamlined body, still fitting into the barrel of the Brown Bess musket and therefore having the same frontal area – it would fly through the air as if its frontal area were only 0.037 square inches, because the air flow would be attached, and there wouldn't be a large wake. (We non-mathematicians are unkindly jubilant when we learn that physicists have yet to agree a definition of drag coefficient, or this would incline us to suggest its drag coefficient to be one-tenth.) The only thing slowing it down would be the friction of the air on the surface of the bullet. The air flow would be laminar flow, and as laminar means leaves, we are required to think of it as sliding through leaves of air next to its skin. It would go a very great deal farther for the same initial velocity. Laminar flow is not very stable, and can quite suddenly burst out behind a streamlined body as a huge wake which is called separated flow, with an enormous increase in drag.

However, a musket ball is not a streamlined shape; it is what aeroplane designers call a bluff body. It has a very horrid drag coefficient, and never goes anywhere near laminar flow. At low speeds, the flow behind the musket-ball also separates, billowing out in a huge separated wake, and it is this that increases its drag so dramatically to about ten times that of a stream-lined body.

But above a certain speed the air remains attached to a musket-ball, not in the beautiful low-drag laminar flow but as turbulent flow. Turbulent flow is where the air is spun off the body in tiny little circles, and it absorbs about double the energy of laminar flow. Nevertheless, this is still five times better than separated flow.

Now (missing out a x10^5 which complicates matters for us) there is a thing called the Reynolds number and it is:

$2/3$ x sphere diameter x velocity

(where the diameter is in metres and the velocity in metres per second)

At any Reynolds number below 3 (again, skipping a x10^5), the air flow behind the musket ball is not turbulent, but separated. It isn't quite as precise as this due to the little x10^5 I have been trying to avoid, so converting to imperial numbers we find that for a Brown Bess musket ball the lowest speed for the attached, turbulent flow is somewhere in the region of 847 fps. Turbulent flow has about double the drag of laminar flow, but it's a lot more stable, and it can be triggered even on a sphere if the surface is roughened, which will make the flow remain attached, if turbulent, at much lower speeds. As golf ball designers found, at some inconvenience to my head, it is possible to extend the range by dimpling the surface, and were it not for the fact that large lead balls went out of fashion among soldiers in the middle of the nineteenth century, one could imagine a dimpled lead ball being of some service.

Anyway, since the half-ounce bullet of Payne-Gallwey has a diameter of .527 inches, we can assume that at the speeds we might expect from a bullet-crossbow or any other of our low-velocity weapons, the drag will be constant and proportional to the square of the velocity. To find the drag, I needed to shoot a ball through two chronographs, and see how much velocity it lost over a given distance.

Calibrating my electronic chronographs with a string of shots, so that they could both measure the identical path of flight of a test shot, revealed that on average the Chrony figures needed to be multiplied by

1.01527 in order to correct them to give a figure which could be compared with those from the Chronotech. The Chronotech consistently registered faster figures, but these were not uniformly faster. I have no idea what the explanation for this might be, but it does emphasise the wisdom of taking a number of shots with any chronograph, and calculating some kind of average. To illustrate the point, the results were the first set of figures.

Chronotech	Chrony
341	-
334	-
335	332
338	330
328	323
316	313
332	326
325	320
340	335
337	330
338	334
338	334 (sic)
332.7	327.7

Using a bag of compressed air and a copper pipe I then shot 11 half-ounce spherical bullets with the two chronographs separated by 10 metres, obtaining the second set of results shown. One shot gave no readings on either chronograph – experiments are fraught with this sort of irritation.

Of these averages, the second was corrected to 273.6 based on the chronograph calibration.

A ½-ounce bullet, therefore, launched at an initial velocity of 281.7 fps has a velocity of 273.6 fps at exactly 10-metres range. At this speed, it therefore loses 6% of its energy every 10 metres.

Chronotech	Chrony
280	271
-	-
274	263
277	275
279	264
286	274
287	272
282	270
279	265
287	270
286	272
281.7	269.6

Calculating the 'muzzle' velocity from this information, though straightforward, required the computation of both the deceleration due to drag and the downwards acceleration due to gravity. Both of these were done by J. R. Wiggins on a computer program he had written. We found that a range of 300 yards, which is that to which Payne-Gallwey's crossbow would shoot, would be reached by a launch velocity of 206 fps and an initial angle of 45°. This surprised us; we had expected a somewhat higher initial velocity, not least because Robins, shooting a ¾-inch ball over water, had said that a muzzle velocity of 400 fps gave distances of 313, 319 and 373 yards. But it bears out the usefulness of experimental data as opposed to speculation. It also suggests that Robins' gunpowder was not as consistent as modern powder, and perhaps that it is hard to measure with any accuracy the splash of a musket bullet 300 yards from the shore.

This is a comparatively high loss of energy but tallies with what we know about smooth musket balls: they have a very high drag. In drag tests on a Brown Bess musket, Martin Pegler found a loss of velocity from 792 – 815 fps at the muzzle to 627 fps at 100 yards (which gives perhaps a 5.5% loss every 10 metres), and 415 fps at 200 yards which might be 8.5% loss every 10 metres. These tie in very roughly with my own measurements of 6% energy loss of a ½-ounce ball at 10 metres at very much lower speeds. The blip of low drag is lower than our Reynolds number calculation seems to predict; it ought not to occur below 847 fps. We may need to include the fine detail of our calculation, recalling that the 10^5 I have been trying to avoid cluttering the calculation with means that the Reynolds number of 3×10^5 is just a mathematician's way of saying 300,000. Were it not for the fact that fluid dynamics makes my brain ache, I would now endeavour to prove to myself that there is plenty of room to accommodate a blip of low, turbulent drag between 792 and 627 fps. As it is, I shall blithely say that we have a final salutary reminder that however intriguing and attractive theories and mathematics might be, reality is often disconcertingly different, and it is the reality that is of rather more concern. But the low drag blip is very real, and can often be found if enough bullet velocity measurements are taken. If we look closely at tables of rifle velocity we can see that a similar blip of low drag appears for the old .303 bullet; its lowest drag point is between the speeds of 1,016 and 978 fps.

Fortunately, given that the very curved trajectory of any slow bullet limits its useful range, the loss of energy through drag is negligible at the distances we might expect to shoot catapults or crossbows. If we generously assume an extreme range of 40 metres, the bullet will still have 85% of its kinetic energy. This is very low drag compared with the energy loss of a conventional, waisted airgun pellet.

Airguns, of course, sometimes venture into the realms of velocities above 800 fps, where the drag is very high. For waisted pellets, any speed above 800 fps results in a loss of around 5 or 6 foot-pounds every 10 metres. Having nothing better to do, I have just shot two samples to prove it to myself.

Shooting light-weight, flat-headed 12-grain Hobby pellets from different rifles:
893.5 fps at the muzzle drops to 760.45 fps 10-metres down-range,
    representing a loss of 5.87 foot-pounds.
But 682 fps at the muzzle only drops to 631 fps at 10 metres, a loss of
    1.8 foot-pounds.

Shooting 14.35-grain, rounded-nose Superdome pellets:
847 fps at the muzzle drops to 755.4 fps at 10 metres, a loss of
    4.68 foot-pounds.
613.7 fps at the muzzle drops to 561 fps at 10 metres, a loss of 2 foot pounds.

As the losses are reasonably constant, the physicist will deduce that a heavier pellet has a lower drag, and this is borne out when we see other tests. Although many people prefer the high velocity of .177 air rifles over heavier calibres, at the higher velocities the drag on any light-weight pellet is three times as great as it is at lower velocities, and while a powerful .22 air rifle shooting a 20-grain pellet at a muzzle velocity of 800 fps may still have half its energy left at 60 metres, a similarly powerful .177 with a muzzle velocity of 1,300 fps dumps most of its kinetic energy within the first 20 metres, and 60 metres out may have only a seventh of its energy left. The velocity of both air rifles is likely to be the same somewhere around the 40-metre mark. But for shooting with a flat trajectory, the best air rifle may still be the .177, which might average a speed of over 800 fps over a 60-metre flight, whereas the .22 may only average 700 fps over the whole 60 metres. The only difficulty is that at very high speeds, some small pellets are reported to tumble and a tumbling pellet is anything but accurate.

* * * * * *

We started this study with an examination of projectiles, and it is appropriate to end on the same subject. It is always the case that it is the bullet that has the effect on the target, and though the means of getting it there is often more interesting, we must never forget that the accurate arrival of the bullet is our first concern. Designing bullets to do adequate work on arrival is important, unless we are those ascetic and well-disposed people who like only to punch holes in paper targets, but we share with them the need for accuracy, and a well-designed bullet with exactly the right velocity, energy and momentum that misses its mark is to be judged, and rightly judged, as of no account at all.

Notes and references

Chapter 1 Ammunition

Helical flight of tracer bullets can be seen in plate 24 *First Flight*, 2002, by Geoffrey Wellum. The subject of lateral drift of spherical and elongated projectiles was gone into in great and fascinating detail by T. F. Fremantle in chapter 12 of *The Book of the Rifle*, 1901. That a round ball fired from a smooth-bore barrel will hit a man-sized target up to about 40 yards and up to 100 yards if from a long smooth barrel and a tight fit is given by Howard Blackmore in *Hunting Weapons* 1970, p. 276. Martin Pegler, *Powder and Ball Small Arms*, 1998, pp. 55-6, tested a Brown Bess and found it gave a 9-inch group with two flyers at 50 yards, a 31-inch group at 100 yards, and no bullet found the target at 200 yards. Robert Bailey describes poisoned arrows among the Efe of Zaire in *National Geographic*, vol. 176 no. 5, November 1989, pp. 664-686. Arthur Credland, *Journal of the Society of Archer Antiquaries* (JSAA), vol. 18, 1975, pp. 13-21 describes the use of clay balls in India for stonebows. Adrian Eliot Hodgkin, *The Archer's Craft*, 1951, starts his chapter on the subject with the outrageous sentence 'Making a bowstring is a jolly business.' I cannot bring myself to admit that so frustrating do I find string-making that once, to my infinite regret, I flung my copy – a signed first edition – across the room and damaged the cover. The velocity and mass of a golf ball can be found in *Encyclopædia Britannica* under 'Golf'. Nelson's accuracy is given by H. A. Baker on p. 274, *Journal of the Arms and Armour Society* (JAAS), June 1985. Michael Glover, *Warfare from Waterloo to Mons*, 1980, p. 56, notes that Nelson's warships were touching one another when the guns were fired. Prof. Sir O. G. Sutton, p. 68, *Mathematics in Action*, 1966, quotes Nelson: 'that our shots cannot miss the object'. Howard Blackmore, *British Military Firearms*, 1961 (revised ed. 1994) p. 274, gives the respective bore and diameter of ball of the Brown Bess musket and on p. 240 the rate of fire. Glover, ibid., p. 25 gives the rate of fire of a muzzle-loading rifle.

Chapter 2 The fibre-glass bullet-shooting crossbow

The Revd. W. B. Daniels (*Rural Sports*, 1801-2), Sir Ralph Payne-Gallwey (*The Crossbow*, 1903), Daniel Higson (*The Bullet Crossbow*, 1922-3) Arthur Graves Credland (JSAA, vol. 15 pp. 22-36 and vol. 28, pp. 24-33) and A. Littler (JSAA vol. 34 1991 pp. 30-41) have all written extensively about the English bullet-shooting crossbow. The nineteenth-century reports of a bullet crossbow being able to hit 'a playing card at 50 yards and kill a dozen pigeons consecutively at 30 yards or more' in *Sporting Magazine*, May 1859, p. 327 is quoted by A. G. Credland, JSAA vol. 15, 1972, p. 34. Page 35 gives the reference to G. Millard shooting six bullets into a two-inch circle at 50 feet, in *Archery World*, vol. 15, Feb 1966. George Agar Hansard, *The Book of Archery*, 1840, p. 238-9 describes the gambler allowing a glass to be shot off his head at 16 paces. G. W. Spearing, *The Craft of the Gunsmith*, 1986, p. 31 describes the tempering of a shotgun lock spring using mutton-fat in a country gun-maker's to gauge the correct temper for the spring-steel. A photograph of a leg transfixed by a crossbow bolt is to be found in the *British Medical Journal*, BMJ 1990:301:70 (7 July). Chinese pellet shooting crossbows are illustrated in Josef Alm's book *European Crossbows: a Survey*, English version 1994, p. 93. Lt. Cdr. W. Paterson describes coxcombing in *A Guide to the Crossbow*, p. 117. Tim Baker wrote a brilliant chapter on strings in Vol. 2 of *The Traditional Bowyer's Bible*. J. E. Gordon on strength of string is on p. 90 of *Structures*, 1978.

Chapter 3 Yew-wood bullet crossbow

The discovery that a bow length of 66-67 inches is the fastest is given by Tim Baker, p. 69-70 of Vol. 1 of *The Traditional Bowyer's Bible*, 1992. Otzi's bow is described in *The Man In The Ice*,1994, Konrad Spindler, p. 87 and his height on p. 160. The Statute of Edward IV in 1465 ordaining that everyone between 16 and 60 should have a bow of his own height plus a fistmele between the nocks is given by Lt. Cdr. W. F. Paterson, JSAA, vol. 24, 1981, p. 5. That doubling the thickness of a bow makes it eight times as stiff but it will recoil only twice as fast is given by Dr. Robert P. Elmer, *Target Archery* 1952, pp. 157 & 162. That the stress cannot be calculated directly as a function of the length of a bow is given by Paul E. Klopsteg, *Turkish Archery* 1934, 3rd edition 1987, p. 197. Blackmore's reference to the slingers of Benjamin's army (Judges, 20.16) is given in *Hunting Weapons*, p. 329. Klopsteg, Hickman and Nagler's finding that one-third the string weight may be considered as arrow weight is in *Archery, the Technical Side*, 1947, p. 208 and that the velocity is inversely related to the cube root of the arrow weight, on p. 167. The Norwegian whaling crossbow is illustrated by Josef Alm, ibid., pp. 8-10, and A. G. Credland, JSAA Vol 26 1983, p. 13. Paul Comstock on leaving a bow strung for a while before shooting it is found in *The Traditional Bowyer's Bible*, Vol. 2, p. 111. Ancient crossbow nuts of the crown of deer antler are described by A. G. Credland, JSAA, vol. 23, 1980, pp. 12-19.

Chapter 4 Catapults
Richard Jefferies' reference to the squire is on p. 296, *Field & Hedgerow*, 1892, *An English Deer Park*. Hodges' rubber-powered weapons are described by Raymond G. Rieser, JSAA, vol 31, pp. 13-19; and by Blackmore, *Hunting Weapons*, pp. 171, 209. Emmanuel E. Papagrigorakis' description of a speargun is in *The Underwater Man, A complete diving manual*, 1980, tr. Philip Ramp. The Special Operations Executive rubber-powered crossbows are described by Arthur G. Credland, JSAA, vol 27, pp. 5-20. John Holden, *Shooting Straight*, 1987, p. 76 describes six archers who achieved velocities ranging from 159 fps to 194 fps using the same bow and the same arrow. J. E. Gordon's reference to Griffith on crack propagation is from p. 99, and that rubber breaks in a brittle manner is on p. 103, ibid. On p. 306 he goes into the end fixings of tension members. A brief reference to the Shanghai in an article by Lee Warner on hunting in East Timor is on pp. 58-63, *Guns & Game* magazine, Number 40, Oct-Dec 2003.

Chapter 5 The hand stonebow
Long arrows are illustrated in countless articles in *National Geographic* magazine on South American and Papua New Guinea tribesmen, and in the whole of E. G. Heath and Vilma Chiara's book *Brazilian Indian Archery* 1977. Sir Anthony Aguecheek's stonebow is in Shakespeare's *Twelfth Night*: Act II, Sc. V. That the inside of a tree is under compression is shown by J. E. Gordon on p. 281, ibid.. Propeller-twist is described on pp. 285-6, *The Traditional Bowyer's Bible*, volume 1. The dial bendmeter is illustrated opposite p. 72, Elmer, ibid. The motion of a hand-held stonebow is described by A. G. Credland in probably the best study of this weapon, in JSAA, vol 18, 1975, pp. 13-21. Edward Morse described five different bow release holds in 1885; they are illustrated on p. 76 of Heath and Chiara's *Brazilian Indian Archery*.

Chapter 6 Blowpipes
H. L. Blackmore, *Hunting Weapons*, London 1971, p. 337, gives the indigenous name 'sumpitan' for this weapon. The indigenous words phonetically spelt out here – 'kelaput', 'tehloh' and 'tahjum' – were noted at the time the weapon was obtained. Blackmore, ibid., p. 339 says the wood was from the Jagang tree and describes boring on p. 340; boring is also described in *Encyclopædia Britannica* under 'Blowpipe', 1957 edition. Poisons are described in E. G. Heath & Vilma Chiara, ibid., p. 92, and the use of Euphorbia in crossbows is described by Alonso Martinez de Espinar, *Arte de Ballesteria y Monteria*, Madrid, 1644. Accuracy of the blowpipe is given by Blackmore, ibid., p. 341. A very full article by A. G. Credland is in the *Journal of the Arms and Armour Society*, vol. X, no.4, December 1981 p119–147.

Chapter 7 Low-pressure airguns – the theory

Reilly's pamphlet was reprinted by W. S. Curtis in 1995. Arne Hoff's *Airguns and other pneumatic arms*, 1972, gives a full description of the Girandoni air rifle on pp. 64-65 including the muzzle velocity of the Danish-built version. *The Construction and Operation of the Air Gun*, vol. 1, by Geoffrey Baker and Colin Currie (privately printed, 2002) gives precise engineering dimensions of all components in the Girandoni repeating air rifle, including (p. 53) the pump. *Air Guns and Air Pistols* by L. Wesley, 1955, is where most of us first read of the Austrian repeating air rifle of 1780, described on pp. 28–32. The highest pressure to which he hand-pumped an air reservoir is given on p. 35. Blackmore's report of the experiment of 1905 in Schloss Pfaffroda in Saxony is in *Hunting Weapons*, p. 321. Wesley's photographs of bullets shot at a steel plate are on pp. 18 and 50, ibid. Hoff, ibid, p. 78, describes the Danish air machine gun. Arrows shot from muskets are described by A. G. Credland, JSAA, Vol 29, 1986, pp. 34-51.Wooden darts, for crossbows, are described by Vernard Foley, George Palmer and Werner Soedel in *Scientific American*, January 1985, vol. 252 (1), p. 85. Blackmore's reference to the burst air reservoir is in *English Pistols*, 1985, p. 27.

Chapter 8 Low-pressure airguns – the practical

If the flow of air along a pipe is laminar, then the velocity at the middle of the pipe is double the average velocity; if turbulent, the velocity in the middle is about one and a quarter the average velocity; these are given in *Transport processes: Momentum, Heat, and Mass*, by Christie J. Geankoplis, 1983, p.94. Illustrations of Venturi tubes showing inlet cones of around 11° and outlet cones of around 6° taper are found in *Flowmeters*, Alan T. J. Hayward, 1979, pp. 22-24. G. V. and G. M. Cardew, *The Airgun from Trigger to Target*, 1995, (reprinted 1996) p. 145, tell us that oil will not explode in a slowly hand-pumped system. A full discussion of Chinese crossbow locks by Dr. Forke is reproduced in JSAA, Vol 29, 1986, pp. 28-33. Howard Blackmore in *Hunting Weapons*, p. 323 records a valve bursting out of a copper ball reservoir killing the man who was pumping it. Colonel Hanger giving the rate of twist of 'the American rifle' as being 1 turn in 39 inches, and the bore never more than 36, is quoted on p. 15 of Fremantle, ibid.. That there were only 35 deaths (including suicides) worldwide from air weapons reported in the English literature in the thirty years since 1956 (*British Medical Journal*, 14 June 1997). By contrast, firearms account for 40,000 deaths, 150,000 intentional and 17,000 unintentional injuries each year in America alone (BMJ, 29 June 1996).

Chapter 9 High-pressure airguns – the theory

Arne Hoff's *Airguns and other Pneumatic Arms* (Plate 45) shows the mechanism of Kolbe's airgun in a publication dated 1744. Anyone proposing to make or even maintain an airgun ought to read and re-read the work of Cardews *père et fils*. Their experiments are of such significance to an understanding of airguns that their book cannot be over-rated. Townsend Whelen's *The Ultimate in Rifle Precision*, 1958, introduces bullet sectional density, and a great deal else too. The mushrooming of airgun pellets was detailed in a website by Ian Pellant. Such is the ephemeral nature of the Internet that details appear, disappear, and reappear and must be hunted down using search engines. Franklin W. Mann's *The Bullet's Flight from Powder to Target*, 1909 is a classic of experimental work and has to be read to understand why rifles are not perfectly accurate. However in drawing 9.2 I have followed Matt and Bruce Grant's clear interpretation (p. 86, *The Sharp Shooter*, 1972) of Mann's work since it is more easily understood than Mann's partially unwound spiral wires (Mann, p. 249-261). Gough Thomas' *Shotguns for Game and Clays* includes information on the striking energy required for small and flying game. Fremantle ibid. notes Wallingford's International score on p. 481. The different spellings of his name are Giradoni in L. Wesley, *Air Guns and Air Pistols*, Girardoni in H. Blackmore, *Hunting Weapons* and Girandoni in Arne Hoff, *Airguns and other Pneumatic Arms*.

Notes & References

Chapter 10 High-pressure airguns – the practical

Engineering textbooks do give working and burst pressures of hydraulic steel tubing but it is wisest to obtain specific details from the steel supplier at the time of purchase of any materials. Dolinek and Durdik, *Encyclopaedia of European Historical Weapons*, 1993, refers to Paul Giffard's patent for the pump-up pneumatic on p. 344. The D-bit is described in the November 30, 1950 issue of *Model Engineer* magazine.

Chapter 11 Compounding and complexity

Edward McEwen's siege compound bow, the 'Bow of the Ox', was described by him in JSAA, volume 28 1985, pp. 15–21. The Koltze crossbow is described by Ulrich Eichstaedt, *Visier* 10/1995, pp.138 to 141. Rex Harpham kindly supplied the information on the crossbows of Robert van House.

Chapter 12 Velocity measurements

Robins' invention and use of the ballistic pendulum is described throughout his book *New Principles of Gunnery*, 1742. W. S. Curtis did the world a great service in republishing his book in 1972. Lt. Cdr. W. Paterson's falling screen chronograph is in *Bowman's Handbook*, ed. Patrick Clover, 1968, p.36. The method of J. D. Seagrave is described on p. 37, ibid. Saxton Pope's penetration of paraffin wax with a longbow is in *Hunting with the Bow and Arrow*, 1923, p. 48. Wendy Hodkinson's flight records are in the introduction to *Turkish Archery* by Klopsteg. Pegler, ibid., pp. 55-6, found that the Brown Bess had a velocity of 792-815 fps, 942 fps being achieved with a ball tightly wrapped in a greased patch. Increasing the charge of powder gave no increase in velocity but just more unburnt powder being blown out of the barrel. But this was using modern powder and the testers declared their fear of using the full military charge. With admirable caution, since revisionism must by its nature open itself to future revisionism, they accepted as fact that at that date a velocity of 1500 fps had been reached. Henry Wilkinson (1852, republished by W. S. Curtis in 1983) on p. 13 of his pamphlet *Observations (Theoretical And Practical) On Muskets, Rifles And Projectiles Together With A Treatise On The Elastic Concave Wadding* – a snappy little title – gives the American musket velocity of 1250 fps. Fremantle's ballistic pendulum is described on pp. 336-8, ibid. The Chatham musket tests of 1846 are described in H. L. Blackmore, *British Military Firearms*, p. 226. George Laycock in *The Deer Hunter's Bible*, 1963 (1986) p. 52, publishes figures for buckshot from a shotgun: the figures indicate that at around 800 fps, a .33-calibre lead ball loses about 8% of its energy every 10 yards, and that it has about half its initial energy at a range of 80 yards. H. A. Baker, JAAS, Vol XI no 5, June 1985, pp. 257-298 gave us the detailed, excellent and entertaining account of the Hutton cannonball experiments. Payne-Gallwey's shooting of Anglesey is documented by A. G. Credland, JAAS, Vol XV, March 1997. I am indebted to Dr. Flewett for all the JAAS references. O. G. Sutton, ibid., p. 74, tells us of the Reverend Francis Bashforth's invention of the electronic chronograph. The extreme range of his English bullet crossbow is given by Sir Ralph Payne-Gallwey, *The Crossbow*, 1903, p. 199. Ascher Shapiro's film was written up as a book, *Shape and Flow*, 1961. Drag coefficients are intelligibly explained by Frank Rowland Whitt & David Gordon Wilson, *Bicycling Science*, 2nd edition, 1982, p. 88. Wiggins' and my drag measurements on crossbow bullets are in JSAA, vol. 44, 2001, pp. 5-11. Robins' ranges over water are on p. 77 of his book. Velocity losses of the .303 rifle are given by Fremantle, ibid., p. 442. They refer to the round-nosed bullet, not the later pointed version which reduced the drag to about 60%. Comparing the 'form factor' of the two, Matt and Bruce Grant, *ibid.*, 1972, p. 6, the round nosed bullet was 1.06 while the pointed version only .64. More air rifle pellet drag figures at 10-metre intervals, measured by Panagiotis Perros, are to be found on p. 25, *Air Gunner*, May 1996.

Index

ACKNOWLEDGEMENTS

Inasmuch as this is not a work of fiction, it owes a great deal directly and indirectly to many people. Often without knowing it, and from giving me valuable insights just in the course of a conversation to translating obscure texts into English, the following have been invaluable:

J Abel, C Boyton, D Elmy,
R Fitzsimmons, Dr W Flewett,
R Harpham, A Holmshaw,
R Knight, Dr G Lambie,
E McEwen, A Middleton,
G Pettingill, Dr W Pienaar,
Dr C Saunders, C Sleath,
Dr A Slovak, A Wells, J Whitaker
Liz Woodall.

Sadly, I must claim paternity over any errors that lie within.

Richard Middleton, 2005